Chef Infrastructure Automation Cookbook

Over 80 delicious recipes to automate your cloud and server infrastructure with Chef

Matthias Marschall

[PACKT] open source*

PUBLISHING   community experience distilled

BIRMINGHAM - MUMBAI

Chef Infrastructure Automation Cookbook

First published: August 2013

Production Reference: 1200813

Published by Packt Publishing Ltd.
Livery Place
35 Livery Street
Birmingham B3 2PB, UK

ISBN 978-1-84951-922-9

www.packtpub.com

Cover Image by Matthias Marschall (mm@agileweboperations.com)

Credits

Author

Matthias Marschall

Reviewers

Robert Curth

Julian C. Dunn

Seth Vargo

Acquisition Editor

Saleem Ahmed

Lead Technical Editor

Azharuddin Sheikh

Technical Editors

Sharvari Baet

Aparna Chand

Dylan Fernandes

Aparna K

Project Coordinator

Anugya Khurana

Proofreader

Jonathan Todd

Indexer

Monica Ajmera Mehta

Production Coordinator

Kirtee Shingan

Cover Work

Kirtee Shingan

Foreword

From the beginning, Chef has been about a group of like-minded practitioners working together to help one another build better infrastructure. We started small—just a few people tinkering and experimenting. As we gained more and more comfort and conviction in the tools we were building, and in one another, we expanded both in the scope of the infrastructures we were automating, and in the scope of the tool we were building.

Writing a book about a technology that moves as quickly as Chef does is a brave endeavor and one that can only really be undertaken by someone who has long been both a practitioner and active member of our community. Matthias is both, and I'm proud that we've come so far together that someone of his caliber would write a book about Chef.

If you're a first-time Chef, welcome to our community. May you build systems you are proud of, and that your users love. If you're a long-time member of our community, congratulations! Matthias has something to teach all of us, and you should take personal pride in the part you've played in getting all of us here.

Best wishes,

Adam Jacob
Co-founder of Opscode and the Creator of Chef

About the Author

Matthias Marschall is a software engineer "Made in Germany". His four children make sure that he feels comfortable in lively environments, and stays in control of chaotic situations. A lean and agile engineering lead, he's passionate about continuous delivery, infrastructure automation, and all things DevOps.

In recent years, Matthias has helped build several web-based businesses, first with Java and then with Ruby on Rails. He quickly grew into system administration, writing his own configuration management tool before moving his whole infrastructure to Chef in its early days.

In 2008, he started a blog (`http://www.agileweboperations.com`) together with Dan Ackerson. There they shared their ideas about DevOps since the early days of the continually emerging movement. You can find him on Twitter as `@mmarschall`.

Matthias is a CTO at gutefrage.net GmbH, helping run Germany's biggest Q&A site among other high-traffic sites. He holds a Master's degree in Computer Science (Dipl.-Inf. (FH)) and teaches courses on Agile Software Development at the University of Augsburg.

When not writing or coding, Matthias enjoys drawing cartoons and playing Go. He lives near Munich, Germany.

My thanks go to my colleagues at gutefrage.net for all those valuable discussions.

I thank Adam Jacob, Joshua Timberman, and all the other great people at Opscode for your help with the book.

Special thanks go to my reviewers Seth Vargo, Julian Dunn, and Robert Curth who made the book so much better.

Finally, thanks to my wife Stephanie. You paid the price when the pressure rose and my thoughts circled around the book. Without you, this book would not have happened. You have my love always!

About the Reviewers

Robert Curth is a simple engineer working at gutefrage.net who reviewed this book through the eyes of a Chef novice.

Julian C. Dunn is a Senior Consultant with Opscode, Inc., the developer of Chef. He has 15 years of experience in software development and infrastructure operations at companies of various sizes across industries as diverse as finance, media/broadcasting, Internet security, and advertising.

Prior to joining Opscode, Julian was a Senior Operations Engineer at SecondMarket, Inc., where he managed infrastructure in Amazon EC2 using Chef. Before SecondMarket, he worked as web operations manager at the Canadian Broadcasting Corporation where he managed content and streaming media delivery systems for Canada's largest website.

When not helping customers with automating all the things, he enjoys traveling, cycling, and stopping his cat from clawing the furniture.

Seth Vargo is a solutions engineer at Opscode, the maker of Chef. Seth created and currently leads the #learnchef campaign–a program designed to interactively teach Chef to new users. A graduate of the Carnegie Mellon Information Systems program, Seth has been a developer and systems administrator for more than 12 years. He is a proponent of open source, and is the author of popular open source tools such as powify, bootstrap_forms, strainer, fauxhai, and many Chef community cookbooks. When he's not at home in Pittsburgh, Pennsylvania, Seth is traveling and evangelizing Chef at conferences, meetup groups, and open training courses.

I'd like to thank Matthias for taking the initiative and making the effort to produce this book.

www.PacktPub.com

Support files, eBooks, discount offers, and more

You might want to visit www.PacktPub.com for support files and downloads related to your book.

Did you know that Packt offers eBook versions of every book published, with PDF and ePub files available? You can upgrade to the eBook version at www.PacktPub.com and as a print book customer, you are entitled to a discount on the eBook copy. Get in touch with us at service@packtpub.com for more details.

At www.PacktPub.com, you can also read a collection of free technical articles, sign up for a range of free newsletters and receive exclusive discounts and offers on Packt books and eBooks.

http://PacktLib.PacktPub.com

Do you need instant solutions to your IT questions? PacktLib is Packt's online digital book library. Here, you can access, read and search across Packt's entire library of books.

Why Subscribe?

- ▸ Fully searchable across every book published by Packt
- ▸ Copy and paste, print, and bookmark content
- ▸ On demand and accessible via web browser

Free Access for Packt account holders

If you have an account with Packt at www.PacktPub.com, you can use this to access PacktLib today and view nine entirely free books. Simply use your login credentials for immediate access.

Table of Contents

Preface

Irrespective of whether you're a systems administrator or a developer, if you're sick and tired of repetitive manual work and not knowing whether you may dare to reboot your server, it's time for you to get your infrastructure automated.

This book has all the required recipes to configure, deploy, and scale your servers and applications, irrespective of whether you manage five servers, 5,000 servers, or 500,000 servers.

It is a collection of easy-to-follow, step-by-step recipes showing you how to solve real-world automation challenges. Learn techniques from the pros and make sure you get your infrastructure automation project right the first time.

This book takes you on a journey through the many facets of Chef. It teaches you simple techniques as well as fully fledged real-world solutions. By looking at easily digestible examples, you'll be able to grasp the main concepts of Chef, which you'll need for automating your own infrastructure. Instead of wasting time trying to get existing community cookbooks running in your environment, you'll get ready-made code examples to get you started.

After describing how to use the basic Chef tools, the book shows you how to troubleshoot your work and explains the Chef language. Then, it shows you how to manage users, applications, and your whole cloud infrastructure. The book concludes by providing you, additional, indispensable tools and giving you an in-depth look into the Chef ecosystem.

Learn the techniques of the pros by walking through a host of step-by-step guides to solve your real-world infrastructure automation challenges.

What this book covers

Chapter 1, *Chef Infrastructure*, helps you to get started with Chef. It explains some key concepts such as cookbooks, roles, and environments and shows you how to use some basic tools such as Git, Knife, Chef Shell, Vagrant, and Berkshelf.

Chapter 2, Evaluating and Troubleshooting Cookbooks and Chef Runs, is all about getting your cookbooks right. It covers logging, debugging, as well as the why-run mode and shows you how to develop your cookbooks totally test driven.

Chapter 3, Chef Language and Style, covers additional Chef concepts such as attributes, templates, libraries, and even Light Weight Resource Providers. It shows you how to use plain old Ruby inside your recipes, and ends with writing your own Ohai and Knife plugins.

Chapter 4, Writing Better Cookbooks, shows you how to make your cookbooks more flexible. It covers ways to override attributes, use data bags and search, and to make your cookbooks idempotent. Writing cross-platform cookbooks is covered as well.

Chapter 5, Working with Files and Packages, covers powerful techniques to manage configuration files and to install and manage software packages. It tells you how to install software from source and how to manage whole directory trees.

Chapter 6, Users and Applications, shows you how to manage user accounts, securing SSH, and configuring sudo. Then, it walks you through installing complete applications such as nginx, MySQL, Wordpress, Ruby on Rails, and Varnish. It ends by showing you how to manage your own OS X workstation with Chef.

Chapter 7, Servers and Cloud Infrastructure, deals with networking and applications spanning multiple servers. You'll learn how to set up high-availability services and load-balancers and how to monitor your whole infrastructure with Nagios. Finally, it'll show you how to manage your Amazon EC2 cloud with Chef.

What you need for this book

To run the examples in this book, you'll need a computer running OS X or Ubuntu Linux 12.04. The examples will use Sublime Text (http://www.sublimetext.com/) as the editor. Make sure you've configured its command-line tool, `subl`, to follow along smoothly.

It helps if you've Ruby 1.9.3 with Bundler (http://bundler.io/) installed on your box as well.

Who this book is for

This book is for system engineers and administrators who have a fundamental understanding of information management systems and infrastructure. It helps if you've already played around with Chef; however, the book covers all the important topics you will need to know. If you don't want to dig through a whole book before you can get started, this book is for you, as it features a set of independent recipes you can try out immediately.

Conventions

In this book, you will find a number of styles of text that distinguish between different kinds of information. Here are some examples of these styles, and an explanation of their meaning.

Code words in text are shown as follows: "The Omnibus Installer will download Ruby and all required Ruby gems into /opt/chef/embedded."

A block of code is set as follows:

```
name "web_servers"
description "This role contains nodes, which act as web servers"
run_list "recipe[ntp]"
default_attributes 'ntp' => {
  'ntpdate' => {
    'disable' => true
  }
}
```

When we wish to draw your attention to a particular part of a code block, the relevant lines or items are set in bold:

```
name "web_servers"
description "This role contains nodes, which act as web servers"
run_list "recipe[ntp]"
default_attributes 'ntp' => {
  'ntpdate' => {
    'disable' => true
  }
}
```

Any command-line input or output is written as follows:

```
mma@laptop:~/chef-repo $ knife role from file web_servers.rb
```

New terms and important words are shown in bold. Words that you see on the screen, in menus or dialog boxes, for example, appear in the text like this: "Clicking the **Next** button moves you to the next screen".

Warnings or important notes appear in a box like this.

Tips and tricks appear like this.

Reader feedback

Feedback from our readers is always welcome. Let us know what you think about this book—what you liked or may have disliked. Reader feedback is important for us to develop titles that you really get the most out of.

To send us general feedback, simply send an e-mail to feedback@packtpub.com, and mention the book title via the subject of your message.

If there is a topic that you have expertise in and you are interested in either writing or contributing to a book, see our author guide on www.packtpub.com/authors.

Customer support

Now that you are the proud owner of a Packt book, we have a number of things to help you to get the most from your purchase.

Downloading the example code

You can download the example code files for all Packt books you have purchased from your account at http://www.packtpub.com. If you purchased this book elsewhere, you can visit http://www.packtpub.com/support and register to have the files e-mailed directly to you.

Errata

Although we have taken every care to ensure the accuracy of our content, mistakes do happen. If you find a mistake in one of our books—maybe a mistake in the text or the code—we would be grateful if you would report this to us. By doing so, you can save other readers from frustration and help us improve subsequent versions of this book. If you find any errata, please report them by visiting http://www.packtpub.com/submit-errata, selecting your book, clicking on the **errata submission form** link, and entering the details of your errata. Once your errata are verified, your submission will be accepted and the errata will be uploaded on our website, or added to any list of existing errata, under the Errata section of that title. Any existing errata can be viewed by selecting your title from http://www.packtpub.com/support.

Piracy

Piracy of copyright material on the Internet is an ongoing problem across all media. At Packt, we take the protection of our copyright and licenses very seriously. If you come across any illegal copies of our works, in any form, on the Internet, please provide us with the location address or website name immediately so that we can pursue a remedy.

Please contact us at `copyright@packtpub.com` with a link to the suspected pirated material.

We appreciate your help in protecting our authors, and our ability to bring you valuable content.

Questions

You can contact us at `questions@packtpub.com` if you are having a problem with any aspect of the book, and we will do our best to address it.

1

Chef Infrastructure

"What made Manhattan Manhattan was the underground infrastructure, that engineering marvel."

- Andrew Cuomo

In this chapter, we will cover the following:

- ▶ Using version control
- ▶ Installing Chef on your workstation
- ▶ Using the Hosted Chef platform
- ▶ Managing virtual machines with Vagrant
- ▶ Creating and using cookbooks
- ▶ Inspecting files on your Chef Server with Knife
- ▶ Defining cookbook dependencies
- ▶ Managing cookbook dependencies with Berkshelf
- ▶ Downloading and integrating cookbooks as vendor branches into your Git repository
- ▶ Using custom Knife plugins
- ▶ Changing organizations based on the current Git branch
- ▶ Deleting a node from the Chef Server
- ▶ Running Chef Solo
- ▶ Using roles
- ▶ Using environments
- ▶ Freezing cookbooks
- ▶ Running Chef Client as a daemon
- ▶ Using the Chef console (Chef Shell)

Introduction

This chapter will cover the basics of Chef, including common terminology, workflow practices, and various tools surrounding Chef. We will explore version control using Git, walk through working with community cookbooks, and running those cookbooks on your own servers to configure them the way you need them.

First, let's talk about the terminology used in the Chef universe.

A cookbook is a collection of recipes – codifying the actual resources, which should be installed and configured on your node – and the files and configuration templates needed.

Once you've written your cookbooks, you need a way to deploy them to the nodes you want to provision. Chef offers multiple ways for this task. The most widely used way is to use a central **Chef Server**. You can either run your own or sign up for Opscode's **Hosted Chef**.

The Chef Server is the central registry where each node needs to get registered. The Chef Server distributes the cookbooks to the nodes based on their configuration settings.

Knife is Chef's command-line tool called to interact with the Chef Server. You use it for uploading cookbooks and managing other aspects of Chef.

On your nodes, you need to install **Chef Client** – the part that retrieves the cookbooks from the Chef Server and executes them on the node.

In this chapter, we'll see the basic infrastructure components of your Chef setup at work and learn how to use the basic tools. Let's get started with having a look at how to use Git as a version control system for your cookbooks.

Using version control

Do you manually back up every file before you change it? And do you invent creative filename extensions like _me and _you when you try to collaborate on a file? If you answer yes to any of the preceding questions, it's time to rethink your process.

A **version control system** (**VCS**) helps you stay sane when dealing with important files and collaborating on them.

Using version control is a fundamental part of any infrastructure automation. There are multiple solutions (some free, some paid) for managing source version control including Git, SVN, Mercurial, and Perforce. Due to its popularity among the Chef community, we will be using Git. However, you could easily use any other version control system with Chef.

 Don't even think about building your **Infrastructure As Code** without using a version control system to manage it!

Getting ready

You'll need Git installed on your box. Either use your operating system's package manager (such as Apt on Ubuntu or Homebrew on OS X), or simply download the installer from `www.git-scm.org`.

Git is a distributed version control system. This means that you don't necessarily need a central host for storing your repositories. But in practice, using **GitHub** as your central repository has proven to be very helpful. In this book, I'll assume that you're using GitHub. Therefore, you need to go to `github.com` and create a (free) account to follow the instructions given in this book. Make sure that you upload your SSH key following the instructions at `https://help.github.com/articles/generating-ssh-keys`, so that you're able to use the SSH protocol to interact with your GitHub account.

As soon as you've created your GitHub account, you should create your repository by visiting `https://github.com/new` and using `chef-repo` as the repository name.

How to do it...

Before you can write any cookbooks, you need to set up your initial Git repository on your development box. Opscode provides an empty Chef repository to get you started. Let's see how you can set up your own Chef repository with Git using Opscode's skeleton.

1. Download Opscode's skeleton Chef repository as a tarball:

   ```
   mma@laptop $ wget http://github.com/opscode/chef-repo/tarball/
   master
   ```

   ```
   ...TRUNCATED OUTPUT...
   2013-07-05 20:54:24 (125 MB/s) - 'master' saved [9302/9302]
   ```

2. Extract the downloaded tarball:

   ```
   mma@laptop $ tar zvf master
   ```

3. Rename the directory. Replace 2c42c6a with whatever your downloaded tarball contained in its name:

   ```
   mma@laptop $ mv opscode-chef-repo-2c42c6a/ chef-repo
   ```

4. Change into your newly created Chef repository:

   ```
   mma@laptop $ cd chef-repo/
   ```

5. Initialize a fresh Git repository:

   ```
   mma@laptop:~/chef-repo $ git init .
   Initialized empty Git repository in /Users/mma/work/chef-repo/.
   git/
   ```

6. Connect your local repository to your remote repository on `github.com`. Make sure to replace `mmarschall` with your own GitHub username:

   mma@laptop:~/chef-repo $ git remote add origin git@github.com:mmarschall/chef-repo.git

7. Add and commit Opscode's default directory structure:

   mma@laptop:~/chef-repo $ git add .

   mma@laptop:~/chef-repo $ git commit -m "initial commit"

   ```
   [master (root-commit) 6148b20] initial commit
    10 files changed, 339 insertions(+), 0 deletions(-)
    create mode 100644 .gitignore
   ...TRUNCATED OUTPUT...
   create mode 100644 roles/README.md
   ```

8. Push your initialized repository to GitHub. This makes it available to all your co-workers to collaborate on it.

   mma@laptop:~/chef-repo $ git push -u origin master

   ```
   ...TRUNCATED OUTPUT...
   To git@github.com:mmarschall/chef-repo.git
    * [new branch]      master -> master
   ```

How it works...

You've downloaded a tarball containing Opscode's skeleton repository. Then, you've initialized your `chef-repo` and connected it to your own repository on GitHub.

After that, you've added all the files from the tarball to your repository and committed them. This makes Git track your files and the changes you make later.

As a last step, you've pushed your repository to GitHub, so that your co-workers can use your code too.

There's more...

Let's assume you're working on the same `chef-repo` repository together with your co-workers. They cloned your repository, added a new cookbook called `other_cookbook`, committed their changes locally, and pushed their changes back to GitHub. Now it's time for you to get the new cookbook down to your own laptop.

Pull your co-workers, changes from GitHub. This will merge their changes into your local copy of the repository.

mma@laptop:~/chef-repo $ git pull

```
From github.com:mmarschall/chef-repo
```

```
* branch            master      -> FETCH_HEAD
...TRUNCATED OUTPUT...
create mode 100644 cookbooks/other_cookbook/recipes/default.rb
```

In the case of any conflicting changes, Git will help you merge and resolve them.

See also

▶ Learn about Git basics at `http://git-scm.com/videos`

▶ Walk through the basic steps using GitHub at `https://help.github.com/categories/54/articles`

▶ The *Downloading and integrating cookbooks as vendor branches into your Git repository* section

Installing Chef on your workstation

If you want to use Chef, you'll need to install it on your local workstation first. You'll have to develop your configurations locally and use Chef to distribute them to your Chef Server.

Opscode provides a fully packaged version, which does not have any external prerequisites. This fully packaged Chef is called the **Omnibus Installer**. We'll see how to use it in this section.

Getting ready

Make sure you've curl installed on your box by following the instructions available at `http://curl.haxx.se/download.html`.

How to do it...

Let's see how to install Chef on your local workstation using Opscode's Omnibus Chef installer:

1. In your local shell, run the following command:

   ```
   mma@laptop:~/chef-repo $ curl -L https://www.opscode.com/chef/
   install.sh | sudo bash

   Downloading Chef...
   ...TRUNCATED OUTPUT...
   Thank you for installing Chef!
   ```

2. Add the newly installed Ruby to your path:

   ```
   mma@laptop:~ $ echo 'export PATH="/opt/chef/embedded/bin:$PATH"'
   >> ~/.bash_profile && source ~/.bash_profile
   ```

How it works...

The Omnibus Installer will download Ruby and all the required Ruby gems into `/opt/chef/embedded`. By adding the `/opt/chef/embedded/bin` directory to your `.bash_profile`, the Chef command-line tools will be available in your shell.

There's more...

If you already have Ruby installed in your box, you can simply install the Chef Ruby gem by running `mma@laptop:~ $ gem install chef`.

See also

▸ Find detailed instructions for OS X, Linux, and Windows at `https://learnchef.opscode.com/quickstart/workstation-setup/`.

Using the Hosted Chef platform

If you want to get started with Chef right away (without the need to install your own Chef Server) or want a third party to give you an **Service Level Agreement** (**SLA**) for your Chef Server, you can sign up for Hosted Chef by Opscode. Opscode operates Chef as a cloud service. It's quick to set up and gives you full control, using users and groups to control the access permissions to your Chef setup. We'll configure **Knife**, Chef's command-line tool to interact with Hosted Chef, so that you can start managing your nodes.

Getting ready

Before being able to use Hosted Chef, you need to sign up for the service. There is a free account for up to five nodes.

Visit `http://www.opscode.com/hosted-chef` and register for a free trial or the free account.

I registered as the user `webops` with an organization short-name of `awo`.

After registering your account, it is time to prepare your organization to be used with your `chef-repo` repository.

How to do it...

Carry out the following steps to interact with the Hosted Chef:

1. Navigate to `http://manage.opscode.com/organizations`. After logging in, you can start downloading your validation keys and configuration file.

2. Select your organization to be able to see its contents using the web UI.

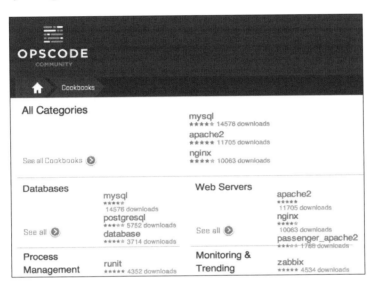

3. Regenerate the validation key for your organization and save it as `<your-organization-short-name>.pem` in the `.chef` directory inside your `chef-repo` repository.

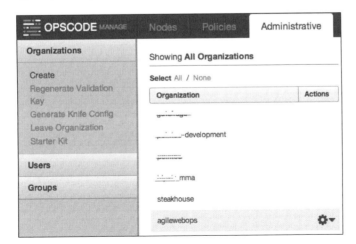

4. Generate the Knife config and put the downloaded `knife.rb` into the `.chef` directory inside your `chef-repo` directory as well. Make sure you replace `webops` with the username you chose for Hosted Chef and `awo` with the short-name you chose for your organization:

```
current_dir = File.dirname(__FILE__)
log_level                  :info
log_location               STDOUT
node_name                  "webops"
client_key                 "#{current_dir}/webops.pem"
validation_client_name     "awo-validator"
validation_key             "#{current_dir}/awo-validator.pem"
chef_server_url            "https://api.opscode.com/organizations/
awo"
cache_type                 'BasicFile'
cache_options( :path =>   "#{ENV['HOME']}/.chef/checksums" )
cookbook_path              ["#{current_dir}/../cookbooks"]
```

5. Use Knife to verify that you can connect to your hosted Chef organization. It should only have your validator client so far. Instead of `awo`, you'll see your organization's short-name:

```
mma@laptop:~/chef-repo $ knife client list

awo-validator
```

How it works...

Hosted Chef uses two private keys (called validators): one for the organization and the other for every user. You need to tell Knife where it can find these two keys in your `knife.rb` file.

The following two lines of code in your `knife.rb` file tells Knife about which organization to use and where to find its private key:

```
validation_client_name     "awo-validator"
validation_key             "#{current_dir}/awo-validator.pem"
```

The following line of code in your `knife.rb` file tells Knife about where to find your users' private key:

```
client_key                 "#{current_dir}/webops.pem"
```

And the following line of code in your `knife.rb` file tells Knife that you're using Hosted Chef. You will find your organization name as the last part of the URL:

```
chef_server_url            "https://api.opscode.com/organizations/awo"
```

Using the `knife.rb` file and your two validators Knife can now connect to your organization hosted by Opscode.

You do not need your own, self-hosted Chef Server, nor do you need to use Chef Solo in this setup.

There's more...

This setup is good for you if you do not want to worry about running, scaling, and updating your own Chef Server and if you're happy with saving all your configuration data in the cloud (under Opscode's control).

If you need to have all your configuration data within your own network boundaries, you might sign up for Private Chef, which is a fully supported and enterprise-ready version of Chef Server.

If you don't need any advanced enterprise features like role-based access control or multi-tenancy, then the open source version of Chef Server might be just right for you.

See also

  ▶ Learn more about the various Chef products at `http://www.opscode.com/chef/#which-chef`

  ▶ You can watch a screencast about how to register for Hosted Chef at `https://learnchef.opscode.com/screencasts/register-for-hosted-chef/`

Managing virtual machines with Vagrant

Developing Chef cookbooks requires you to run your work-in-progress cookbooks multiple times on your nodes. To make sure they work, you need a clean, initial state of your nodes every time you run them. You can achieve this by using **Virtual Machines** (**VM**). But manually setting up and destroying VMs is tedious and breaks your development flow.

Vagrant is a command-line tool that provides you with a configurable, reproducible, and portable development environment by enabling you to manage VMs. It lets you define and use preconfigured disk images to create new VMs. Also, you can configure Vagrant to use provisioners such as Shell scripts, Puppet, or Chef to bring your VM into the desired state.

In this recipe, we will see how to use Vagrant to manage VMs using VirtualBox and Chef Client as the provisioner.

Getting ready

Download and install VirtualBox at `https://www.virtualbox.org/wiki/Downloads`.

Download and install Vagrant at `http://downloads.vagrantup.com/`.

Install the Vagrant Omnibus plugin to enable Vagrant to install Chef Client on your VM by running the following commands:

```
mma@laptop:~/chef-repo $ vagrant plugin install vagrant-omnibus

    Installing the 'vagrant-omnibus' plugin. This can take a few
    minutes...
    Installed the plugin 'vagrant-omnibus (1.1.0)'!
```

How to do it...

Let's create and boot a virtual node by using Vagrant:

1. Visit `https://github.com/opscode/bento` and choose a Vagrant box for basing your VMs on. We'll use `opscode-ubuntu-12.04` in this example.

2. The URL of the `opscode-ubuntu-12.04` box is `https://opscode-vm-bento.s3.amazonaws.com/vagrant/opscode_ubuntu-12.04_provisionerless.box`.

3. Edit your new `Vagrantfile`. Make sure that you replace `<YOUR-ORG>` with the name of your organization on the Chef Server. Use the name and URL of the box file you noted down in the first step as `config.vm.box` and `config.vm.box_url`:

    ```
    mma@laptop:~/chef-repo $ subl Vagrantfile
    ```

    ```
    Vagrant.configure("2") do |config|
      config.vm.box = "opscode-ubuntu-12.04"
      config.vm.box_url = https://opscode-vm-bento.s3.amazonaws.com/
    vagrant/opscode_ubuntu-12.04_provisionerless.box
      config.omnibus.chef_version = :latest

      config.vm.provision :chef_client do |chef|
        chef.provisioning_path = "/etc/chef"
        chef.chef_server_url = "https://api.opscode.com/
    organizations/<YOUR_ORG>"
        chef.validation_key_path = "/.chef/<YOUR_ORG>-validator.pem"
        chef.validation_client_name = "<YOUR_ORG>-validator"
        chef.node_name = "server"
      end
    end
    ```

4. Create your virtual node using Vagrant:

```
mma@laptop:~/chef-repo $ vagrant up

Bringing machine 'server' up with 'virtualbox' provider...
...TRUNCATED OUTPUT...
[server] Importing base box 'opscode-ubuntu-12.04'...
...TRUNCATED OUTPUT...
[server] Installing Chef 11.4.4 Omnibus package...
[server] Running provisioner: chef_client...
Creating folder to hold client key...
Uploading chef client validation key...
Generating chef JSON and uploading...
Running chef-client...
  [2013-05-27T20:06:04+00:00] INFO: *** Chef 11.4.4 ***
...TRUNCATED OUTPUT...
```

5. Log in to your virtual node using SSH:

```
mma@laptop:~/chef-repo $ vagrant ssh

Welcome to Ubuntu 12.04.2 LTS (GNU/Linux 3.5.0-23-generic x86_64)

 * Documentation:  https://help.ubuntu.com/
Last login: Wed Apr 24 07:30:09 2013 from 10.0.2.2
vagrant@server:~$
```

How it works...

The `Vagrantfile` is written in a Ruby **Domain Specific Language** (**DSL**) for configuring the Vagrant virtual machines. We want to boot a simple Ubuntu VM. Let's go through the `Vagrantfile` step-by-step.

First, we create a `config` object. Vagrant will use this `config` object to configure the VM:

```
Vagrant.configure("2") do |config|
  ...
end
```

Inside the `config` block, we tell Vagrant which VM image to use, in order to boot the node:

```
config.vm.box = "opscode-ubuntu-12.04"
config.vm.box_url = "https://opscode-vm-bento.s3.amazonaws.com/
vagrant/opscode_ubuntu-12.04_provisionerless.box"
```

We want to boot our VM using a so-called Bento Box provided by Opscode. We use Ubuntu version 12.04 here.

 If you have never used the box before, Vagrant will download the image file (a few hundred megabytes) when you run `vagrant up` for the first time.

As we want our VM to have Chef Client installed, we tell the Vagrant Omnibus plugin to use the latest version of Chef Client:

```
config.omnibus.chef_version = :latest
```

After selecting the VM image to boot, we configure how to provision the box using Chef. The Chef configuration happens in a nested Ruby block:

```
config.vm.provision :chef_client do |chef|
...
end
```

Inside this chef block, we need to instruct Vagrant on how to hook up our virtual node to the Chef Server. First, we need to tell Vagrant where to store all the Chef stuff on your node:

```
chef.provisioning_path = "/etc/chef"
```

Vagrant needs to know the API endpoint of your Chef Server. If you use Hosted Chef, it is `https://api.opscode.com/organizations/<YOUR_ORG>`. You need to replace `<YOUR_ORG>` with the name of the organization you created in your account on Hosted Chef. If you are using your own Chef Server, change the URL accordingly:

```
chef.chef_server_url = "https://api.opscode.com/
organizations/<YOUR_ORG>"
```

While creating your organization on Hosted Chef, you must have downloaded your private key. Tell Vagrant where to find this file:

```
chef.validation_key_path = /.chef/<YOUR_ORG>-validator.pem"
```

Also, you need to tell Vagrant as which client it should validate itself against the Chef Server:

```
chef.validation_client_name = "<YOUR_ORG>-validator"
```

Finally, you should tell Vagrant how to name your node:

```
chef.node_name = "server"
```

After configuring your `Vagrantfile`, all you need to do is run the basic Vagrant commands like `vagrant up`, `vagrant provision`, and `vagrant ssh`. To stop your VM, just run the `vagrant halt` command.

There's more...

If you want to start from scratch again, you will have to destroy your VM as well as delete both the client and the node from your Chef Server by running the following commands:

```
mma@laptop:~/chef-repo $ vagrant destroy
```

```
mma@laptop:~/chef-repo $ knife node delete server -y && knife client delete server -y
```

Alternatively, you may use the Vagrant Butcher plugin found at `https://github.com/cassianoleal/vagrant-butcher`.

See also

- ▶ Find the Vagrant documentation at `http://docs.vagrantup.com/v2/getting-started/index.html`
- ▶ You can use a Vagrant plugin for VMware instead of VirtualBox and find it at `http://www.vagrantup.com/vmware`
- ▶ You can use a Vagrant plugin for Amazon AWS instead of VirtualBox and find the same at `https://github.com/mitchellh/vagrant-aws`

Creating and using cookbooks

Cookbooks are an essential part of Chef. You can easily create them using Knife, Chef's command-line tool. In this section (and many of the following sections), I will assume that you're using a Chef Server to manage your infrastructure. You can either set up your own or use the Hosted Chef as described previously.

In this section, we'll create and apply a simple cookbook using Knife.

Getting ready

Make sure you've Chef installed and a node available for testing. Check out the installation instructions at `http://learnchef.com` if you need help here.

Edit your `knife.rb` file and add the following three lines to it, filling in your own values:

```
cookbook_copyright "your company"
cookbook_license "apachev2"
cookbook_email "your email address"
```

The Apache 2 license is the most commonly found in cookbooks, but you're free to choose whichever suits your needs. If you put none as the `cookbook_license`, Knife will put "All rights reserved" into your recipe's metadata file.

Knife will use the preceding values as default whenever you create a new cookbook.

How to do it...

Carry out the following steps to create and use cookbooks:

1. Create a cookbook by running the following with the name `my_cookbook`:

   mma@laptop:~/chef-repo $ knife cookbook create my_cookbook

   ```
   ** Creating cookbook my_cookbook
   ** Creating README for cookbook: my_cookbook
   ** Creating CHANGELOG for cookbook: my_cookbook
   ** Creating metadata for cookbook: my_cookbook
   ```

2. Upload your new cookbook to the Chef Server:

   mma@laptop:~/chef-repo $ knife cookbook upload my_cookbook

   ```
   Uploading my_cookbook      [0.1.0]
   Uploaded 1 cookbook.
   ```

3. Add the your node's run list. In this example, the name of the node is `server`:

   mma@laptop:~/chef-repo $ knife node run_list add server recipe[my_cookbook]

   ```
   server:
     run_list:  recipe[my_cookbook]
   ```

4. Run Chef Client on your node:

   user@server:~$ sudo chef-client

How it works...

Knife is the command-line interface for the Chef Server. It uses the RESTful API exposed by the Chef Server to do its work and helps you to interact with the Chef Server.

The `knife` command supports a host of commands structured like the following:

```
knife <subject> <command>
```

The `<subject>` used in this section is either a `cookbook` or a `node`. The commands we use are `create` or `upload` for the cookbook, and `run_list add` for the node.

See also

► The *Using the Hosted Chef platform* section

Inspecting files on your Chef Server with Knife

Sometimes, you may want to peek into the files stored on your Chef Server. You might not be sure about an implementation detail of that specific cookbook version, which is currently installed on your Chef Server, and would want to look it up. Knife can help you out by letting you show various aspects of the files stored on your Chef Server.

Getting ready

Make sure you have the `iptables` cookbook installed locally and uploaded to your Chef Server.

1. Install the `iptables` community cookbook by executing the following command:

    ```
    mma@laptop:~/work/chef_helpster $ knife cookbook site install
    iptables
    ```

    ```
    Installing iptables to /Users/mma/work/chef-repo/cookbooks
    ...TRUNCATED OUTPUT...
    ```

2. Upload the `iptables` cookbook to your Chef Server by executing the following command:

    ```
    mma@laptop:~/work/chef_helpster $ knife cookbook
    ```

    ```
    Uploading iptables        [0.12.0]
    Uploaded 1 cookbook.
    ```

How to do it...

Let's find out how Knife can help you to look into a cookbook stored on your Chef Server:

1. First, you want to find out the current version of the cookbook you're interested in. In our case, we're interested in the `iptables` cookbook:

    ```
    mma@laptop:~/work/chef_helpster $ knife cookbook show iptables
    ```

    ```
    iptables    0.12.0
    ```

2. Then, you can look up the definitions of the `iptables` cookbook:

```
mma@laptop:~/work/chef_helpster $ knife cookbook show iptables
0.12.0 definitions
```

```
checksum:      189188109499d68612a5b95b6809b580
name:          iptables_rule.rb
path:          definitions/iptables_rule.rb
specificity:   default
url:           https://s3.amazonaws.com/opscode-platform...
```

3. Now, you can even show the contents of the `iptables_rule.rb` definition file as stored on the Chef Server:

```
mma@laptop:~/work/chef_helpster $ knife cookbook show iptables
0.12.0 definitions iptables_rule.rb
```

```
#
# Cookbook Name:: iptables
# Definition:: iptables_rule
#
#
define :iptables_rule, :enable => true, :source => nil, :variables
=> {} do
...TRUNCATED OUTPUT...
end
```

How it works...

The `knife show` sub-command helps you understand what exactly is stored on the Chef Server. It let's you drill down into specific sections of your cookbooks and see the exact content of the files stored on your Chef Server.

There's more...

Using Chef 11, you can pass patterns to the `knife show` command to tell it what exactly you want to see. Showing the contents of the `iptables_rule` definition can be done like this, in addition to the way we used previously:

```
mma@laptop:~/work/chef_helpster $ knife show cookbooks/iptables/
definitions/*
```

```
cookbooks/iptables/definitions/iptables_rule.rb:
#
# Cookbook Name:: iptables
# Definition:: iptables_rule
#
#
```

```
define :iptables_rule, :enable => true, :source => nil, :variables =>
{} do
...TRUNCATED OUTPUT...
end
```

See also

▶ To find some more examples on `knife show`, visit `http://docs.opscode.com/knife_show.html`

Defining cookbook dependencies

Quite often, you might want to use features of other cookbooks in your own cookbooks. For example, if you want to make sure that all packages required for compiling the C software are installed, you might want to include the `build-essential` cookbook that does just that. When using Chef Server, it needs to know about such dependencies in your cookbooks. You need to declare them in the cookbook's metadata.

Getting ready

Make sure you've a cookbook named `my_cookbook` and the `run_list` command of your node includes `my_cookbook`, as described in the *Creating and using cookbooks* recipe.

How to do it...

Edit the metadata of your cookbook in the file `cookbooks/my_cookbook/metadata.rb` to add a dependency to the `build-essential` cookbook:

```
mma@laptop:~/chef-repo $ subl cookbooks/my_cookbook/metadata.rb

...
depends 'build-essential'
depends 'apache2', '>= 1.0.4'
```

How it works...

If you want to use a feature of another cookbook inside your cookbook, you will need to include the other cookbook in your recipe.

```
include_recipe 'build-essential'
```

To tell the Chef Server that your cookbook requires the `build-essential` cookbook, you need to declare that dependency in the `metadata.rb` file. If you've uploaded all the dependencies on your Chef Server, the Chef Server will then send all the required cookbooks to the node.

Declaring dependencies is not necessary, if you're using Chef Solo.

The first `depends` call tells the Chef Server that your cookbook depends on the latest version of the `build-essential` cookbook.

The second `depends` call tells the Chef Server that your cookbook depends on a version of the `apache2` cookbook, which is greater or equal to the version `1.0.4`. You may use any of these version constraints with your depends calls:

- `<` (less than)
- `<=` (less than or equal to)
- `=` (equal to)
- `>=` (greater than or equal to)
- `~>` (approximately greater than)
- `>` (greater than)

There's more...

If you're using the `foodcritic` gem and include another recipe inside your recipe, without declaring the cookbook dependency in your `metadata.rb` file, `foodcritic` will warn you:

mma@laptop:~/chef-repo $ foodcritic my_cookbook

```
FC007: Ensure recipe dependencies are reflected in cookbook metadata:
cookbooks/my_cookbook/recipes/default.rb:9
```

Additionally, you can declare conflicting cookbooks through the `conflicts` call:

```
conflicts "nginx"
```

Of course, you can use version constraints exactly the way you did with `depends`.

See also

- The *Inspecting files on your Chef Server with Knife* section
- Find out how to use `foodcritic` in the *Flagging problems in your Chef cookbooks* section in *Chapter 2, Evaluating and Troubleshooting Cookbooks and Chef Runs*

Managing cookbook dependencies with Berkshelf

It's a pain to manually ensure that you've installed all the cookbooks, which another cookbook depends on. You've to download each and every one of them manually only to find out that with each downloaded cookbook, you inherit another set of dependent cookbooks.

And even if you use `knife cookbook site install`, which installs all the dependencies locally for you, your cookbook directory and your repository get cluttered with all those cookbooks. Usually, you don't really care about all those cookbooks and don't want to see or even manage them.

This is where Berkshelf comes into play. It works like Bundler for Ruby gems, managing cookbook dependencies for you. It downloads all the defined dependencies recursively.

Instead of polluting your Chef repository, it stores all the cookbooks in a central location. You just commit your Berkshelf dependency file (called `Berksfile`) to your repository, and every colleague or build server can download and install all those dependent cookbooks based on it.

Let's see how to use Berkshelf to manage the dependencies of your cookbook.

Getting ready

Make sure you've a cookbook named `my_cookbook` and the `run_list` of your node includes `my_cookbook` as described in the *Creating and using cookbooks* section.

How to do it...

Berkshelf helps you to keep those utility cookbooks out of your Chef repository. This makes it much easier to maintain the cookbooks, which really matter.

Let's see how to write a cookbook running a bunch of utility recipes and manage the required cookbooks with Berkshelf:

1. Create a `Gemfile` containing the `berkshelf` gem:

   ```
   mma@laptop:~/chef-repo $ subl Gemfile

   source 'https://rubygems.org'
   gem 'berkshelf'
   ```

2. Run Bundler to install the gem:

   ```
   mma@laptop:~/chef-repo $ bundler install

   Fetching gem metadata from https://rubygems.org/
   ...TRUNCATED OUTPUT...
   ```

```
Installing berkshelf (2.0.7)
Using bundler (1.3.5)
Your bundle is complete!
```

3. Edit your cookbook's metadata:

mma@laptop:~/chef-repo $ subl cookbooks/my_cookbook/metadata.rb

```
...
depends "chef-client"
depends "apt"
depends "ntp"
```

4. Edit your cookbook's default recipe:

mma@laptop:~/chef-repo $ subl cookbooks/my_cookbook/recipes/default.rb

```
...
include_recipe "chef-client"
include_recipe "apt"
include_recipe "ntp"
```

5. Create your `Berksfile`:

mma@laptop:~/chef-repo $ subl Berksfile

```
site :opscode

metadata
```

6. Run Berkshelf to install all the required cookbooks:

mma@laptop:~/chef-repo $ cd cookbooks/my_cookbook

mma@laptop:~/chef-repo/cookbooks/my_cookbook $ berks install

```
Using my_cookbook (0.1.0) from metadata
Installing chef-client (3.0.4) from site: 'http://cookbooks.
opscode.com/api/v1/cookbooks'
Installing cron (1.2.4) from site: 'http://cookbooks.opscode.com/
api/v1/cookbooks'
Installing apt (2.0.0) from site: 'http://cookbooks.opscode.com/
api/v1/cookbooks'
Installing ntp (1.3.2) from site: 'http://cookbooks.opscode.com/
api/v1/cookbooks'
```

7. Upload all the cookbooks on the Chef Server:

mma@laptop:~/chef-repo/cookbooks/my_cookbook $ berks upload

```
Using my_cookbook (0.1.0)
...TRUNCATED OUTPUT...
Uploading ntp (1.3.2) to: 'https://api.opscode.com:443/
organizations/agilewebops'
```

How it works...

Berkshelf comes as a Ruby gem, which we need to install first.

Then, we create our cookbook and tell it to use a few other cookbooks.

Instead of manually installing all the cookbooks using `knife cookbook site install`, we create a Berksfile besides the `metadata.rb` file.

The `Berksfile` is pretty simple. We tell Berkshelf to use the Opscode community site as the default source for all cookbooks:

```
site :opscode
```

And we tell Berkshelf to read the `metadata.rb` file to find all the required cookbooks. This is the simplest way when working inside a single cookbook. Please see the following *There's more...* section to find an example of a more advanced usage of the `Berksfile`.

After telling Berkshelf where to find all the required cookbook names, we use it to install all those cookbooks:

berks install

Berkshelf stores cookbooks in `~/.berkshelf/cookbooks` by default. This keeps your Chef repository clutter free. Instead of having to manage all the required cookbooks inside your own Chef repository, Berkshelf takes care of them. You simply need to check in `Berksfile` with your cookbook, and everyone using your cookbook can download all the required cookbooks using Berkshelf.

To make sure that there's no mix-up with different cookbook versions when sharing your cookbook, Berkshelf creates a file called `Berksfile.lock` alongside `Berksfile`. There you'll find the exact versions of all the cookbooks that Berkshelf installed:

```
{
  "sha": "b7d5bda18ccfaffe88a7b547420c670b8f922ff1",
  "sources": {
    "my_cookbook": {
      "path": "."
    },
    "chef-client": {
      "locked_version": "3.0.4"
    },
    "cron": {
      "locked_version": "1.2.4"
    },
    "apt": {
      "locked_version": "2.0.0"
    },
```

```
      "ntp": {
        "locked_version": "1.3.2"
      }
    }
  }
}
```

Berkshelf will only use the exact versions specified in the `Berksfile.lock` file, if it finds this file.

Finally, we use Berkshelf to upload all the required cookbooks on the Chef Server:

```
berks upload
```

There's more...

Berkshelf integrates tightly with Vagrant via the `vagrant-berkshelf` plugin. You can set up Berkshelf and Vagrant in such a way that Berkshelf installs and uploads all the required cookbooks on your Chef Server whenever you execute `vagrant up` or `vagrant provision`. You'll save all the work of running `berks install` and `berks upload` manually before creating your node with Vagrant.

Let's see how you can integrate Berkshelf and Vagrant.

First, you need to install the Berkshelf plugin for Vagrant:

```
mma@mma-mbp:~/work/chef-repo (master)$ vagrant plugin install vagrant-berkshelf

    Installing the 'vagrant-berkshelf' plugin. This can take a few
    minutes...
    Installed the plugin 'vagrant-berkshelf (1.3.2)'!
```

Then, you need to tell Vagrant that you want to use the plugin. You do this by enabling the plugin in your `Vagrantfile`:

```
mma@mma-mbp:~/work/chef-repo (master)$ subl Vagrantfile

    ...
    config.berkshelf.enabled = true
    ...
```

Then, you need a `Berksfile` in the root directory of your Chef repository, to tell Berkshelf which cookbooks to install on each Vagrant run:

```
    cookbook 'my_cookbook', path: 'cookbooks/my_cookbook'
```

Eventually, you can start your VM using Vagrant. Berkshelf will first download and install all the required cookbooks in the Berkshelf, and upload them to the Chef Server. Only after all the cookbooks are made available on the Chef Server by Berkshelf, will Vagrant go on:

```
mma@mma-mbp:~/work/chef-repo $ vagrant up

    Bringing machine 'server' up with 'virtualbox' provider...
    ...TRUNCATED OUTPUT...
     [Berkshelf] Uploading cookbooks to 'https://api.opscode.com/
    organizations/agilewebops'
    ...TRUNCATED OUTPUT...
```

This way, using Berkshelf together with Vagrant, you save a lot of manual steps and get faster cycle times for your cookbook development.

See also

▸ For the full documentation of Berkshelf, please visit `http://berkshelf.com/`

▸ Please find the Berkshelf source code at: `https://github.com/RiotGames/berkshelf`

▸ Please find the Vagrant Berkshelf plugin source code at: `https://github.com/riotgames/vagrant-berkshelf`

▸ The *Managing virtual machines with Vagrant* section

Downloading and integrating cookbooks as vendor branches into your Git repository

The Opscode community offers a wide variety of ready-made cookbooks for many major software packages. They're a great starting point for your own infrastructure. But, usually you need to modify these cookbooks to suit your needs. Modifying your local copy of a community cookbook leaves you in the dilemma of not being able to update to the latest version of the community cookbook without losing your local changes.

Getting ready

You'll need to make sure that your local Git repository is clean and does not have any uncommitted changes:

```
mma@laptop:~/chef-repo $ git status

    # On branch master
    nothing to commit (working directory clean)
```

How to do it...

Carry out the following steps:

1. Go to `http://community.opscode.com/cookbooks` and search for the cookbook you need. In our example, we will use the **mysql** cookbook, which is featured right there on top under the **All Categories** list as well as above the **Databases** section. All we need is to note down the exact name of the cookbook in this case it's simply `mysql`.

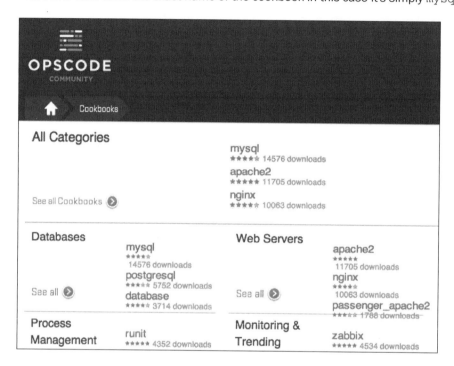

2. Use Knife to pull down the cookbook and to integrate it with your local repository:

   ```
   mma@laptop:~/chef-repo $ knife cookbook site install mysql

   Installing mysql to /Users/mma/work/chef-repo/cookbooks
   ...TRUNCATED OUTPUT...
   Cookbook build-essential version 1.2.0 successfully installed
   ```

3. Verify the downloaded cookbooks:

   ```
   mma@laptop:~/chef-repo $ cd cookbooks

   mma@laptop:~/chef-repo/cookbooks $ ls -l

   total 8
   -rw-r--r--   1 mma   staff   3064 23 Nov 22:02 README.md
   ```

```
drwxr-xr-x  12 mma    staff    408 28 Nov 20:40 build-essential
drwxr-xr-x  13 mma    staff    442 28 Nov 20:34 my_cookbook
drwxr-xr-x  15 mma    staff    510 28 Nov 20:39 mysql
drwxr-xr-x   7 mma    staff    238 28 Nov 20:39 openssl
```

4. Validate the Git status:

    mma@laptop:~/chef-repo/cookbooks $ git status

    ```
    # On branch master
    # Your branch is ahead of 'origin/master' by 3 commits.
    #
    nothing to commit (working directory clean)
    ```

5. You might have noticed that your local branch has received three commits. Let's have a look at those:

    mma@laptop:~/chef-repo/cookbooks $ git log

    ```
    commit 766bd4098184f4d188c75daa49e12abb5b1fd360
    Author: Matthias Marschall <mm@agileweboperations.com>
    Date:   Wed Nov 28 20:40:01 2012 +0100
    commit 766bd4098184f4d188c75daa49e12abb5b1fd360
    Author: Matthias Marschall <mm@agileweboperations.com>
    Date:   Wed Nov 28 20:40:01 2012 +0100


        Import build-essential version 1.2.0


    commit 6ad70f1fbbb96df1fc55c3237966c60d156d6026
    Author: Matthias Marschall <mm@agileweboperations.com>
    Date:   Wed Nov 28 20:39:59 2012 +0100


        Import openssl version 1.0.0


    commit d03dd06f3c931078c2a9943a493955780e39bf22
    Author: Matthias Marschall <mm@agileweboperations.com>
    Date:   Wed Nov 28 20:39:58 2012 +0100


        Import mysql version 2.0.2
    ```

The `knife` command successfully downloaded and imported the `mysql` cookbook as well as its dependencies: the `build-essential` and `openssl` cookbooks.

How it works...

Knife executes a set of commands to download the desired cookbook and to integrate it with your local repository.

Let's have a look at the output of the `knife cookbook site install` command again and go through it step-by-step.

First, the command makes sure that you're on the master branch of your repository:

```
Checking out the master branch.
```

The next step is to create a new vendor branch for the `mysql` cookbook if none exists so far:

```
Creating pristine copy branch chef-vendor-mysql.
```

Then it downloads the tarball, removes any older version, uncompresses the new tarball, and removes it after successfully extracting its contents into a new cookbook directory:

```
Downloading mysql from the cookbooks site at version 2.0.2 to /Users/
mma/work/chef-repo/cookbooks/mysql.tar.gz
Cookbook saved: /Users/mma/work/chef-repo/cookbooks/mysql.tar.gz
Removing pre-existing version.
Uncompressing mysql version 2.0.2.
Removing downloaded tarball
```

Now, it's time to commit the newly extracted files to the vendor branch:

```
1 files updated, committing changes
```

Finally, it tags it with the current version of the cookbook:

```
Creating tag cookbook-site-imported-mysql-2.0.2
```

The `knife cookbook site install` command executes all the previous mentioned steps for all the cookbooks the desired cookbook depends on, by default.

Eventually, you end up with a separate branch, the so-called vendor branch, for every downloaded cookbook integrated into your master branch and nicely tagged. This approach enables you to change whatever you like in your master branch and still pull down newer versions of the community cookbook. Git will automatically merge both the versions or will ask you to remove conflicts manually; all the standard Git procedures.

Downloading the example code

You can download the example code files for all Packt books you have purchased from your account at http://www.packtpub.com. If you purchased this book elsewhere, you can visit http://www.packtpub.com/support and register to have the files e-mailed directly to you.

There's more...

If you want to integrate the desired cookbook into another branch, use the `--branch`
`BRANCH_NAME` parameter.

```
mma@laptop:~/chef-repo [experimental] $ knife cookbook site install mysql
--branch experimental
    Installing mysql to /Users/mma/work/chef-repo/cookbooks
    Checking out the experimental branch.
    Pristine copy branch (chef-vendor-mysql) exists, switching to it.
    Downloading mysql from the cookbooks site at version 2.0.2 to /Users/
    mma/work/chef-repo/cookbooks/mysql.tar.gz
    Cookbook saved: /Users/mma/work/chef-repo/cookbooks/mysql.tar.gz
    Removing pre-existing version.
    Uncompressing mysql version 2.0.2.
    removing downloaded tarball
    No changes made to mysql
    Checking out the experimental branch.
    ...TRUNCATED OUTPUT...
```

As you can see, instead of checking out the master branch, the `knife cookbook site
install` command uses the experimental branch now.

You can use the `-D` switch when running the command to avoid downloading all the
cookbooks your desired cookbook depends on.

```
mma@laptop:~/chef-repo $ knife cookbook site install mysql -D
    Installing mysql to /Users/mma/work/chef-repo/cookbooks
    Checking out the master branch.
    Pristine copy branch (chef-vendor-mysql) exists, switching to it.
    Downloading mysql from the cookbooks site at version 2.0.2 to /Users/
    mma/work/chef-repo/cookbooks/mysql.tar.gz
    Cookbook saved: /Users/mma/work/chef-repo/cookbooks/mysql.tar.gz
    Removing pre-existing version.
    Uncompressing mysql version 2.0.2.
    removing downloaded tarball
    No changes made to mysql
    Checking out the master branch.
```

You see that the command stopped after dealing with the `mysql` cookbook. It did not get
the other cookbooks yet.

See also

▸ You can use Berkshelf to manage cookbooks and their dependencies for you, which makes the preceding approach obsolete. See the *Managing cookbook dependencies with Berkshelf* section.

Using custom Knife plugins

Knife comes with a set of commands out of the box. The built-in commands deal with the basic elements of Chef like cookbooks, roles, data bags, and so on. But, it would be nice to use Knife for more than just the basic stuff. Fortunately, Knife comes with a plugin API, and there are already a host of useful Knife plugins built by Opscode and the Chef community.

Getting ready

Make sure that you've Bundler installed on your local workstation:

```
mma@laptop:~/chef-repo $ gem install bundler

    Fetching: bundler-1.3.5.gem (100%)
    Successfully installed bundler-1.3.5
    1 gem installed
```

Make sure you've got an account at Amazon AWS if you want to follow along and try out the knife-ec2 plugin. There are Knife plugins available for most cloud providers. Go through the *There's more...* section of this section for the list.

How to do it...

Let's see which Knife plugins are available, and try to use one for managing Amazon EC2 instances:

1. List the Knife plugins that are shipped as Ruby gems:

```
mma@laptop:~/chef-repo $ gem search -r knife-

*** REMOTE GEMS ***
knife-audit (0.2.0)
knife-azure (1.0.2)
...TRUNCATED OUTPUT...
knife-ec2 (0.6.4)
...TRUNCATED OUTPUT...
```

2. Create a Gemfile containing the EC2 plugin:

```
mma@laptop:~/chef-repo $ subl Gemfile
```

```
source 'https://rubygems.org'
gem 'knife-ec2', '~>0.6.4'
```

3. Install the EC2 plugin for managing servers in the Amazon AWS cloud:

```
mma@laptop:~/chef-repo $ bundle install
```

```
Fetching gem metadata from https://rubygems.org/
...TRUNCATED OUTPUT...
Installing knife-ec2 (0.6.4)
Using bundler (1.3.5)
Your bundle is complete!
```

4. List all the available instance types in AWS using the `knife ec2` plugin. Please use your own AWS credentials instead of XXX and YYYYY:

```
mma@laptop:~/chef-repo $ knife ec2 flavor list --aws-access-key-id
XXX --aws-secret-access-key YYYYY
```

ID	Name	Arch	RAM
Disk	Cores		
c1.medium	High-CPU Medium	32-bit	
1740.8	350 GB	5	
...TRUNCATED OUTPUT...			
m2.xlarge	High-Memory Extra Large	64-bit	
17510.	420 GB	6.5	
t1.micro	Micro Instance	0-bit	613
0 GB	2		

How it works...

Knife looks for plugins at various places.

First, it looks into the `.chef` directory located inside your current Chef repository, to find the plugins specific to this repository:

```
./.chef/plugins/knife/
```

Then, it looks into the `.chef` directory located in your home directory, to find the plugins that you want to use in all your Chef repositories:

```
~/.chef/plugins/knife/
```

Finally, it looks for installed gems. Knife will load all the code from any `chef/knife/` directory found in your installed Ruby gems. This is the most common way of using plugins developed by Opscode or the Chef community.

There's more...

There are Knife plugins for most of the major cloud providers as well as for most of the major virtualization technologies.

At the time of the writing of this book, the following cloud providers were supported by Knife plugins:

- ▶ Microsoft Azure
- ▶ BlueBox
- ▶ Brightbox
- ▶ Amazon EC2
- ▶ Eucalyptus
- ▶ HP Cloud Services
- ▶ OpenStack
- ▶ Rackspace Cloud
- ▶ Terremark
- ▶ VSphere
- ▶ Apache CloudStack

Virtualization technologies supported by Knife plugins are listed as follows:

- ▶ KVM
- ▶ VMware ESX
- ▶ Vagrant
- ▶ Xenserver

See also

- ▶ The *Creating custom Knife plugins* recipe in *Chapter 2, Evaluating and Troubleshooting Cookbooks and Chef Runs*
- ▶ Find a list of supported cloud providers at `http://docs.opscode.com/plugin_knife.html`

Changing organizations based on the current Git branch

Chef has this notion of environments to separate, for example, a staging environment from a production environment. You can define specific cookbook versions to be used only in a specific environment and a few more things.

But for development, you might want to give everyone a separate organization on Hosted Chef, to make sure that no one is stepping on one another's toes while doing heavy refactoring. This is not possible by solely using the environments feature.

 Please note that this is not a condoned behavior and has proven to be difficult to manage. It fails for many companies supported directly by Opscode. But, if this is the way to go for you, here you'll learn how.

If you're using separate organizations for each developer, you can automate choosing the right organization, by making your `knife.rb` aware of your current Git branch. I assume that you use the `master` branch for maintaining your production-ready cookbooks and the `development` branch for playing around with your stuff.

Let's see how to let Knife autoselect the correct organization.

Getting ready

Additionally to your default organization in your Hosted Chef account, you need to create a new organization for every totally sandboxed environment.

1. Create a new organization called `YOUR_ORG-development`, for example, `awo-development`, using the Opscode management console at `http://manage.opscode.com`.

2. Create a separate Git branch named `development`:

   mma@laptop:~/chef-repo $ git checkout -b development

   mma@laptop:~/chef-repo $ subl Gemfile

   ```
   ...
   gem 'grit'
   ```

3. Run Bundler to install the Grit gem:

   mma@laptop:~/chef-repo $ bundle install

   ```
   ...TRUNCATED OUTPUT...
   Installing grit (2.5.0)
   ```

How to do it...

Let's create a `knife.rb` file, which evaluates your current Git branch and switches the Hosted Chef organization accordingly.

1. Put the following lines at the top of your `knife.rb` file. Replace `"awo"` with the value you used for `YOUR_ORG` while getting ready:

   ```
   organization_base_name = "awo"
   require 'grit'
   ```

```
repository = Grit::Repo.new(Dir.pwd)
current_branch = Grit::Head.current(repository).name
organization = organization_base_name
organization << "-#{current_branch}" unless current_branch ==
'master'
```

2. Make sure that you set the `chef_server_url` correctly:

    ```
    chef_server_url          "https://api.opscode.com/
    organizations/#{organization}"
    ```

3. Run the `knife` command off your Git master branch, replacing `"awo"` with your chosen short-name for your organization:

    mma@laptop:~/chef-repo $ knife node list

    ```
    awo
    ```

4. Switch to your development branch:

    mma@laptop:~/chef-repo $ git checkout development

5. And, run the `knife` command again:

    mma@laptop:~/chef-repo [development]$ knife node list

    ```
    awo-development
    ```

How it works...

To be able to use `grit` for getting the current branch name, we require the `grit` gem.

Next, we instantiate a `Grit::Repo` object from the current working directory. We then use this `Grit::Repo` object to retrieve the current branch. From the current branch, simply take the name and store it in the `current_branch` variable.

Now, it's time to set our organization name to the name of our default organization.

After that, we amend the organization name with a - symbol along with the branch name, unless the branch name equals master. This means that if we're currently in the master branch, Knife will use our default organization (without any suffix). If it is on a `git` branch, it will attach the suffix `-branch_name` to our organization name.

Further down, we use the constructed organization name to connect to the Chef Server by calling `chef_server_url`:

```
chef_server_url          "https://api.opscode.com/
organizations/#{organization}"
```

There's more...

Your `knife.rb` file is a plain Ruby file. You can put any Ruby code inside it using any gems you want.

To be a little more flexible, we made our `knife.rb` file even read an environment variable, `CHEF_ORG`, which overrides the `git` branch magic:

```
organization = ENV['CHEF_ORG'] || begin
  require 'grit'
  repository = Grit::Repo.new(Dir.pwd)
  current_branch = Grit::Head.current(repository).name
  chef_org = "awo"
  chef_org << "-#{current_branch}" unless current_branch == 'master'
  chef_org
end
```

As long as you don't set the environment variable `CHEF_ORG`, everything works as before. But if you call Knife in the following manner, it will use the given environment variable as the organization name directly.

```
mma@laptop:~/chef-repo $ CHEF_ORG=experimental knife node list
  experimental
```

See also

▸ The *Using the Hosted Chef platform* section

Deleting a node from the Chef Server

Bootstrapping a node not only installs Chef on that node but also creates a client object on the Chef Server as well. The client object is used by the Chef Client to authenticate against the Chef Server on each run.

Additionally to registering a client, a node object is created. The node object is the main data structure, which is used by the Chef Client to converge the node to the desired state.

Getting ready

Make sure you've at least one node registered at your Chef Server, which is safe to remove.

How to do it...

Let's delete the node and the client object to completely remove your node from the Chef Server.

1. Delete the node object:

   mma@laptop:~/chef-repo $ knife node delete my_node

   ```
   Do you really want to delete my_node? (Y/N) y
   Deleted node[my_node]
   ```

2. Delete the client object:

   mma@laptop:~/chef-repo $ knife node client my_node

   ```
   Do you really want to delete my_node? (Y/N) y
   Deleted client[my_node]
   ```

How it works...

To keep your Chef Server clean, it's important to not only manage your node objects but also take care of your client objects.

Knife connects to the Chef Server and deletes the node object with the given name using the Chef Server RESTful API.

The same happens while deleting the client object on the Chef Server.

After deleting both the objects, your node is totally removed from the Chef Server. Now, you can reuse the same node name with a new box or virtual machine.

There's more...

It is a bit tedious and error prone when you have to issue two commands. To simplify things, you can use a Knife plugin called playground.

1. Add the knife-playground plugin to your Gemfile:

   mma@laptop:~/chef-repo $ subl Gemfile

   ```
   ...
   gem 'knife-playground'
   ```

2. Run Bundler to install the Knife plugin:

   mma@laptop:~/chef-repo $ bundle install

   ```
   ...TRUNCATED OUTPUT...
   Installing knife-playground (0.2.2)
   ```

3. Run the `knife pg clientnode delete` sub-command:

    mma@laptop:~/chef-repo $ knife pg clientnode delete my_node

    ```
    Deleting CLIENT my_node...
    Do you really want to delete my_node? (Y/N) y
    Deleted client[my_node]
    Deleting NODE my_node...
    Do you really want to delete my_node? (Y/N) y
    Deleted node[my_node]
    ```

See also

▶   The *Managing Virtual Machines with Vagrant* section

▶   The *Using the Hosted Chef platform* section

Running Chef Solo

If running your own Chef Server seems like overkill and you're not comfortable with using Hosted Chef, you can use Chef Solo to execute cookbooks on your server.

Getting ready

Before you're able to run Chef Solo on your servers, you will need to add two files to your local Chef repository: `solo.rb` and `node.json`.

The `solo.rb` file tells Chef Solo where to find the cookbooks, roles, and data bags.

The `node.json` file sets the run list (and any other node-specific attributes if required).

1. Create a `solo.rb` file inside your Chef repository with the following contents:

    ```
    current_dir = File.expand_path(File.dirname(__FILE__))
    file_cache_path "#{current_dir}"
    cookbook_path "#{current_dir}/cookbooks"
    role_path "#{current_dir}/roles"
    data_bag_path "#{current_dir}/data_bags"
    ```

2. Add the file to Git:

    mma@laptop:~/chef-repo $ git add solo.rb

3. Create a file called `node.json` inside your Chef repository with the following contents:

```
{
  "run_list": [ "recipe[ntp]" ]
}
```

4. You might need to get the `ntp` cookbook into your Chef repository:

mma@laptop:~/chef-repo $ knife cookbook site install ntp

```
Installing ntp to /Users/mma/work/chef-repo/cookbooks
...TRUNCATED OUTPUT...
Cookbook ntp version 1.3.0 successfully installed
```

5. Add the `node.json` file to Git:

mma@laptop:~/chef-repo $ git add node.json

6. Commit and push your changes to GitHub so that your server will be able to pull them:

mma@laptop:~/chef-repo $ git commit -m "initial setup for Chef Solo"

mma@laptop:~/chef-repo $ git push

```
Counting objects: 4, done.
Delta compression using up to 4 threads.
...TRUNCATED OUTPUT...
To git@github.com:mmarschall/chef-repo.git
   b930647..5bcfab6  master -> master
```

Now you should be ready to install NTP on your server using Chef Solo.

How to do it...

Let's install NTP on your node using Chef Solo:

1. Log in to your remote server, which you want to provision with Chef Solo.

2. Clone your Chef repository. Please replace `mmarschall` with your own GitHub username:

user@server:~$ git clone git://github.com/mmarschall/chef-repo.git

3. Change into your Chef repository:

user@server:~$ cd chef-repo

4. Run Chef Solo to converge the node:

```
user@server:~/chef-repo$ sudo chef-solo -c solo.rb -j node.json

[2012-12-08T22:54:13+01:00] INFO: *** Chef 11.0.0 ***
[2012-12-08T22:54:13+01:00] INFO: Setting the run_list to
["recipe[ntp]"] from JSON
...TRUNCATED OUTPUT...
  [2012-12-08T22:54:16+01:00] INFO: Chef Run complete in 2.388374
seconds
[2012-12-08T22:54:16+01:00] INFO: Running report handlers
[2012-12-08T22:54:16+01:00] INFO: Report handlers complete
```

How it works...

`solo.rb` configures Chef Solo to look for its cookbooks, roles, and data bags inside the current directory: the Chef repository.

Chef Solo takes its node configuration from a JSON file, in our example we simply called it `node.json`. If you're going to manage multiple servers, you'll need a separate file for each node.

Then, Chef Solo just executes a Chef run based on the configuration data found in `solo.rb` and `node.json`.

> Chef Solo has limited functionality when compared to a Chef Server:
> - No node data storage
> - No search inside recipes
> - No environments to manage cookbook versions (you could use Git branches instead)

There's more...

Instead of cloning a GitHub repository on your server, you can collect your cookbooks into one file by using `tar` and make the resulting tarball available via HTTP. Your server can then download the cookbooks tarball if you tell it where the tarball lives, by using the `-r` parameter to Chef Solo.

To circumvent the limitations of Chef Solo, there exist various other tools such as `little-chef` or `knife-solo`.

See also

- Read more about Chef Solo at `http://docs.opscode.com/chef_solo.html`.

Using roles

Roles are the Chef way to group nodes. Typical cases are to have roles for web servers, database servers, and so on.

You can set custom run lists for all the nodes in your roles and override attribute values from within your roles.

Let's see how to create a simple role.

Getting ready

For the following examples, I assume that you have a node named `server` and that you have at least one cookbook (I'll use the `ntp` cookbook) registered with your Chef Server.

How to do it...

Let's create a role and see what we can do with it.

1. Create a role:

   ```
   mma@laptop:~/chef-repo $ subl roles/web_servers.rb
   ```

   ```
   name "web_servers"
   description "This role contains nodes, which act as web servers"
   run_list "recipe[ntp]"
   default_attributes 'ntp' => {
     'ntpdate' => {
       'disable' => true
     }
   }
   ```

2. Upload the role to the Chef Server:

   ```
   mma@laptop:~/chef-repo $ knife role from file web_servers.rb
   ```

   ```
   Updated Role web_servers!
   ```

3. Assign the role to a node called `server`:

   ```
   mma@laptop:~/chef-repo $ knife node edit server
   ```

   ```
   "run_list": [
     "role[web_servers]"
   ]
   Saving updated run_list on node server
   ```

4. Run Chef Client:

```
user@server:~$ sudo chef-client

...TRUNCATED OUTPUT...
[2013-07-25T13:28:24+00:00] INFO: Run List is [role[web_servers]]
[2013-07-25T13:28:24+00:00] INFO: Run List expands to [ntp]
...TRUNCATED OUTPUT...
```

How it works...

You define a role in a Ruby file inside the `roles` folder of your Chef repository. A role consists of a `name` and a `description` attribute. Additionally, a role usually contains a role-specific run list and role-specific attribute settings.

Every node, that has a role in its run list will have the role's run list expanded into its own. This means all the recipes (and roles) that are in the role's run list will be executed on your nodes.

You need to upload your role to your Chef Server using the `knife role from file` command.

Only then can you add the role to your node's run list.

Running Chef Client on a node having your role in its run list will execute all the recipes listed in the role.

The attributes you define in your role will be merged with attributes from environments and cookbooks according to the precedence rules described at `http://docs.opscode.com/essentials_roles.html#attribute-precedence`.

See also

▶   The *Using search to find nodes* section in *Chapter 4, Writing Better Cookbooks*

▶   The *Overriding attributes* section in *Chapter 4, Writing Better Cookbooks*

▶   Read everything about roles at `http://docs.opscode.com/essentials_roles.html`

Using environments

Having separate environments for development, testing, and production is a good idea to be able to develop and test cookbook updates and other configuration changes in isolation. Chef enables you to group your nodes into separate environments to support an ordered development flow.

Getting ready

For the following examples, I assume that you have a node named `my_server` in the `_default` environment and that you have at least one cookbook (I'll use the `ntp` cookbook) registered with your Chef Server.

How to do it...

Let's see how to manipulate environments using Knife.

 This is only a good idea if you want to play around. For serious work, please create files describing your environments and put them under version control as described in the *There's more...* section.

1. Create your environment on the fly using Knife. The following command will open your shell's default editor so that you can modify the environment definition:

   mma@laptop:~/chef-repo $ knife environment create book

   ```
   {
     "name": "book",
     "description": "",
     "cookbook_versions": {
     },
     "json_class": "Chef::Environment",
     "chef_type": "environment",
     "default_attributes": {
     },
     "override_attributes": {
     }
   }
   Created book
   ```

2. List the available environments:

   mma@laptop:~/chef-repo $ knife environment list

   ```
   _default
   book
   ```

3. List the nodes for all the environments:

   mma@laptop:~/chef-repo $ knife node list

   ```
   my_server
   ```

4. Verify that the node `my_server` is not in the `book` environment yet by listing nodes in the `book` environment only:

```
mma@laptop:~/chef-repo $ knife node list -E book

mma@laptop:~/chef-repo $
```

5. Change the environment of the `my_server` node by editing the node data and changing the value of `chef_environment` from `_default` to `book`:

```
mma@laptop:~/chef-repo $ knife node edit my_server
{
  "name": "my_server",
  "chef_environment": "book",
  "normal": {
  },
  "run_list": [
    "recipe[ntp]"
  ]
}
Saving updated chef_environment on node my_server
```

6. List the nodes of the `book` environment again:

```
mma@laptop:~/chef-repo $ knife node list -E book

my_server
```

7. Use specific cookbook versions and override certain attributes for the environment:

```
mma@laptop:~/chef-repo $ knife environment edit book
{
  "name": "book",
  "description": "",
  "cookbook_versions": {
    "ntp": "1.3.2"
  },
  "json_class": "Chef::Environment",
  "chef_type": "environment",
  "default_attributes": {
  },
  "override_attributes": {
    "ntp": {
      "servers": ["0.europe.pool.ntp.org", "1.europe.pool.ntp.
org", "2.europe.pool.ntp.org", "3.europe.pool.ntp.org"]
    }
  }
}
Saved book
```

How it works...

A common use of environments is to promote cookbook updates from development to staging and then into production. Additionally, they enable you to use different cookbook versions on separate sets of nodes and also to use environment-specific attributes. You might have nodes with lesser memory in your staging environment as in your production environment. By using environment-specific default attributes, you can, for example, configure your MySQL service to consume lesser memory on staging than on production.

 The Chef Server always has an environment called `_default` which cannot be edited or deleted. All the nodes go in there if you don't specify any other environment.

Be aware that roles are not environment specific. You may use environment-specific run lists, though.

The node's environment can be queried using the `node.chef_environment` method inside your cookbooks.

There's more...

If you want your environments to be under version control (and you should!), a better way to create a new environment is to create a new Ruby file in the `environments` directory inside your Chef repository:

```
mma@laptop:~/chef-repo $ cd environments
mma@laptop:~/chef-repo $ subl book.rb
    name "book"
```

You should add, commit, and push your new environment file to GitHub:

```
mma@laptop:~/chef-repo $ git add environments/book.rb
mma@laptop:~/chef-repo $ git commit -a -m "the book env"
mma@laptop:~/chef-repo $ git push
```

Now, you can create the environment on the Chef Server from the newly created file using Knife:

```
mma@laptop:~/chef-repo $ knife environment from file book.rb
    Created Environment book
```

There is a way to migrate all the nodes from one environment to another using `knife exec`:

```
mma@laptop:~/chef-repo $ knife exec -E 'nodes.transform("chef_
environment:_default") { |n| n.chef_environment("book") }
```

You can limit your search for nodes in a specific environment:

```
mma@laptop:~/chef-repo $ knife search node "chef_environment:book"
    1 item found
```

See also

▶ The *Managing virtual machines with Vagrant* section

▶ Read more about environments at `http://docs.opscode.com/essentials_environments.html`

Freezing cookbooks

Uploading broken cookbooks overriding your working ones is a major pain and can result in widespread outrage throughout your infrastructure. If you've a cookbook version known to work, it is a good idea to freeze this version so that no one can overwrite the same version with broken code. When used together with environments, freezing cookbooks can keep your production servers safe.

Getting ready

Make sure you've at least one cookbook (I'll use the `ntp` cookbook) registered with your Chef Server.

How to do it...

Let's see what happens if we freeze a cookbook.

1. Upload a cookbook and freeze it:

   ```
   mma@laptop:~/chef-repo $ knife cookbook upload ntp --freeze

   Uploading ntp              [1.3.2]
   Uploaded 1 cookbook.
   ```

2. Try to upload the same cookbook version again:

   ```
   mma@laptop:~/chef-repo $ knife cookbook upload ntp

   Uploading ntp              [1.3.2]
   Conflict: The cookbook ntp at version 1.3.2 is frozen. Use the
   'force' option to override.
   ```

3. Change the cookbook version:

   ```
   mma@laptop:~/chef-repo $ subl cookbooks/ntp/metadata.rb

   ...
   version              "1.3.3"
   ```

4. Upload the cookbook again:

```
mma@laptop:~/chef-repo $ knife cookbook upload ntp

Uploading ntp              [1.3.2]
Uploaded 1 cookbook.
```

How it works...

By using the `--freeze` option when uploading a cookbook, you tell the Chef Server that it should not accept any changes to the same version of the cookbook anymore. This is important if you're using environments and want to make sure that your production environment cannot be broken by uploading a corrupted cookbook with the same version number as used on your production servers.

By changing the version number of your cookbook, you can upload the new version. Then you can make, for example, your staging environment use that new cookbook version.

There's more...

For supporting a more elaborate workflow, you can use the `knife-spork` Knife plugin. It helps multiple developers work on the same Chef Server and repository without treading on each other's toes. You can find more on it at `https://github.com/jonlives/knife-spork`.

See also

▶ Check out Seth Vargo's talk about Chef + Environments = Safer Infrastructure at `https://speakerdeck.com/sethvargo/chef-plus-environments-equals-safer-infrastructure`

Running Chef Client as a daemon

While you can run Chef Client on your nodes manually whenever you change something in your Chef repository, it's sometimes preferable to have Chef Client run automatically ever so often. Letting Chef Client run automatically makes sure that no box misses any updates.

Getting ready

You need to have a node registered with your Chef Server. It needs to be able to run `chef-client` without any errors.

How to do it...

Let's see how to start Chef Client in daemon mode so that it runs automatically.

1. Start Chef Client in daemon mode, running every 30 minutes:

```
user@server:~$ sudo chef-client -i 1800
```

2. Validate that the Chef Client is running as a daemon:

```
user@server:~$ ps auxw | grep chef-client
```

How it works...

The -i parameter will start Chef Client as a daemon. The given number is the seconds between each Chef Client run. In the previous example, we specified 1,800 seconds, which results in Chef Client running every 30 minutes.

You can use the same command in a service startup script.

There's more...

Instead of running Chef Client as a daemon, you can use a cron job to run it every so often:

```
user@server:~$ subl /etc/cron.d/chef_client
```

```
PATH=/usr/local/bin:/usr/bin:/bin
# m h dom mon dow user command
*/15 * * * * root chef-client -l warn | grep -v 'retrying [1234]/5 in'
```

This cron job will run Chef Client every 15 minutes and swallow the first four retrying warning messages. This is important to avoid cron sending out e-mails if the Chef Server is a little slow and the Chef Client needs a few retries.

 It is possible to initiate a Chef Client run at any time by sending the SIGUSR1 signal to the Chef Client daemon:

```
user@server:~$ sudo killall -USR1 chef-client
```

Using the Chef console (Chef Shell)

Writing cookbooks is hard. What makes it even harder is the long feedback cycle of uploading them to the Chef Server, provisioning a Vagrant VM, checking how they failed there, rinse, and repeat. It would be so much easier if we could try out some pieces of the recipes we're writing before we've to do all this heavy lifting.

Chef comes with Chef Shell, which is essentially an interactive Ruby session with Chef. In the Chef Shell, you can create attributes, write recipes, and initialize Chef runs, among other things. It's there to evaluate parts of your recipes on the fly before you upload them to your Chef Server and execute complete cookbooks on your nodes.

How to do it...

Running the Chef Shell is straightforward.

1. Start the Chef Shell in standalone mode:

```
mma@laptop:~/chef-repo $ chef-shell

loading configuration: none (standalone chef-shell session)
Session type: standalone
Loading...[2012-12-12T20:48:01+01:00] INFO: Run List is []
[2012-12-12T20:48:01+01:00] INFO: Run List expands to []
done.

This is chef-shell, the Chef Shell.
 Chef Version: 11.0.0
 http://www.opscode.com/chef
 http://wiki.opscode.com/display/chef/Home

run `help' for help, `exit' or ^D to quit.

Ohai2u mma@laptop!

chef >
```

2. Switch to the attributes mode in the Chef Shell:

```
chef > attributes_mode
```

3. Set an attribute value to be used inside the recipe later:

```
chef:attributes > set[:title] = "Chef Cookbook"

 => "Chef Cookbook"

chef:attributes > quit

 => :attributes

chef >
```

4. Switch to the recipe mode:

```
chef > recipe_mode
```

5. Create a `file` resource, using the title attribute as content:

```
chef:recipe > file "/tmp/book.txt" do
chef:recipe >      content node.title
chef:recipe ?> end
 => <file[/tmp/book.txt] @name: "/tmp/book.txt" @noop: nil @
before: nil @params: {} @provider: Chef::Provider::File @allowed_
actions: [:nothing, :create, :delete, :touch, :create_if_missing]
@action: "create" @updated: false @updated_by_last_action: false
@supports: {} @ignore_failure: false @retries: 0 @retry_delay:
2 @source_line: "(irb#1):1:in `irb_binding'" @elapsed_time: 0 @
resource_name: :file @path: "/tmp/book.txt" @backup: 5 @diff: nil
@cookbook_name: nil @recipe_name: nil @content: "Chef Cookbook">

chef:recipe >
```

6. Initiate a Chef run to create the file with the given content:

```
chef:recipe > run_chef
[2012-12-12T21:07:49+01:00] INFO: Processing file[/tmp/book.txt]
action create ((irb#1) line 1)
--- /var/folders/1r/_35fx24d0y5g08qs131c33nw0000gn/T/chef-
tempfile20121212-11348-dwp1zs     2012-12-12 21:07:49.000000000
+0100
+++ /var/folders/1r/_35fx24d0y5g08qs131c33nw0000gn/T/chef-
diff20121212-11348-hdzcp1 2012-12-12 21:07:49.000000000 +0100
@@ -0,0 +1 @@
+Chef Cookbook
\ No newline at end of file
[2012-12-12T21:07:49+01:00] INFO: entered create
[2012-12-12T21:07:49+01:00] INFO: file[/tmp/book.txt] created file
/tmp/book.txt
```

How it works...

The Chef Shell starts an **interactive Ruby** (**IRB**) session enhanced with some Chef specific features. It offers certain modes such as `attributes_mode` or `recipe_mode`, which enable you to write commands like you would put them into an attributes file or recipe.

Entering a resource command into the recipe context will create the given resource, but not run it yet. It's like Chef reading your recipe files and creating the resources but not yet running them. You can run all the resources you created within the recipe context using the `run_chef` command. This will execute all the resources on your local box and physically change your system. For playing around with temporary files, your local box might do, but if you're going to do more invasive stuff such as installing or removing packages, installing services, and so on, you might want to use the Chef Shell from within a Vagrant VM.

There's more...

You can not only run the Chef Shell in standalone mode but also in Chef Solo mode and Chef Client mode. If you run it in Chef Client mode, it will load the complete run list of your node and you'll be able to tweak it inside the Chef Shell. You start the Chef Client mode by using the `--client` parameter:

```
mma@laptop:~/chef-repo $ chef-shell --client
```

You can configure which client your Chef Shell shall act as, as well as the Chef Server to connect to in a file called `chef_shell.rb`.

Additionally to evaluating recipe code within your Chef Shell, you can even use it to manage your Chef Server, for example, listing all nodes:

```
chef > nodes.list

   => [node[my_server]]
```

See also

  ▸   Read more about the Chef Shell at `http://docs.opscode.com/ chef_shell.html`.

2

Evaluating and Troubleshooting Cookbooks and Chef Runs

"Most people spend more time and energy going around problems than in trying to solve them."

> *- Henry Ford*

In this chapter, we'll cover the following:

- ▶ Testing your Chef cookbooks
- ▶ Flagging problems in your Chef cookbooks
- ▶ Test Driven Development for cookbooks using ChefSpec
- ▶ Integration testing your Chef cookbooks with Test Kitchen
- ▶ Showing affected nodes before uploading cookbooks
- ▶ Overriding a node's run list to execute a single recipe
- ▶ Using why-run mode to find out what a recipe might do
- ▶ Debugging Chef Client runs
- ▶ Inspecting results of your last Chef Client run
- ▶ Raising and logging exceptions in recipes
- ▶ Diffing cookbooks with Knife
- ▶ Using community exception and report handlers
- ▶ Creating custom handlers

Introduction

Developing cookbooks and making sure your nodes converge to the desired state is a complex endeavor. You need transparency about what is really happening. This chapter will cover a lot of ways to see what's going on and to make sure that everything is going smoothly.

Testing your Chef cookbooks

You know how annoying this is: you tweak a cookbook, upload it to your Chef Server, start a Chef run on your node and, boom! it fails. What's even more annoying is that it only fails because you missed a mundane comma in the default recipe of the cookbook you just tweaked, not because a black hole absorbed your node and the whole data center that node lives in. Fortunately, there's a very quick and easy way to find such simple glitches before you go all in and try to run your cookbooks on real nodes.

Getting ready

Install the `ntp` cookbook by running:

```
mma@laptop:~/chef-repo $ knife cookbook site install ntp
```

```
Installing ntp to /Users/mma/work/chef-repo/cookbooks
...TRUNCATED OUTPUT...
Cookbook ntp version 1.3.2 successfully installed
```

How to do it...

Carry out the following steps to test your cookbooks:

1. Run `knife cookbook test` on a working cookbook, for example, the `ntp` cookbook:

    ```
    mma@laptop:~/chef-repo $ knife cookbook test ntp
    ```

    ```
    checking ntp
    Running syntax check on ntp
    Validating ruby files
    Validating templates
    ```

2. Now, let's break something in the `ntp` cookbook's default recipe by removing the comma at the end of the `node['ntp']['varlibdir']`, line:

    ```
    mma@laptop:~/chef-repo $ subl cookbooks/ntp/recipes/default.rb
    ```

    ```
    ...
    [ node['ntp']['varlibdir']
    ```

```
    node['ntp']['statsdir'] ].each do |ntpdir|
    directory ntpdir do
      owner node['ntp']['var_owner']
      group node['ntp']['var_group']
      mode 0755
    end
  end
  ...
```

3. Run the test command again:

   mma@laptop:~/chef-repo $ knife cookbook test ntp

```
checking ntp
Running syntax check on ntp
Validating ruby files
FATAL: Cookbook file recipes/default.rb has a ruby syntax error:
FATAL: cookbooks/ntp/recipes/default.rb:25: syntax error,
unexpected tIDENTIFIER, expecting ']'
FATAL:    node['ntp']['statsdir'] ].each do |ntpdir|
FATAL:            ^
FATAL: cookbooks/ntp/recipes/default.rb:25: syntax error,
unexpected ']', expecting $end
FATAL:    node['ntp']['statsdir'] ].each do |ntpdir|
FATAL:                              ^
```

How it works...

`knife cookbook test` executes a Ruby syntax check on all Ruby files within the cookbook as well as on all ERB templates. It loops through all Ruby files and runs `ruby -c` against each of them. `ruby -c` causes Ruby to check the syntax of the script and quit without running it.

After going through all Ruby files, `knife cookbook test` goes through all ERB templates and pipes the rendered version created by `erubis -x` through `ruby -c`.

There's more...

`knife cookbook test` does only a very simple syntax check on the Ruby files and ERB templates. There exists a whole eco-system of additional tools such as Foodcritic (a lint check for Chef cookbooks), ChefSpec, and Test Kitchen, and many more. You can go fully test driven if you want!

See also

▸ The *Test Driven Development for cookbooks using ChefSpec* section

▸ The *Integration testing your cookbooks with Test Kitchen* section

Flagging problems in your Chef cookbooks

Writing solid Chef recipes can be quite challenging. There are a couple of pitfalls, which you can easily overlook. And writing cookbooks in a consistent style is even harder. You might wonder what the proven ways to write cookbooks are. **Foodcritic** tries to identify possible issues with the logic and style of your cookbooks.

In this section we'll learn how to use Foodcritic on some existing cookbooks.

Getting ready

1. Add the `foodcritic` gem to your Gemfile:

   mma@laptop:~/chef-repo $ subl Gemfile

   ```
   source 'https://rubygems.org'
   gem 'foodcritic', '~>2.2.0'
   ```

2. Run Bundler to install the `foodcritic` gem:

   mma@laptop:~/chef-repo $ bundle install

   ```
   Fetching gem metadata from https://rubygems.org/
   ...TRUNCATED OUTPUT...
   Installing foodcritic (2.2.0)
   ```

3. Install the `mysql` cookbook by running:

   mma@laptop:~/chef-repo $ knife cookbook site install mysql

   ```
   Installing mysql to /Users/mma/work/chef-repo/cookbooks
   ...TRUNCATED OUTPUT...
   Cookbook mysql version 3.0.2 successfully installed
   ```

How to do it...

Let's see how Foodcritic reports findings:

1. Run `foodcritic` on your cookbook:

   mma@laptop:~/chef-repo $ foodcritic ./cookbooks/mysql

   ```
   FC002: Avoid string interpolation where not required: ./cookbooks/
   mysql/attributes/server.rb:220
   ...TRUNCATED OUTPUT...
   FC024: Consider adding platform equivalents: ./cookbooks/mysql/
   recipes/server.rb:132
   ```

2. Get a detailed list of the reported sections inside the `mysql` cookbook by using the `-C` flag:

   mma@laptop:~/chef-repo $ foodcritic -C ./cookbooks/mysql

   ```
   cookbooks/mysql/attributes/server.rb
   FC002: Avoid string interpolation where not required
   [...]
     85|   default['mysql']['conf_dir'] = "#{mysql['basedir']}"
   [...]
   cookbooks/mysql/recipes/client.rb
   FC007: Ensure recipe dependencies are reflected in cookbook
   metadata
     40|   end
     41|when "mac_os_x"
     42|   include_recipe 'homebrew'
     43|end
     44|
   [...]
   ```

How it works...

Foodcritic defines a set of rules and checks your recipes against each of them. It comes with rules concerning various areas: style, correctness, attributes, strings, portability, search, services, files, metadata, and so on. Running Foodcritic against a cookbook tells you which of its rules matched a certain part of your cookbook. By default it gives you a short explanation of what you should do along the concerned file and line number.

If you run `foodcritic -C`, it displays the excerpts of the places where it found the rules to match.

In the preceding example, Foodcritic raised the issue that the `mysql` cookbook uses string interpolation where it is not required:

```
85|    default['mysql']['conf_dir'] = "#{mysql['basedir']}"
```

This could be re-written as:

```
85|    default['mysql']['conf_dir'] = mysql['basedir']
```

directly using the attribute value.

There's more...

Some of the rules, especially the ones from the styles section, are opinionated. You're able to exclude certain rules or complete sets of rules, such as the style rules when running Foodcritic.

```
mma@laptop:~/chef-repo $ foodcritic -t ~style ./cookbooks/mysql

   FC007: Ensure recipe dependencies are reflected in cookbook
      metadata: ./cookbooks/mysql/recipes/client.rb:42
   FC024: Consider adding platform equivalents:
      ./cookbooks/mysql/recipes/server.rb:132
   FC024: Consider adding platform equivalents:
      ./cookbooks/mysql/recipes/server.rb:134
   FC028: Incorrect #platform? usage:
      ./cookbooks/mysql/attributes/server.rb:120
```

In this case, the tilde negates the tag selection to exclude all rules with the `style` tag. Running without tilde would run the style rules exclusively:

```
mma@laptop:~/chef-repo $ foodcritic -t style ./cookbooks/mysql

   FC002: Avoid string interpolation where not required:
      ./cookbooks/mysql/attributes/server.rb:85
   FC019: Access node attributes in a consistent manner:
      cookbooks/mysql/libraries/helpers.rb:24
   FC019: Access node attributes in a consistent manner:
      cookbooks/mysql/libraries/helpers.rb:28
   FC023: Prefer conditional attributes:
      ./cookbooks/mysql/recipes/server.rb:157
```

If you want to run `foodcritic` in a **continuous integration** (**CI**) environment, you can use the `-f` parameter to indicate on which rules the build should fail:

```
mma@laptop:~/chef-repo $ foodcritic -f style ./cookbooks/mysql

   FC001: Use strings in preference to symbols to access node
      attributes: ./cookbooks/mysql/templates/default/grants.sql.erb:1
      ...TRUNCATED OUTPUT...
```

```
FC028: Incorrect #platform? usage:
  ./cookbooks/mysql/attributes/server.rb:120
```

```
mma@laptop:~/chef-repo $ echo $?
```

```
3
```

In this example, we tell `foodcritic` to fail if any rule of the `style` group fails. In our case, it returns a non zero exit code instead of zero, as it would if either no rule matches or we omit the `-f` parameter.

See also

▸ The *Testing your Chef cookbooks* section

▸ Check out strainer, a tool to test multiple things such as Foodcritic and Knife test as well as other stuff at once at: `http://github.com/customink/strainer`.

Test Driven Development for cookbooks using ChefSpec

Test Driven Development (**TDD**) is a way to write unit tests before writing any recipe code. By writing the test first, you design what your recipe should do and you ensure that your test is for real because it should fail as long as you haven't written your recipe code.

As soon as you've done your recipe, your unit tests should pass.

ChefSpec is built on the popular **RSpec** framework and offers a tailored syntax for testing Chef recipes.

Let's develop a very simple recipe using the TDD approach with ChefSpec.

Getting started..

Make sure you've a cookbook called `my_cookbook` and the `run_list` of your node includes `my_cookbook` as described in the *Creating and using cookbooks* section in *Chapter 1, Chef Infrastructure*.

How to do it...

Let's write a failing test first and then a recipe, which makes the test pass:

1. Create a `Gemfile` containing the `chefspec` gem:

    ```
    mma@laptop:~/chef-repo $ subl Gemfile
    ```

```
source 'https://rubygems.org'
gem 'chefspec'
```

2. Run `bundler` to install the gem:

    mma@laptop:~/chef-repo $ bundler install

    ```
    Fetching gem metadata from https://rubygems.org/
    ...TRUNCATED OUTPUT...
    Installing chefspec (1.3.1)
    Using bundler (1.3.5)
    Your bundle is complete!
    ```

3. Create the `spec` directory for your cookbook:

    mma@laptop:~/chef-repo $ mkdir cookbooks/my_cookbook/spec

4. Create your `spec`:

    **mma@laptop:~/chef-repo $ subl
      cookbooks/my_cookbook/spec/default_spec.rb**

    ```
    require 'chefspec'

    describe 'my_cookbook::default' do
      let(:chef_run) {
        ChefSpec::ChefRunner.new(
          platform:'ubuntu', version:'12.04'
        ).converge(described_recipe)
      }

      it 'creates a greetings file, containing the platform
        name' do
        expect(chef_run).to
          create_file_with_content('/tmp/greeting.txt','Hello!
          ubuntu!')
      end
    end
    ```

5. Run `rspec` to validate, that your `spec` fails (you've not written your recipe yet):

    **mma@laptop:~/chef-repo $ rspec
      cookbooks/my_cookbook/spec/default_spec.rb**

    ```
    F

    Failures:

      1) my_cookbook::default creates a greetings file, containing the
    platform name
        Failure/Error: expect(chef_run.converge(described_recipe)).to
    create_file_with_content('/tmp/greeting.txt','Hello! ubuntu!')
    ```

```
        File content:
          does not match expected:
        Hello! ubuntu!
      # ./cookbooks/my_cookbook/spec/default_spec.rb:11:in `block
(2 levels) in <top (required)>'

Finished in 0.11152 seconds
1 example, 1 failure

Failed examples:

rspec ./cookbooks/my_cookbook/spec/default_spec.rb:10 # my_
cookbook::default creates a greetings file, containing the
platform name
```

6. Edit your cookbook's default recipe:

mma@laptop:~/chef-repo $ subl
cookbooks/my_cookbook/recipes/default.rb

```
template '/tmp/greeting.txt' do
  variables greeting: 'Hello!'
end
```

7. Create the `template` file:

mma@laptop:~/chef-repo $ subl
cookbooks/my_cookbook/recipes/default.rb

```
<%= @greeting %> <%= node['platform'] %>!
```

8. Run `rspec` again to see whether your test succeeds now:

mma@laptop:~/chef-repo $ rspec
cookbooks/my_cookbook/spec/default_spec.rb

```
.

Finished in 0.10142 seconds
1 example, 0 failures
```

How it works...

First, you need to set up the basic infrastructure for using RSpec with Chef. You need the `chefspec` Ruby gem and your cookbook needs a directory called `spec` where all your tests will live.

When everything is set up, we're ready to start. Following the **Test First** approach of TDD, we create our spec before we write our recipe.

Every spec needs to require the `chefspec` gem:

```
require 'chefspec'
```

The main part of every spec is a `describe` block, where you tell RSpec that you want to test the `default` recipe of your cookbook:

```
describe 'my_cookbook::default' do
  ...
end
```

Now it's time to create the object simulating the Chef run. Note that ChefSpec will not really run your recipe, but simulate a Chef run so that you can verify whether certain expectations you have about your recipe hold true.

By using RSpec's `let` call, you create a variable called `chef_run`, which you can use later to define your expectations.

The `chef_run` variable is a `ChefSpec::ChefRunner` object. We want to simulate a Chef run on Ubuntu 12.04. The parameters `platform` and `version`, which we pass to the constructor during the `ChefSpec::ChefRunner.new` call, populate the automatic node attributes so that it looks like we do our simulated Chef run on an Ubuntu 12.04 node. ChefSpec uses **Fauxhai** to simulate the automatic node attributes as they would occur on various operating systems:

```
let(:chef_run) {
    ChefSpec::ChefRunner.new(
      platform:'ubuntu', version:'12.04'
    ).converge(described_recipe)
}
```

You can retrieve the recipe under test using the `described_recipe` call instead of typing `my_cookbook::default` again. Using `described_recipe` instead of the recipe name will keep you from repeating the recipe name in every `it`-block. It will keep your spec **DRY**:

```
ChefSpec::ChefRunner.new(...).converge(described_recipe)
```

Finally, we define what we expect our recipe to do.

We describe what we expect our recipe to do with `it`-statements. Our description of the `it`-call will show up in the error message, if this test fails:

```
it 'creates a greetings file, containing the platform name' do
  ...
end
```

Now it's finally time to formulate our exact expectations. We use standard RSpec syntax to define our expectations:

```
expect(...).to ...
```

Every expectation works on the simulated Chef run object, defined previously.

We use a ChefSpec specific matcher called `create_file_with_content` with the filename and the content as parameters to tell our spec what our recipe should do.

```
... create_file_with_content('/tmp/greeting.txt','Hello! ubuntu!')
```

On the ChefSpec site you find the complete list of custom matchers you can use to test your recipes in the ChefSpec README at:

```
https://github.com/acrmp/chefspec#making-assertions
```

After defining our spec, it's time to run it and see it fail:

```
$ rspec cookbooks/my_cookbook/spec/default_spec.rb
```

Then we write our recipe. We use the template resource to create a file with the contents as specified in the spec.

Finally, we run `rspec` again to see our spec pass!

There's more...

You can modify your node attributes before simulating the Chef run:

```
it 'uses a node attribute as greeting text' do
  chef_run.node.override['my_cookbook']['greeting'] = "Go!"
  expect(chef_run).to
    create_file_with_content('/tmp/greeting.txt','Go! ubuntu!')
end
```

Running `rspec` after adding the preceding test to our spec fails as expected, because our recipe does not handle the node parameter `['my_cookbook']['greeting']` yet:

```
.F

Failures:

  1) my_cookbook::default uses a node attribute as greeting text
     Failure/Error: expect(chef_run.converge(described_recipe)).to
       create_file_with_content('/tmp/greeting.txt','Go! ubuntu!')
       File content:
       Hello! ubuntu! does not match expected:
       Go! ubuntu!
```

```
# ./cookbooks/my_cookbook/spec/default_spec.rb:16:in `block
  (2 levels) in <top (required)>'

Finished in 0.25295 seconds
2 examples, 1 failure

Failed examples:

rspec ./cookbooks/my_cookbook/spec/default_spec.rb:14 #
  my_cookbook::default uses a node attribute as greeting text
```

Now, we modify our recipe to use the `node` attribute:

```
node.default['my_cookbook']['greeting'] = "Hello!"

template '/tmp/greeting.txt' do
  variables greeting: node['my_cookbook']['greeting']
end
```

And now, our tests pass again:

```
..

Finished in 0.25078 seconds
2 examples, 0 failures
```

See also

▶ The ChefSpec repository on GitHub:

   https://github.com/acrmp/chefspec

▶ The source code of Fauxhai:

   https://github.com/customink/fauxhai

▶ A talk by Seth Vargo showing an example developing a cookbook test-driven:

   http://www.confreaks.com/videos/2364-mwrc2013-tdding-tmux

▶ The RSpec website:

   http://rspec.info/

Integration testing your cookbooks with Test Kitchen

Verifying that your cookbooks really work when converging a node is essential. Only if you can trust your cookbooks are you ready to run them any time on your production servers.

Test Kitchen is Chef's integration testing framework. It enables you to write tests, which run after a VM is instantiated and converged using your cookbook. Your tests run in that VM and can verify that everything works as expected.

This is in contrast to ChefSpec, which only simulates a Chef run. Test Kitchen boots up a real node and runs Chef on it. Your tests see the real thing.

Let's see how you can write such integration tests for your cookbooks.

Getting started

Make sure you have a cookbook named `my_cookbook` as described in the *Creating and using cookbooks* section in *Chapter 1, Chef Infrastructure*.

Make sure you have Vagrant installed as described in the *Managing virtual machines with Vagrant* section in *Chapter 1, Chef Infrastructure*.

Make sure you have Berkshelf installed and hooked up with Vagrant as described in the *Managing cookbook dependencies with Berkshelf* section in *Chapter 1, Chef Infrastructure*.

How to do it...

Let's create a very simple recipe and use Test Kitchen and **Minitest** to run a full integration test with Vagrant:

1. Edit your cookbook's default recipe:

   ```
   mma@laptop:~/chef-repo $ subl
     cookbooks/my_cookbook/recipes/default.rb

   file "/tmp/greeting.txt" do
     content node['my_cookbook']['greeting']
   end
   ```

2. Edit your cookbook's default attributes:

   ```
   mma@laptop:~/chef-repo $ subl
     cookbooks/my_cookbook/attributes/default.rb

   default['my_cookbook']['greeting'] = "Ohai, Chefs!"
   ```

3. Edit your `Gemfile` to install the necessary Ruby gems:

   `mma@laptop:~/chef-repo $ subl Gemfile`

   ```
   gem 'test-kitchen', '~> 1.0.0.alpha.7'
   gem 'kitchen-vagrant'
   ```

4. Install necessary Ruby gems:

   `mma@laptop:~/chef-repo $ bundle install`

   ```
   ...TRUNCATED OUTPUT...
   Installing test-kitchen (1.0.0.alpha.7)
   Installing kitchen-vagrant (0.10.0)
   ...TRUNCATED OUTPUT...
   ```

5. Change into your cookbook directory:

   `mma@laptop:~/chef-repo $ cd cookbooks/my_cookbook`

6. Create a `.kitchen.yml` file in your cookbook:

   `mma@laptop:~/chef-repo/cookbooks/my_cookbook $ subl .kitchen.yml`

   ```
   ---
   driver_plugin: vagrant
   driver_config:
     require_chef_omnibus: true

   platforms:
   - name: ubuntu-12.04
     driver_config:
       box: opscode-ubuntu-12.04
       box_url: https://opscode-vm.s3.amazonaws.com/vagrant/opscode_
   ubuntu-12.04_provisionerless.box

   suites:
   - name: default
     run_list:
     - recipe[minitest-handler]
     - recipe[my_cookbook_test]
     attributes: { my_cookbook: { greeting: 'Ohai, Minitest!'} }
   ```

7. Create the `test` directory inside your main cookbook:

   `mma@laptop:~/chef-repo/cookbooks/my_cookbook $ mkdir test`

8. Create a test cookbook for the integration test:

   `mma@laptop:~/chef-repo/cookbooks/my_cookbook $ cd test`

```
mma@laptop:~/chef-repo/cookbooks/my_cookbook/test $ knife
  cookbook create my_cookbook_test
** Creating cookbook my_cookbook_test
** Creating README for cookbook: my_cookbook_test
** Creating CHANGELOG for cookbook: my_cookbook_test
** Creating metadata for cookbook: my_cookbook_test
```

9. Exit the test directory:

```
mma@laptop:~/chef-repo/cookbooks/my_cookbook/test $ cd ..
```

10. Edit your test cookbook's default recipe:

```
mma@laptop:~/chef-repo/cookbooks/my_cookbook $ subl
  test/cookbooks/my_cookbook_test/recipes/default.rb
```

```
include_recipe 'my_cookbook::default'
```

11. Create a Minitest Spec in your test cookbook:

```
mma@laptop:~/chef-repo/cookbooks/my_cookbook $ mkdir -p
  test/cookbooks/my_cookbook_test/files/default/tests/minitest
```

```
mma@laptop:~/chef-repo/cookbooks/my_cookbook $ subl
  test/cookbooks/my_cookbook_test/files/default/tests/
  minitest/default_test.rb
```

```
require 'minitest/spec'

describe_recipe 'my_cookbook::default' do

  describe "greeting file" do

    it "creates the greeting file" do
      file("/tmp/greeting.txt").must_exist
    end

    it "contains what's stored in the 'greeting' node
      attribute" do
      file('/tmp/greeting.txt').must_include 'Ohai,
        Minitest!'
    end
  end
end
```

12. Edit your main cookbook's `Berksfile`:

```
mma@laptop:~/chef-repo/cookbooks/my_cookbook $ subl Berksfile
```

```
site :opscode

metadata
```

```
cookbook "apt"
cookbook "minitest-handler"
cookbook "my_cookbook_test", path:
    "./test/cookbooks/my_cookbook_test"
```

13. Run Test Kitchen:

mma@laptop:~/chef-repo/cookbooks/my_cookbook $ kitchen test

```
-----> Starting Kitchen (v1.0.0.alpha.7)
...TRUNCATED OUTPUT...
-----> Converging <default-ubuntu-1204>
-----> Installing Chef Omnibus (true)
...TRUNCATED OUTPUT...
Starting Chef Client, version 11.4.4
[2013-06-29T18:33:57+00:00] INFO: *** Chef 11.4.4 ***
[2013-06-29T18:33:58+00:00] INFO: Setting the run_list to
  ["recipe[minitest-handler]", "recipe[my_cookbook_test]"]
  from JSON
...TRUNCATED OUTPUT...
# Running tests:

recipe::my_cookbook::default::greeting
  file#test_0001_creates the greeting file = 0.00 s = .
recipe::my_cookbook::default::greeting
  file#test_0002_contains what's stored in the 'greeting'
  node attribute = 0.00 s = .


Finished tests in 0.011190s, 178.7277 tests/s, 178.7277
  assertions/s.

2 tests, 2 assertions, 0 failures, 0 errors, 0 skips
...TRUNCATED OUTPUT...
-----> Kitchen is finished. (2m5.69s)
```

How it works...

First, we create a very simple recipe, which writes the value of a node attribute to a file.

Then, we install the test-kitchen Ruby gem and the kitchen-vagrant gem to enable Test Kitchen to use Vagrant for spinning up its test VMs.

Then, it's time to configure Test Kitchen. You do this by creating a `.kitchen.yml` file in your cookbook directory. It consists of three parts:

Part one defines that you want to use Vagrant to spin up VMs and that you want Test Kitchen to install Chef using its Omnibus installer. This is necessary, because we'll use provisionerless Vagrant boxes in part two.

```
driver_plugin: vagrant
driver_config:
  require_chef_omnibus: true
```

Part two defines on which platforms you want to test your cookbook. To keep things simple, we only define Ubuntu 12.04 here. Test Kitchen will always create and destroy new instances. You do not have to fear any side effects with Vagrant VMs you spin up using your Vagrant file.

```
platforms:
- name: ubuntu-12.04
  driver_config:
    box: opscode-ubuntu-12.04
    box_url: https://opscode-
      vm.s3.amazonaws.com/vagrant/opscode_ubuntu-
      12.04_provisionerless.box
```

Part three defines the test suites. We define only one called `default`. We tell Test Kitchen that we want to use the Minitest handler to run our specs and that it should use the `my_cookbook_test` cookbook to converge the node. As we'll see below, we're only including our `my_cookbook::default` recipe there so that we're able to test what that one does. As the last part of our test suite, we define the cookbook attribute's value so that we can make sure it is used:

```
suites:
- name: default
  run_list:
  - recipe[minitest-handler]
  - recipe[my_cookbook_test]
  attributes: { my_cookbook: { greeting: 'Ohai, Minitest!'} }
```

Now it's time to create our test cookbook, which will contain our specs and run our main cookbook.

The test cookbook is very simple in our case; it just calls our main cookbook. No further setup for running reasonable tests is necessary in our simple example.

Then, we write our Minitest spec to verify that the `/tmp/greeting.txt` file exists after the Chef run and that it contains the attribute value we defined when we described our test suite in `.kitchen.yml`.

To make sure that Test Kitchen has all required cookbooks available, we need to add them to our cookbook's Berksfile.

Finally, we can run Test Kitchen. It will first make sure that no old VMs are around and then create a new one. It installs Chef on that brand new VM and starts a Chef run. The Minitest handler hooks itself into the Chef run and executes our specs after the node converged.

If everything worked, Test Kitchen destroys the VM again.

If something fails, Test Kitchen keeps the VM around and you can poke around by running `kitchen login`.

There's more...

Test Kitchen does not only support Vagrant but also a host of other cloud providers such as OpenStack, Amazon EC2, and so on. Just install the `kitchen-<YOUR_CLOUD_PROVIDER>` gem instead of the `kitchen-vagrant` gem and make sure you put the corresponding configuration into your `.kitchen.yml`.

You can define multiple different platforms such as other Ubuntu versions or CentOS, and so on by adding to the platforms definition in `.kitchen.yml`:

```
platforms:
...
- name: centos-6.3
  driver_config:
    box: opscode-centos-6.3
    box_url: https://opscode-vm-
      bento.s3.amazonaws.com/vagrant/opscode_centos-
      6.4_provisionerless.box
```

 You find Test Kitchen's log files inside your cookbook in the directory `.kitchen/logs`.

See also

- ▸ Read the official Getting Started guide for Test Kitchen here: `https://github.com/opscode/test-kitchen/wiki/Getting-Started`

- ▸ Find the Test Kitchen source code on GitHub: `https://github.com/opscode/test-kitchen`

- ▸ Read Joshua Timberman's detailed blog post explaining Test Kitchen using the bluepill cookbook as an example: `http://jtimberman.housepub.org/blog/2013/03/19/anatomy-of-a-test-kitchen-1-dot-0-cookbook-part-1/`

```
http://jtimberman.housepub.org/blog/2013/03/19/anatomy-of-a-
test-kitchen-1-dot-0-cookbook-part-2/
```

▶ You can find a detailed example featuring all kinds of Minitest specs here: `https://github.com/calavera/minitest-chef-handler/blob/v1.0.0/examples/spec_examples/files/default/tests/minitest/default_test.rb`

▶ The source code of the Minitest handler is available on GitHub as well: `https://github.com/calavera/minitest-chef-handler`

Showing affected nodes before uploading cookbooks

You know how it goes. You tweak a cookbook to support your new server and upload it to your Chef Server. Your new node converges just fine and you're a happy pal. Well, until your older production server picks up your modified cookbook during an automated Chef Client run and spits its guts at you. Obviously, you forgot that your old production server was still using the cookbook you tweaked. Luckily, there is the `knife preflight` command, which can show you all nodes using a certain cookbook before you upload it to your Chef Server.

Getting ready

For the following example, we assume that you've at least one role using the `ntp` cookbook in its run list and that you've multiple servers having this role and/or having the `ntp` cookbook in their run list directly.

1. Add the `knife-preflight` gem to your `Gemfile`:

   mma@laptop:~/chef-repo $ subl Gemfile

   ```
   source 'https://rubygems.org'

   gem 'knife-preflight'
   ```

2. Run Bundler to install the `knife-preflight` gem:

   mma@laptop:~/chef-repo $ bundle install

   ```
   Fetching gem metadata from https://rubygems.org/
   ...TRUNCATED OUTPUT...
   Installing knife-preflight (0.1.6)
   ```

How to do it...

Let's see how `preflight` works on the `ntp` cookbook:

Run the `preflight` command to find out which nodes and roles have the `ntp` cookbook in their expanded run lists. You'll obviously see *your* nodes and roles in the output instead of the exact ones listed below:

```
mma@laptop:~/chef-repo $ knife preflight ntp
    Searching for nodes containing ntp OR ntp::default in their
        expanded run_list...
    2 Nodes found

    www-staging.example.com
    cms-staging.example.com
    Searching for roles containing ntp OR ntp::default in their
        expanded run_list...
    3 Roles found

    your_cms_role
    your_www_role
    your_app_role

    Found 6 nodes and 3 roles using the specified search
        criteria
```

How it works...

There are multiple ways for a cookbook to get executed on a node:

- ▶ You can assign the cookbook directly to a node by adding it to the node's run list
- ▶ You can add a cookbook to a role and add the role to the node's run list
- ▶ You can add a role to the run list of another role and add that other role to the node's run list
- ▶ A cookbook can be a dependency of another used cookbook
- ▶ And many more...

No matter how a cookbook ended up in a node's run list, the `knife preflight` command will catch it because Chef stores all expanded lists of roles and recipes in node attributes. The `knife preflight` command issues a search for exactly those node attributes.

Eventually, the `knife preflight` command is a nicer way to run `knife search node recipes:ntp -a name` and `knife search node roles:ntp -a name`.

> When using the `knife preflight` command (or trying to search for the `recipes` and `roles` attributes of a node) it is important to be aware of the fact that those attributes are only filled after a Chef Client run. If you change anything in your run lists but do not run Chef Client, neither `knife preflight` nor `knife search` will pick up your changes.

See also

▶ The _Using custom knife plugins_ section in _Chapter 1, Chef Infrastructure_

▶ The source code of the knife-preflight plugin is available on GitHub:

`https://github.com/jonlives/knife-preflight`

Overriding a node's run list to execute a single recipe

We all have those snowflake environments that are built using Chef but we're not comfortable with running Chef Client anymore. We know that some cookbooks have been enhanced but never tested against this specific environment. The risk of bringing it down by a Chef Client run is pretty high.

But, even though we do not dare to do a full Chef Client run we might need to run, for example, the **users** cookbook to add a new colleague to our snowflake environment. This is where Chef Client's feature to override a run list to execute a single recipe comes in very handy.

> Don't overuse this feature! Make sure you fix your environment so that you're comfortable to run Chef Client whenever you need to!

Getting ready

To follow along with the next example, you'll need a node hooked up to your Chef Server having multiple recipes and/or roles in its run list.

How to do it...

Let's see how to run a single recipe out of a bigger run list on your node:

1. Show the data for your node. In this example, my node has the role `base` in its run list. Depending on your setup, you'll find other data here of course:

   mma@laptop:~/chef-repo $ knife node show www.example.com

   ```
   ...TRUNCATED OUTPUT...
   Run List:    role[base]
   Roles:       base
   Recipes:     chef-client::delete_validation, runit, chef-client
   ...TRUNCATED OUTPUT...
   ```

2. Run `chef-client`, overriding its run list. In our example, we want to run the default recipe of the users cookbook. Please replace `recipe[users]` with whatever you want to run on your node:

   user@server:~$ chef-client -o "recipe[users]"

   ```
   [Wed, 19 Dec 2012 22:27:02 +0100] INFO: *** Chef 11.2.0 ***
   [Wed, 19 Dec 2012 22:27:09 +0100] INFO: Run List is [users]
   [Wed, 19 Dec 2012 22:27:09 +0100] INFO: Run List expands to
   [users]
   ...TRUNCATED OUTPUT...
   ```

How it works...

Usually, the node uses the run list stored on the Chef Server. The `-o` parameter simply ignores the node's run list and uses whatever the value of the `-o` parameter is, as the run list for the current Chef run. It will not persist the passed-in run list. The next Chef Client run (without the `-o` parameter) will use the run list stored on the Chef Server again.

See also

▸ Read more about Chef run lists at:

  http://docs.opscode.com/essentials_node_object_run_lists.html

▸ The *Showing affected nodes before uploading cookbooks* section

Using why-run mode to find out what a recipe might do

`why-run` lets each resource tell you, what it would do right now assuming certain prerequisites. This is great because it gives you a glimpse about what might really happen on your node when you run your recipe for real.

But, because Chef converges a lot of resources to a desired state, `why-run` will never be accurate for a complete run. Nevertheless, it might help you during development while you're adding resources step-by-step to build the final recipe.

In this section, we'll try out `why-run` to see what it tells us about our Chef runs.

Getting ready

To try out `why-run` mode you need a node where you can execute Chef Client and at least one cookbook available to that node.

How to do it...

Let's try to run the `ntp` cookbook in `why-run` mode:

1. Override the current run list to run the `ntp` recipe in `why-run` mode on a brand new box:

    ```
    user@server:~$ sudo chef-client -o recipe['ntp'] --why-run
    ```

    ```
    Converging 7 resources
    Recipe: ntp::default
      * package[ntp] action install[2012-12-22T20:27:44+00:00]
        INFO: Processing package[ntp] action install
        (ntp::default line 21)

        - Would install version 1:4.2.6.p3+dfsg-1ubuntu3.1 of
          package ntp
      * package[ntpdate] action install[2012-12-
        22T20:27:46+00:00] INFO: Processing package[ntpdate]
        action install (ntp::default line 21)
      (up to date)
      * directory[/var/lib/ntp] action create[2012-12-
        22T20:27:46+00:00] INFO: Processing
        directory[/var/lib/ntp] action create (ntp::default
        line 26)
    ```

```
      - Would create new directory /var/lib/ntp
      - Would change mode from '' to '0755'
...TRUNCATED OUTPUT...
Chef Client finished, 8 resources updated
```

2. Install the `ntp` package manually, to see the difference in a `why-run`:

   user@server:~$ sudo apt-get install ntp

   ```
   ...TRUNCATED OUTPUT...
   0 upgraded, 3 newly installed, 0 to remove and 3 not
     upgraded.
   ...TRUNCATED OUTPUT...
    * Starting NTP server ntpd [ OK ]
   Processing triggers for libc-bin ...
   ldconfig deferred processing now taking place
   ```

3. Run `why-run` for the `ntp` recipe again (now with installed `ntp` package):

   user@server:~$ sudo chef-client -o recipe['ntp'] --why-run

   ```
   ...TRUNCATED OUTPUT...
   Converging 7 resources
   Recipe: ntp::default
     * package[ntp] action install[2012-12-22T20:45:22+00:00]
       INFO: Processing package[ntp] action install
       (ntp::default line 21)
     (up to date)
     * package[ntpdate] action install[2012-12-
       22T20:45:22+00:00] INFO: Processing package[ntpdate]
       action install (ntp::default line 21)
     (up to date)
     * directory[/var/lib/ntp] action create[2012-12-
       22T20:45:22+00:00] INFO: Processing
       directory[/var/lib/ntp] action create (ntp::default
       line 26)
     (up to date)
   ...TRUNCATED OUTPUT...
   Chef Client finished, 3 resources updated
   ```

How it works...

The `why-run` mode is the no-op mode for Chef Client. Instead of providers modifying the system, it tries to tell what the Chef Client run would attempt to do.

It's important to know that `why-run` makes certain assumptions; if it cannot find the command needed to find out about the current status of a certain service, it assumes that an earlier resource would have installed the needed package for that service and that therefore the service would be started. We see this when the `ntp` cookbook tries to enable the `ntp` service:

```
* Service status not available. Assuming a prior action would
  have installed the service.
* Assuming status of not running.
- Would enable service service[ntp]
```

Additionally, `why-run` shows diffs of modified files. In our example, those diffs show the whole files as those files do not exist yet. This feature is more helpful if you already have `ntp` installed and your next Chef run would only change a few configuration parameters.

> why-run mode will execute `not_if` and `only_if` blocks. It is assumed that the code within `not_if` and `only_if` blocks is only there to find out whether a resource should be executed and it is not there to modify the system.

See also

▸ Read more about the issues with dry runs in configuration management at:

http://blog.afistfulofservers.net/post/2012/12/21/promises-lies-and-dryrun-mode/

Debugging Chef Client runs

Your Chef Client run fails and you don't know why. You get obscure error messages and you've a hard time to find any clue about where to look for the error. Is your cookbook broken? Do you have a networking issue? Is your Chef Server down? Only by looking at the most verbose log output have you a chance to find out.

Getting ready

You need a Chef Client configured to use Hosted Chef or your own Chef Server.

How to do it...

Let's see how we can ask Chef Client to print debug messages:

1. Run Chef Client with debug output:

```
user@server:~$ sudo chef-client -l debug

...TRUNCATED OUTPUT...
Hashed Path:A+WOcvvGu160cBO7IFKLYPhh9fI=
X-Ops-Content-Hash:2jmj7l5rSw0yVb/vlWAYkK/YBwk=
X-Ops-Timestamp:2012-12-27T11:14:07Z
X-Ops-UserId:vagrant'
Header hash: {"X-Ops-Sign"=>"algorithm=sha1;version=1.0;",
  "X-Ops-Userid"=>"vagrant", "X-Ops-Timestamp"=>"2012-12-
  27T11:14:07Z", "X-Ops-Content-
  Hash"=>"2jmj7l5rSw0yVb/vlWAYkK/YBwk=", "X-Ops-
  Authorization-
  1"=>"HQmTt9U/
  LJJVAJXWtyOu3GW8FbybxAIKp4rhiw9O9O3wtGYVHyVGuoilWDao",
  "X-Ops-Authorization-
  2"=>"2/uUBPWX+YAN0g1/
  fD2854QAU2aUcnSaVM0cPNNrldoOocmA0U5HXkBJTKok",
  "X-Ops-Authorization-
  3"=>"6EXPrEJg5T+
  ddWd5qHAN6zMqYc3untb41t+eBpigGHPhtn1LLInMkPeIYwBm",
  "X-Ops-Authorization-
  4"=>"B0Fwbwz2HVP3wEsYdBGu7yOatq7fZBXHfIpeOi0kn/
  Vn0P7HrucnOpONmMgU", "X-Ops-Authorization-
  5"=>"RBmmbetFSKCYsdg2v2mW/
  ifLIVemhsHyOQjffPYPpNIB3U2n7vji37NxRnBY",
  "X-Ops-Authorization-
  6"=>"Pb3VM7FmY60xKvWfZyahM8y8WVV9xPWsD1vngihjFw=="}
[2012-12-27T11:14:07+00:00] DEBUG: Sending HTTP Request via
  GET to api.opscode.com:443/organizations/agilewebops/
  nodes/vagrant
[2012-12-27T11:14:09+00:00] DEBUG: ---- HTTP Status and
  Header Data: ----
[2012-12-27T11:14:09+00:00] DEBUG: HTTP 1.1 200 OK
[2012-12-27T11:14:09+00:00] DEBUG: server: nginx/1.0.5
[2012-12-27T11:14:09+00:00] DEBUG: date: Thu, 27 Dec 2012
  11:14:09 GMT
```

```
[2012-12-27T11:14:09+00:00] DEBUG: content-type:
  application/json
[2012-12-27T11:14:09+00:00] DEBUG: transfer-encoding:
  chunked
[2012-12-27T11:14:09+00:00] DEBUG: connection: close
[2012-12-27T11:14:09+00:00] DEBUG: content-encoding: gzip
[2012-12-27T11:14:09+00:00] DEBUG: ---- End HTTP
  Status/Header Data ----
...TRUNCATED OUTPUT...
```

How it works...

The `-l` option on the Chef Client run sets the log level to `debug`. In `debug` log level the Chef Client shows more or less everything it does including every request to the Chef Server.

There's more...

The `debug` log level is the most verbose one. You're free to use any of these: `debug`, `info`, `warn`, `error`, `fatal` with the `-l` switch.

See also

▸　The *Raising and logging exceptions in recipes* section

Inspecting results of your last Chef Client run

More often than we like to admit Chef Client runs fail. Especially when developing new cookbooks we need to know what exactly went wrong.

Even though Chef prints all the details to `stdout`, you might want to look at it again, for example, after clearing your shell window.

Getting ready

You need to have a broken cookbook in your node's run list.

How to do it...

Carry out the following steps:

1. Run Chef Client with your broken cookbook:

```
user@server:~$ sudo chef-client
======================================================================
==============


Recipe Compile Error in /srv/chef/file_store/cookbooks/my_
cookbook/recipes/default.rb


======================================================================
==============




NoMethodError


------------


undefined method `each' for nil:NilClass




Cookbook Trace:


---------------


  /srv/chef/file_store/cookbooks/my_cookbook/recipes/default.
rb:9:in `from_file'


Relevant File Content:


----------------------


/srv/chef/file_store/cookbooks/my_cookbook/recipes/default.rb:
```

```
2:  # Cookbook Name:: my_cookbook

3:  # Recipe:: default

4:  #

5:  # Copyright 2013, YOUR_COMPANY_NAME

6:  #

7:  # All rights reserved - Do Not Redistribute

8:  #

9>> nil.each {} 10:
```

2. Look into the `stracktrace` file to find out what happened in more detail:

```
user@server:~$ less /srv/chef/file_store/chef-stacktrace.out

Generated at 2013-07-21 18:34:05 +0000

NoMethodError: undefined method `each' for nil:NilClass

/srv/chef/file_store/cookbooks/my_cookbook/recipes/default.rb:9:in
`from_file'

/opt/chef/embedded/lib/ruby/gems/1.9.1/gems/chef-11.4.4/lib/chef/
mixin/from_file.rb:30:in `instance_eval'

/opt/chef/embedded/lib/ruby/gems/1.9.1/gems/chef-11.4.4/lib/chef/
mixin/from_file.rb:30:in `from_file'

/opt/chef/embedded/lib/ruby/gems/1.9.1/gems/chef-11.4.4/lib/chef/
cookbook_version.rb:346:in `load_recipe'
```

How it works...

Chef Client reports errors to `stdout` by default. If you missed that output, you need to look into the files Chef generated to find out what went wrong.

There's more...

If you provision a node using Vagrant, you'll find an additional file after a failed provisioning run: `/srv/chef/file_store/failed-run-data.json`. It contains detailed information on the node attributes as well as the backtrace to the error location.

See also

▶ The *Logging debug messages* section

Raising and logging exceptions in recipes

Running your own cookbooks on your nodes might lead to situations where it does not make any sense to continue the current Chef run. If a critical resource is offline or a mandatory configuration value cannot be determined, it is time to bail out.

But, even if things are not that bad, you might want to log certain events while executing your recipes. Chef offers the possibility to write your custom log messages and to exit the current run, if you choose to do so.

In this section, we'll learn how to add log statements and stop Chef runs using exceptions.

Getting ready

You need to have at least one cookbook you can modify and run on a node. The following example will use the `ntp` cookbook.

How to do it...

Let's see how to add our custom log message to a recipe:

1. Add log statements to the `ntp` cookbook's default recipe:

   ```
   mma@laptop:~/chef-repo $ subl cookbooks/ntp/recipes/default.rb
   ```

   ```
   Chef::Log.info('** Going to install the ntp service
     now...')

   service node['ntp']['service'] do
     supports :status => true, :restart => truetrue
     action [ :enable, :start ]
   end

   Chef::Log.info('** ntp service installed and started
     successfully!')
   ```

2. Upload the modified cookbook to the Chef Server:

   ```
   mma@laptop:~/chef-repo $ knife cookbook upload ntp
   ```

   ```
   Uploading ntp                [1.3.2]
   Uploaded 1 cookbook.
   ```

3. Run Chef Client on the node:

   ```
   user@server:~$ sudo chef-client
   ```

   ```
   ...TRUNCATED OUTPUT...
   ```

```
[2012-12-27T13:53:19+00:00] INFO: Storing updated cookbooks/ntp/
TESTING.md in the cache.
[2012-12-27T13:53:19+00:00] INFO: ** Going to install the ntp
service now...
[2012-12-27T13:53:19+00:00] INFO: ** ntp service installed and
started successfully!
[2012-12-27T13:53:19+00:00] INFO: Processing package[ntp] action
install (ntp::default line 21)
...TRUNCATED OUTPUT...
```

4. Raise an exception from within the ntp default recipe:

   mma@laptop:~/chef-repo $ subl cookbooks/ntp/recipes/default.rb

   ```
   ...
   Chef::Application.fatal!('Ouch!!! Bailing out!!!')
   ...
   ```

5. Upload the modified cookbook to the Chef Server:

   mma@laptop:~/chef-repo $ knife cookbook upload ntp

   ```
   Uploading ntp            [1.3.2]
   Uploaded 1 cookbook.
   ```

6. Run Chef Client on the node again:

   user@server:~$ sudo chef-client

   ```
   ...TRUNCATED OUTPUT...
   [2013-02-21T11:09:44+00:00] FATAL: 'Ouch!!! Bailing out!!!



   ================================================================
   ==============

   Recipe Compile Error in
     /srv/chef/file_store/cookbooks/my_cookbook/recipes/
     default.rb


   ================================================================
   ==============




   SystemExit
   ----------
   exit
   ```

```
Cookbook Trace:
---------------
  /srv/chef/file_store/cookbooks/my_cookbook/recipes/default.
  rb:9:in `from_file'


Relevant File Content:
----------------------
/srv/chef/file_store/cookbooks/my_cookbook/recipes/default.
  rb:

  2:  # Cookbook Name:: my_cookbook
  3:  # Recipe:: default
  4:  #
  5:  # Copyright 2013, YOUR_COMPANY_NAME
  6:  #
  7:  # All rights reserved - Do Not Redistribute
  8:  #
  9>> Chef::Application.fatal!("'Ouch!!! Bailing out!!!")
  10:
```

```
[2013-02-21T11:09:44+00:00] ERROR: Running exception
  handlers
[2013-02-21T11:09:44+00:00] FATAL: Saving node information
  to /srv/chef/file_store/failed-run-data.json
[2013-02-21T11:09:44+00:00] ERROR: Exception handlers
  complete
```

How it works...

The `fatal!(msg)` method logs the given error message through `Chef::Log.fatal(msg)` and then exits the Chef Client process using `Process.exit`.

There's more...

You might want to exit the Chef Client run without logging a `fatal` message. You can do so by using the `exit!(msg)` method in your recipe. It will log the given message as `debug` and exit the Chef Client.

▸ Read the documentation for the `fatal!` method here:

  `http://rdoc.info/gems/chef/Chef/Application#fatal%21-class_ method`

▸ Find a detailed description about how to abort a Chef Client run here:

  `http://stackoverflow.com/questions/14290397/how-do-you-abort- end-a-chef-run`

Diffing cookbooks with knife

When working with a Chef Server you often need to know what exactly is already uploaded to it. You edit files like recipes or roles locally, and commit and push them to GitHub.

But, before you're ready to upload your edits to the Chef Server, you want to verify your changes. To do that you want to run a **diff** between the local version of your files against the version already uploaded to the Chef Server.

Getting ready

If you're using Chef 10.x or 0.10.x you need to install the `knife-essentials` gem by adding it to your `Gemfile` and running `bundle` install.

How to do it...

After changing a recipe, you can diff it against the current version stored on the Chef Server.

Let Knife show you the differences between your local version of `my_cookbook` and the version stored on the Chef Server by running:

```
mma@laptop:~/chef-repo $ knife diff cookbooks/my_cookbook

    diff --knife remote/cookbooks/my_cookbook/recipes/default.rb
      cookbooks/my_cookbook/recipes/default.rb
    --- remote/cookbooks/my_cookbook/recipes/default.rb      2012-11-26
      21:39:06.000000000 +0100
    +++ cookbooks/my_cookbook/recipes/default.rb       2012-11-26
      21:39:06.000000000 +0100
    @@ -6,3 +6,4 @@
     #
     # All rights reserved - Do Not Redistribute
     #
    +group "my_group"
```

```
\ No newline at end of file
Only in cookbooks/my_cookbook: attributes
Only in cookbooks/my_cookbook: definitions
Only in cookbooks/my_cookbook: files
Only in cookbooks/my_cookbook: libraries
Only in cookbooks/my_cookbook: providers
Only in cookbooks/my_cookbook: resources
Only in cookbooks/my_cookbook: templates
```

How it works...

The `diff` verb for `knife` treats the Chef Server like a file server mirroring your local file system. That way you can run diffs comparing your local files against files stored on the Chef Server.

There's more...

If you want to show diffs of multiple cookbooks at once, you can use wildcards when running `knife diff`:

mma@laptop:~/chef-repo $ knife diff cookbooks/*

```
diff --knife remote/cookbooks/backup_gem/recipes/default.rb
  cookbooks/backup_gem/recipes/default.rb
...TRUNCATED OUTPUT...
diff --knife remote/cookbooks/backup_gem/metadata.rb
  cookbooks/backup_gem/metadata.rb
...TRUNCATED OUTPUT...
```

In addition to the `diff` verb, `knife` understands the verbs `download`, `list`, `show`, and `upload`. And it does not only offer these verbs for cookbooks but for everything that is stored on the Chef Server, such as roles, data bags, and so on.

See also

▸ Find some more examples on how to use `knife diff` here:

`http://docs.opscode.com/knife_diff.html`

▸ The `knife-essentials` gem lives here:

`https://github.com/jkeiser/knife-essentials`

Using community exception and report handlers

When running your Chef Client as daemon on your nodes, you usually have no idea whether everything works as expected. Chef comes with a feature named **Handler**, which helps you to find out what's going on during your Chef Client runs.

There are a host of community handlers available, for example, for reporting Chef Client run results to IRC, via e-mail, to Campfire, Nagios, Graphite, you name it.

In this section, we'll see how to install an IRC handler as an example. The same method is applicable to all other available handlers.

 For a full list of available community handlers go to:

```
http://docs.opscode.com/essentials_handlers_available_
handlers.html
```

Getting ready...

1. In order to install community exception and report handlers, you need to get the `chef_handler` cookbook first:

   mma@laptop:~/chef-repo $ knife cookbook site install chef_handler

   ```
   ...TRUNCATED OUTPUT...
   Cookbook chef_handler version 1.1.2 successfully installed
   ```

2. Upload the `chef_handler` cookbook to your Chef Server:

   mma@laptop:~/chef-repo $ knife cookbook upload chef_handler

   ```
   Uploading chef_handler    [1.1.2]
   Uploaded 1 cookbook.
   ```

How to do it...

Let's see how to install and use one of the community handlers:

1. Create your own cookbook for installing community exception and report handlers:

   mma@laptop:~/chef-repo $ knife cookbook create my_handlers

   ```
   ** Creating cookbook my_handlers
   ** Creating README for cookbook: my_handlers
   ** Creating CHANGELOG for cookbook: my_handlers
   ** Creating metadata for cookbook: my_handlers
   ```

2. Make your `my_handlers` cookbook aware of the fact that it needs the `chef_handler` cookbook by adding the dependency to its metadata:

```
mma@laptop:~/chef-repo $ subl
  cookbooks/my_handlers/metadata.rb

...
depends 'chef_handler'
```

3. Add the IRC handler to your `my_handlers` cookbook (make sure you use your own URI for the `irc_uri` argument):

```
mma@laptop:~/chef-repo $ subl
  cookbooks/my_handlers/recipes/default.rb

include_recipe 'chef_handler'

chef_gem "chef-irc-snitch"

chef_handler 'Chef::Handler::IRCSnitch' do
  action :enable
  arguments :irc_uri => "irc://nick:password@irc.example.
    com:6667/#admins"
  source File.join(Gem::Specification.find{|s| s.name ==
    'chef-irc-snitch'}.gem_dir,
    'lib', 'chef-irc-snitch.rb')
end
```

4. Upload your `my_handlers` cookbook to your Chef Server:

```
mma@laptop:~/chef-repo $ knife cookbook upload my_handlers

Uploading my_handlers    [0.1.0]
Uploaded 1 cookbook.
```

5. Run Chef Client on your node to install your handlers:

```
user@server:~$ sudo chef-client

...TRUNCATED OUTPUT...
 [2012-12-28T11:02:57+00:00] INFO: Enabling chef_handler[Chef::Han
dler::IRCSnitch] as a report handler
[2012-12-28T11:02:57+00:00] INFO: Enabling chef_handler[Chef::Hand
ler::IRCSnitch] as a exception handler
[2012-12-28T11:02:58+00:00] INFO: Chef Run complete in 3.762220162
seconds
[2012-12-28T11:02:58+00:00] INFO: Running report handlers
[2012-12-28T11:02:58+00:00] INFO: Report handlers complete
```

How it works...

The `chef_handler` **Light Weight Resource Provider** (**LWRP**) provided by the `chef_handler` cookbook helps you enable and configure any custom handler without the need to manually modify the `client.rb` on all your nodes.

Typically, you install the desired community handler as a gem. You do this using the `chef_gem` resource.

You can pass an attributes hash to the `Handler` class and you need to tell the LWRP where it can find the `Handler` class. The default should be `chef/handlers/...` but more often than not, this is not the case. We're searching through all our installed Ruby gems to find the right one and append the path to the `.rb` file where the `Handler` class is defined.

The LWRP will take care of enabling the handler, if you tell it so using `enable true`.

There's more...

If you want, you can install your handler manually by editing `client.rb` on your nodes.

If your desired handler is not available as a Ruby gem, you can install it into `/var/chef/handlers` and use this directory as the source when using the `chef_handler` LWRP.

See also

▶ Read more about exception and report handlers at:

  `http://docs.opscode.com/essentials_handlers.html`

Creating custom handlers

Chef handlers can be very helpful to integrate Chef with your tool chain. If there is no handler readily available for the tools you use, it's pretty simple to write your own.

We'll have a look how to create an exception handler reporting Chef Client run failures to **Flowdock**, a web-based team inbox and chat tool.

Getting ready...

As we want to publish information to a Flowdock inbox, you need to sign up for an account at `http://www.flowdock.com`. And we need to install the API client as a Ruby gem to be able to post to our team inbox from Chef.

Install the `flowdock` gem on your local development box:

```
mma@laptop:~/chef-repo $ subl Gemfile
```

```
...
gem 'flowdock'
```

```
mma@laptop:~/chef-repo $ bundle install
```

```
Fetching gem metadata from https://rubygems.org/
...TRUNCATED OUTPUT...
Installing flowdock (0.3.1)
```

How to do it...

Carry out the following steps to create a custom handler to post Chef run failures to Flowdock:

1. Create your handler class:

   ```
   mma@laptop:~/work/chef-handler-flowdock $ mkdir -p
     lib/chef/handler
   ```

   ```
   mma@laptop:~/work/chef-handler-flowdock $ subl
     lib/chef/handler/flowdock_handler.rb
   ```

   ```ruby
   require 'chef/handler'
   require 'flowdock'

   class Chef
     class Handler
       class FlowdockHandler < Chef::Handler

         def initialize(options = {})
           @from = options[:from] || nil
           @flow = Flowdock::Flow.new(:api_token =>
             options[:api_token],
             :source => options[:source] || "Chef Client")
         end

         def report
           if run_status.failed?
             content = "Chef Client raised an exception:<br/>"
             content << run_status.formatted_exception
             content << "<br/>"
             content << run_status.backtrace.join("<br/>")

             @from = {:name => "root", :address =>
               "root@#{run_status.node.fqdn}"} if @from.nil?
   ```

```
          @flow.push_to_team_inbox(:subject => "Chef Client
             run on #{run_status.node} failed!",
              :content => content,
              :tags => ["chef",
                run_status.node.chef_environment,
                run_status.node.name], :from => @from)
          end
        end
      end
    end
  end
```

2. Copy the handler to your node:

    user@server:~$ sudo mkdir -p /var/chef/handlers

    **mma@laptop:~/work/chef-handler-flowdock $ scp
    lib/chef/handler/flowdock_handler.rb
    user@server:/var/chef/handlers/flowdock_handler.rb**

3. Enable the handler in your client.rb on your node. Replace FLOWDOCK_API_
    TOKEN with your own token:

    user@server:~$ subl /etc/chef/client.rb

    ```
    require '/var/chef/handlers/flowdock_handler'
    exception_handlers <<
      Chef::Handler::FlowdockHandler.new(:api_token =>
      "FLOWDOCK_API_TOKEN")
    ```

If you've a failing Chef Client run on your node, your handler will report it to your Flowdock flow.

How it works...

To create a Chef handler your class needs to extend Chef::Handler. It should have two methods: initialize and report. Chef will call the report method at the end of every Chef Client run.

The handler class can access the run_status of the Chef Client run to retrieve information about the run, for example, the current node object, success? or failure?, and the exception (if any). You can find a full list of supported attributes here: http://docs. opscode.com/essentials_handlers_properties.html

As we only want to report exceptions, we execute our logic inside the report method only if the Chef run failed.

There's more...

Instead of manually installing the handler on all your nodes, you can create a cookbook (see the *Using community exception and report handlers* section in this chapter).

In our example, we create the Flowdock API client in the `initialize` method. If you use the LWRP to install the handler, the `initialize` method will receive an options Hash from the `attributes` call inside the `chef_handler` provider.

See also

▸   The *Using community exception and report handlers* section

3
Chef Language and Style

"Style is what separates the good from the great."

– Bozhidar Batsov

In this chapter, we will cover the following:

- ▶ Using community Chef style
- ▶ Using attributes to dynamically configure recipes
- ▶ Using templates
- ▶ Mixing plain Ruby with Chef DSL
- ▶ Installing Ruby gems and using them in recipes
- ▶ Using libraries
- ▶ Using definitions
- ▶ Creating your own Lightweight Resources and Providers (LWRP)
- ▶ Extending community cookbooks by using application wrapper cookbooks
- ▶ Creating custom Ohai plugins
- ▶ Creating custom Knife plugins

Introduction

If you want to automate your infrastructure, you will end up using most of Chef's language features. In this chapter, we will have a look at how to use the Chef **Domain Specific Language** (**DSL**) from basic to advanced. We will end the chapter with creating custom plugins for Ohai and Knife.

Using community Chef style

It's easier to read code that adheres to a coding style guide. Especially when sharing cookbooks with the Chef community it is really important to deliver consistently styled code.
On the following pages, you'll find some of the most important rules (out of many more—enough to fill a short book on its own) to apply to your own cookbooks.

Getting ready

As you're writing cookbooks in Ruby, it's a good idea to follow general Ruby principles for readable (and therefore maintainable) code.

Opscode proposes Ian Macdonald's *Ruby Style Guide* (`http://www.caliban.org/ruby/rubyguide.shtml#style`) in its *Cookbook Style Guide Draft* (`http://wiki.opscode.com/display/chef/Cookbook+Style+Guide+Draft`).

But, to be honest, I prefer Bozhidar Batsov's *Ruby Style Guide* (`https://github.com/bbatsov/ruby-style-guide`) due to its clarity.

Let's have a look at the most important rules for Ruby in general and for cookbooks specifically.

How to do it...

Let's walk through a few Chef styling guideline examples:

1. Use two spaces per indentation level:

```
remote_directory node['nagios']['plugin_dir'] do
  source 'plugins'
end
```

2. Use Unix-style line endings. Avoid Windows line endings by configuring Git accordingly:

```
mma@laptop:~/chef-repo $ git config --global core.autocrlf true
```

 For more options on how to deal with line endings in Git read `https://help.github.com/articles/dealing-with-line-endings`.

3. Align parameters spanning more than one line:

```
variables(
  mon_host: 'monitoring.example.com',
  nrpe_directory: "#{node['nagios']['nrpe']['conf_dir']}/nrpe.d"
)
```

4. Describe your cookbook in `metadata.rb` (you should always use the Ruby DSL as the JSON version will be automatically generated from it).

5. Version your cookbook using Semantic Versioning (`http://semver.org`):

```
version          "1.1.0"
```

6. List supported operating systems looping through an array using each:

```
%w(redhat centos ubuntu debian).each do |os|
  supports os
end
```

7. Declare dependencies in your `metadata.rb`:

```
depends "apache2", ">= 1.0.4"
depends "build-essential"
```

8. Construct strings from variable values and static parts using string expansion:

```
my_string = "This resource changed #{counter} files"
```

9. Download temporary files to `Chef::Config[:file_cache_path]` instead of `/tmp` or some local directory.

10. Use strings to access node attributes instead of Ruby symbols:

```
node['nagios']['users_databag_group']
```

11. Set attributes in `my_cookbook/attributes/default.rb` by using `default`:

```
default['my_cookbook']['version']     = "3.0.11"
```

12. Create an attribute namespace by using your cookbook name as a first level in your `my_cookbook/attributes/default.rb`:

```
default['my_cookbook']['version']     = "3.0.11"
default['my_cookbook']['name']        = "Mine"
```

How it works...

Using community Chef style helps to increase the readability of your cookbooks. Your cookbooks will be read much more often than changed. Because of that, it usually pays off to put a little extra effort into following a strict style guide when writing cookbooks.

There's more...

Using Semantic Versioning (see: `http://semver.org`) for your cookbooks helps to manage dependencies. If you change anything, which might break cookbooks depending on your cookbook, you need to consider this as a backwards-incompatible API change. Semantic Versioning demands in that case that you increase the major number of your cookbook, for example, from `1.1.3` to `2.0.0`, resetting minor and patch levels.

Using Semantic Versioning helps to keep your production systems stable if you freeze your cookbooks (see the *Freezing Cookbooks* section in *Chapter 1, Chef Infrastructure*).

See also

  ▸ The *Flagging problems in your Chef cookbooks* section in *Chapter 2, Evaluating and Troubleshooting Cookbooks and Chef Runs*.

Using attributes to dynamically configure recipes

Imagine some cookbook author has hardcoded the path where the cookbook puts a configuration file—but in a place, that does not comply with your rules. Now you're in trouble! You can either patch the cookbook or rewrite it from scratch. Both options leave you with a lot of work and headache.

Attributes are there to avoid such headaches. Instead of hardcoding values inside cookbooks, attributes enable authors to make their cookbooks configurable. By overriding default values set in cookbooks, users can inject their own values. Suddenly, it's next to trivial to obey your own rules.

In the next section, we'll see how to use attributes in your cookbooks.

Getting ready

Make sure you have a cookbook called `my_cookbook`, and the `run_list` of your node includes `my_cookbook` as described in the *Creating and Using Cookbooks* section in *Chapter 1, Chef Infrastructure*.

How to do it...

Let's see how to define and use a simple attribute:

1. Create a default file for your cookbook attributes:

   mma@laptop:~/chef-repo $ subl cookbooks/my_cookbook/attributes/ default.rb

2. Add a default attribute:

   ```
   default['my_cookbook']['message'] = 'hello world!'
   ```

3. Use the attribute inside a recipe:

   mma@laptop:~/chef-repo $ subl cookbooks/my_cookbook/recipes/ default.rb

   ```
   message = node['my_cookbook']['message']
   Chef::Log.info("** Saying what I was told to say: #{message}")
   ```

4. Upload the modified cookbook to the Chef Server:

   mma@laptop:~/chef-repo $ knife cookbook upload my_cookbook

   ```
   Uploading my_cookbook      [0.1.0]
   ```

5. Run Chef Client on your node:

   user@server:~$ sudo chef-client

   ```
   ...TRUNCATED OUTPUT...
   [2013-01-13T20:48:21+00:00] INFO: ** Saying what I was told to
   say: hello world!
   ...TRUNCATED OUTPUT...
   ```

How it works...

Chef loads all attributes from the attribute files before it executes the recipes. The attributes are stored with the node object. You can access all attributes stored with the node object from within your recipes and retrieve their current values.

Chef has a strict order of precedence for attributes: default being the lowest, then comes normal (which is aliased with set), and then override. Additionally, attribute levels set in recipes have precedence over the same level set in an attribute file. And attributes defined in roles and environments have highest precedence since Chef 11.

There's more...

You can set and override attributes within roles and environments as well. Since Chef 11 attributes defined in roles or environments have the highest precedence (on their respective levels: `default`, `normal`, `override`).

1. Create a role:

   mma@laptop:~/chef-repo $ subl roles/german_hosts.rb

   ```
   name "german_hosts"
   description "This Role contains hosts, which should print out
   their messages in German"
   run_list "recipe[my_cookbook]"
   default_attributes "my_cookbook" => { "message" => "Hallo Welt!" }
   ```

2. Upload the role to the Chef Server:

   mma@laptop:~/chef-repo $ knife role from file german_hosts.rb

   ```
   Updated Role german_hosts!
   ```

3. Assign the role to a node called `server`:

   mma@laptop:~/chef-repo $ knife node edit server

   ```
     "run_list": [
       "role[german_hosts]"
     ]
   Saving updated run_list on node server
   ```

4. Run the Chef Client:

   user@server:~$ sudo chef-client

   ```
   ...TRUNCATED OUTPUT...
   [2013-01-13T20:49:49+00:00] INFO: ** Saying what I was told to
   say: Hallo Welt!
   ...TRUNCATED OUTPUT...
   ```

Calculating values in attribute files

Since Chef 11, attributes set in roles and environments (as shown earlier) have the highest precedence, and they're already available when the attribute files get loaded. This enables you to calculate attribute values based on role or environment-specific values.

1. Set an attribute within a role:

   mma@laptop:~/chef-repo $ subl roles/german_hosts.rb

   ```
   name "german_hosts"
   description "This Role contains hosts, which should print out
   their messages in German"
   run_list "recipe[my_cookbook]"
   ```

```
default_attributes "my_cookbook" => {
  "hi" => "Hallo",
  "world" => "Welt"
}
```

2. Calculate the message attribute based on the two attributes `hi` and `world`:

   **mma@laptop:~/chef-repo $ subl cookbooks/my_cookbook/attributes/
   default.rb**

   ```
   default['my_cookbook']['message'] = "#{node['my_cookbook']['hi']}
   #{node['my_cookbook']['world']}!"
   ```

3. Upload the modified cookbook to your Chef Server and run the Chef Client on your node to see that it works as shown in the preceding example.

See also

▸ Read more about attributes in Chef at: `http://docs.opscode.com/chef_ overview_attributes.html`

▸ Learn all about how Chef 11 changed the way to deal with attributes here: `http://www.opscode.com/blog/2013/02/05/chef-11-in-depth- attributes-changes/`

Using templates

Configuration Management is all about, well, configuring your hosts. Usually, configuration is carried out using configuration files. Chef is using templates to be able to fill configuration files with dynamic values. It offers `template` as a resource you can use in your recipes.

You can retrieve such dynamic values from **data bags**, attributes, or even calculate them on the fly before passing them into the template.

Getting ready

Make sure you have a cookbook called `my_cookbook` and the `run_list` of your node includes `my_cookbook` in the *Creating and using cookbooks* section in *Chapter 1, Chef Infrastructure*.

How to do it...

Let's see how to create and use a template to dynamically generate a file on your node.

1. Add a template to your recipe:

   **mma@laptop:~/chef-repo $ subl cookbooks/my_cookbook/recipes/
   default.rb**

   ```
   template '/tmp/message' do
     source 'message.erb'
     variables(
       hi: 'Hallo',
       world: 'Welt',
       from: node['fqdn']
     )
   end
   ```

2. Add the **ERB** template file:

   **mma@laptop:~/chef-repo $ subl cookbooks/my_cookbook/templates/
   default/message.erb**

   ```
   <%- 4.times do %>
   <%= @hi %>, <%= @world %> from <%= @from %>!
   <%- end %>
   ```

3. Upload the modified cookbook to the Chef Server:

   mma@laptop:~/chef-repo $ knife cookbook upload my_cookbook

   ```
   Uploading my_cookbook        [0.1.0]
   Run Chef Client on your node:
   user@server:~$ sudo chef-client
   ...TRUNCATED OUTPUT...
   [2013-01-14T20:41:21+00:00] INFO: Processing template[/tmp/
   message] action create (my_cookbook::default line 9)
   [2013-01-14T20:41:22+00:00] INFO: template[/tmp/message] updated
   content
   ...TRUNCATED OUTPUT...
   ```

4. Validate the content of the generated file:

   user@server:~$ sudo cat /tmp/message

   ```
   Hallo, Welt from vagrant.vm!
   Hallo, Welt from vagrant.vm!
   Hallo, Welt from vagrant.vm!
   Hallo, Welt from vagrant.vm!
   ```

How it works...

Chef uses **Erubis** as its template language. It allows embedding pure Ruby code inside special symbols inside your templates.

You use <%= %> if you want to print the value of a variable or Ruby expression into the generated file.

You use <%- %> if you want to embed Ruby logic into your template file. We used it to loop our expression four times.

When you use the `template` resource, Chef makes all the variables you pass in available as instance variables when rendering the template. We used @hi, @world, and @from in our earlier example.

There's more...

The node object is available in a template as well. Technically, you could access node attributes directly from within your template:

```
<%= node['fqdn'] %>
```

But, this is not a good idea because it will introduce hidden dependencies to your template. It is better to make dependencies explicit, for example, by declaring the FQDN as a variable for the `template` resource inside your cookbook:

```
template '/tmp/fqdn' do
  source 'fqdn.erb'
  variables(
    fqdn:node['fqdn']
  )
end
```

 Avoid using the node object directly inside your templates because this introduces hidden dependencies to node variables in your templates.

If you need a different template for a specific host or platform, you can put those specific templates into various subdirectories of the `templates` directory. Chef will try to locate the correct template by searching through these directories from most specific (host) to least (default).

You could put your `message.erb` into the directory `cookbooks/my_cookbook/templates/host-server.vm ("host-#{node[:fqdn]}")` if it would be host specific. If it would be specific to a certain platform version, you could put it into `cookbooks/my_cookbook/templates/ubuntu-12.04 ("#{node[:platform]}-#{node[:platorm_version]}")`, and if it would only be platform specific, you would put it into `cookbooks/my_cookbook/templates/ubuntu ("#{node[:platform]}")`. Only if your template is the same for any host or platform would you put it into the `default` directory.

> Be aware of the fact that the `templates/default` directory means that a template file is the same for all hosts and platforms—it does not correspond to a recipe name.

See also

> ▸ Read more about templates at: `http://docs.opscode.com/essentials_cookbook_templates.html`

Mixing plain Ruby with Chef DSL

For creating simple recipes you only need to use resources such as `template`, `remote_file`, and `service`. But as your recipes become more elaborate, you'll discover the need to do more advanced things such as conditionally executing parts of your recipe, looping, or even complex calculations.

Instead of declaring the `gem_package` resource 10 times simply using different name attributes, it is so much easier to loop through an array of gem names creating the `gem_package` resources on the fly.

This is the power of mixing plain Ruby with Chef Domain Specific Language (DSL). We'll see a few tricks in the following sections.

Getting ready

Start a Chef Shell on any of your nodes in *client mode* to be able to access your Chef Server:

```
user@server:~$ sudo chef-shell --client

    loading configuration: /etc/chef/client.rb
    Session type: client
    ...TRUNCATED OUTPUT...
    run `help' for help, `exit' or ^D to quit.

    Ohai2u user@server!
    chef >
```

How to do it...

Let's play around with some Ruby constructs in Chef Shell to get a feel for what's possible:

1. Get all nodes from the Chef Server using `search` from the Chef DSL:

   ```
   chef > nodes = search(:node, "hostname:[* TO *]")
   ```

   ```
   => [node[server],node[alice]]
   ```

2. Sort your nodes by name using plain Ruby:

   ```
   chef > nodes.sort! {|a,b| a.name <=> b.name }
   ```

   ```
   => [node[alice],node[server]]
   ```

3. Loop through the nodes printing their operating systems:

   ```
   chef > nodes.each do |n|
   chef > puts n['os']
   chef ?> end
   ```

   ```
   linux
   windows
    => [node[server], node[alice]]
   ```

4. Log only if there are no nodes:

   ```
   chef > Chef::Log.warn("No nodes found") if nodes.empty?
   ```

   ```
   => nil
   ```

5. Install multiple Ruby gems using an array, a loop, and string expansion to construct the gem names:

   ```
   chef > %w{ec2 essentials}.each do |gem|
   chef > gem_package "knife-#{gem}"
   chef ?> end
   ```

   ```
   => ["ec2", "essentials"]
   ```

How it works...

Chef recipes are Ruby files, which get evaluated in the context of a Chef run. They can contain plain Ruby code such as `if` statements and loops as well as Chef **Domain Specific Language** (**DSL**) elements such as resources (`remote_file`, `service`, `template`, and so on).

Inside your recipes you can simply declare Ruby variables and assign them any values. We used the Chef DSL method `search` to retrieve an array of `Chef::Node` instances and stored that array in the variable `nodes`.

Because `nodes` is a plain Ruby array, we can use all methods the array class provides, such as `sort!` or `empty?`.

And we can iterate through the array by using plain Ruby `each`, as we did in the third example explained earlier.

Another common thing is to use `if`, `else`, or `case` for conditional execution. In the preceding fourth example, we used `if` to only write a warning to the logfile, if the `nodes` array is empty.

In the last example, we combined an array of strings (holding parts of gem names) and the `each` iterator with the Chef DSL `gem_package` resource to install two Ruby gems. To take things one step further we used plain Ruby string expansion to construct the full gem names (`knife-ec2` and `knife-essentials`) on the fly.

There's more...

You can use the full power of Ruby combined with the Chef DSL in your recipes. Here is an excerpt from the `server.rb` recipe from Opscode's `nagios` cookbook, which shows what's possible:

```
# Load search defined Nagios hostgroups from the nagios_hostgroups
data bag and find nodes
begin
  hostgroup_nodes= Hash.new
  hostgroup_list = Array.new
  search(:nagios_hostgroups, '*:*') do |hg|
    hostgroup_list << hg['hostgroup_name']
    temp_hostgroup_array= Array.new
    if node['nagios']['multi_environment_monitoring']
      search(:node, "#{hg['search_query']}") do |n|
        temp_hostgroup_array << n['hostname']
      end
    else
      search(:node, "#{hg['search_query']} AND chef_
environment:#{node.chef_environment}") do |n|
        temp_hostgroup_array << n['hostname']
      end
    end
    hostgroup_nodes[hg['hostgroup_name']] = temp_hostgroup_array.
join(",")
  end
rescue Net::HTTPServerException
  Chef::Log.info("Search for nagios_hostgroups data bag failed, so
we'll just move on.")
end
```

First, they declare a few Ruby variables to use them later.

Then, they try to retrieve data from a data bag called `nagios_hostgroups`. To avoid the recipe failing if that data bag is not available, they wrap their logic with `begin`, `rescue`, and `end`—Ruby's way of exception handling.

Inside that block, you see a mix of plain Ruby stuff such as `hostgroup_nodes = Hash.new` and Chef DSL such as the usage of attributes or `search`.

See also

▸ Find out more about how to use Ruby in recipes here: `http://docs.opscode.com/chef/dsl_recipe.html`

▸ The *Using community Chef style* section

▸ The *Using attributes to dynamically configure recipes* section

Installing Ruby gems and using them in recipes

Recipes are plain Ruby files. It is possible to use all of Ruby's language features inside your recipes. Most of the time the built-in Ruby functionality is enough but sometimes you might want to use additional Ruby gems, for example, to connect to an external application via an API or simply to access a MySQL database from within your recipe.

Chef lets you install Ruby gems from within a recipe so that you can use them inside the very same recipe.

Getting ready

Make sure you've a cookbook named `my_cookbook`, which is in your node's run list in the Creating and using cookbooks section in *Chapter 1, Chef Infrastructure*.

How to do it...

Let's see how we can use the `ipaddress` gem in our recipe:

1. Edit the default recipe of your cookbook, installing a gem to be used inside the recipe:

   mma@laptop:~/chef-repo $ subl

   ```
   cookbooks/my_cookbook/recipes/default.rb
   chef_gem 'ipaddress'
   require 'ipaddress'
   ```

```
ip = IPAddress("192.168.0.1/24")
Chef::Log.info("Netmask of #{ip}: #{ip.netmask}")
```

2. Upload the modified cookbook to the Chef Server:

   mma@laptop:~/chef-repo $ knife cookbook upload my_cookbook

   ```
   Uploading my_cookbook     [0.1.0]
   ```

3. Run Chef Client on your node to see whether it works:

   user@server $ sudo chef-client

   ```
   ...TRUNCATED OUTPUT...
   [2013-01-18T14:02:02+00:00] INFO: Netmask of 192.168.0.1:
   255.255.255.0
   ...TRUNCATED OUTPUT...
   ```

How it works...

A Chef run consists of a compile phase where it instantiates all resources and an execution phase where Chef runs the resource providers to converge the node.

If you want to use the functionality of a Ruby gem inside your cookbook, you need to install that gem during the compile phase. Otherwise it will not be available during the execute phase (only afterwards).

The chef_gem resource will exactly do that. And, if you're using Chef Omnibus, this is the only way to make gems available to Chef itself.

The gem_package resource, in contrast, installs the gem into the system Ruby. It does that during the converge phase of the Chef run. This means that gems installed by gem_package can not be used inside your recipes.

See also

▸ The *Mixing plain Ruby with Chef DSL* section

Using libraries

While you can use arbitrary Ruby code within your recipes, this might quickly get messy if you're doing more complicated stuff like integrating existing infrastructure or doing complicated API calls.

Libraries provide a place to encapsulate complicated logic so that your recipes stay clean and neat.

In this section, we'll create a simple library to see how this works out.

Getting ready

Make sure you have a cookbook called my_cookbook and the run_list of your node includes my_cookbook in the *Creating and using cookbooks* section in *Chapter 1, Chef Infrastructure*.

How to do it...

Let's create a library and use it in a cookbook:

1. Create a helper method in your own cookbook's library:

   mma@laptop:~/chef-repo $ subl cookbooks/my_cookbook/libraries/ipaddress.rb

   ```
   class Chef::Recipe
     def netmask(ipaddress)
       IPAddress(ipaddress).netmask
     end
   end
   ```

2. Use your helper method:

   mma@laptop:~/chef-repo $ subl cookbooks/my_cookbook/recipes/default.rb

   ```
   ip = '10.10.0.0/24'
   mask = netmask(ip) # here we use the library method
   Chef::Log.info("Netmask of #{ip}: #{mask}")
   ```

3. Upload the modified cookbook to the Chef Server:

   mma@laptop:~/chef-repo $ knife cookbook upload my_cookbook

   ```
   Uploading my_cookbook      [0.1.0]
   ```

4. Run the Chef Client on your node to see whether it works:

   user@server $ sudo chef-client

   ```
   ...TRUNCATED OUTPUT...
   [2013-01-18T14:38:26+00:00] INFO: Netmask of 10.10.0.0/24:
   255.255.255.0
   ...TRUNCATED OUTPUT...
   ```

How it works...

In your library code you can open the Chef::Recipe class and add your new methods.

 This isn't the cleanest, but the simplest way of doing it. The following paragraphs will help you to find out a cleaner way.

```
class Chef::Recipe
  def netmask(ipaddress)
    ...
  end
end
```

Chef automatically loads your library code in the compile phase that enables you to use the methods you declare there inside your recipes:

```
mask = netmask(ip)
```

There's more...

Opening a class and adding methods pollutes the class' namespace. This might lead to name clashes, for example, if you define a method inside a library of your own cookbook and someone else defines a method with the same name in the library of another cookbook. Another clash would happen if you accidentally use a method name, which Chef defines in its `Chef::Recipe` class.

It's cleaner to introduce your own subclasses inside your libraries and define your methods as class methods. This avoids polluting the `Chef::Recipe` namespace.

mma@laptop:~/chef-repo $ subl cookbooks/my_cookbook/libraries/ipaddress. rb

```
class Chef::Recipe::IPAddress
  def self.netmask(ipaddress)
    IPAddress(ipaddress).netmask
  end
end
```

You can use the method inside your recipes like this:

```
IPAddress.netmask(ip)
```

You can define library methods in Chef Shell directly in the root context:

user@server $ chef-shell --client

```
chef > class Chef::Recipe::IPAddress
chef ?> def self.netmask(ipaddress)
chef ?>     IPAddress(ipaddress).netmask
chef ?>   end
chef ?> end
```

Now you can use the library method inside the recipe context:

```
chef > recipe
chef:recipe > IPAddress.netmask('10.10.0.0/24')
 => "255.255.255.0"
```

See also

▸ The *Using the Chef console (Chef Shell)* section in *Chapter 1, Creating and Using Cookbooks*

▸ The *Mixing plain Ruby with Chef DSL* section

Using definitions

Your cookbooks grow and get pretty long. Silently some duplication sneak in as well. You'll come to the point where it is time to group resources and give them names to regain readability for your cookbook. And if you use the same set of resources again and again it is a good idea to refactor this group of resources into a **definition**.

In this section, we'll group a set of resources into a definition to make it reusable.

Getting ready

Make sure you have a cookbook called `my_cookbook` and the `run_list` of your node includes `my_cookbook` in the *Creating and using cookbooks* section in *Chapter 1, Chef Infrastructure*.

How to do it...

Let's see how to create and use a definition:

1. Create a definition in a new file in your cookbook's `definitions` folder:

   ```
   mma@laptop:~/chef-repo $ subl cookbooks/my_cookbook/definitions/
   capistrano_deploy_dirs.rb
   ```

   ```
   define :capistrano_deploy_dirs, :deploy_to => '' do
     directory "#{params[:deploy_to]}/releases"
     directory "#{params[:deploy_to]}/shared"
     directory "#{params[:deploy_to]}/shared/system"
   end
   ```

2. Use the definition inside your cookbook's default recipe:

   ```
   mma@laptop:~/chef-repo $ subl cookbooks/my_cookbook/recipes/
   default.rb
   ```

   ```
   capistrano_deploy_dirs do
     deploy_to "/srv"
   end
   ```

3. Upload the modified cookbook to the Chef Server:

   ```
   mma@laptop:~/chef-repo $ knife cookbook upload my_cookbook
   ```

   ```
   Uploading my_cookbook    [0.1.0]
   ```

4. Run Chef Client on your node to see whether it works:

user@server $ sudo chef-client

```
...TRUNCATED OUTPUT...
[2013-01-18T16:31:11+00:00] INFO: Processing directory[/srv/
releases] action create (my_cookbook::default line 2)
[2013-01-18T16:31:11+00:00] INFO: directory[/srv/releases] created
directory /srv/releases
[2013-01-18T16:31:11+00:00] INFO: Processing directory[/srv/
shared] action create (my_cookbook::default line 3)
[2013-01-18T16:31:11+00:00] INFO: directory[/srv/shared] created
directory /srv/shared
[2013-01-18T16:31:11+00:00] INFO: Processing directory[/srv/
shared/system] action create (my_cookbook::default line 4)
[2013-01-18T16:31:11+00:00] INFO: directory[/srv/shared/system]
created directory /srv/shared/system
...TRUNCATED OUTPUT...
```

How it works...

Definitions in Chef are like macros: you group a collection of resources and give this group a name. Chef reads the definition and expands its contents into the recipe during the compile phase.

A definition has a name (here `capistrano_deploy_dirs`) by which you can call it from your recipe. And a definition has a list of parameters (here `deploy_to`):

```
define :capistrano_deploy_dirs, :deploy_to => '' do
  ...
end
```

The code inside the definition has access to a hash called `params`. It contains all the keys you defined after the definition name. Here, Chef will add the three `directory` resources to the execution list:

```
define ...
  directory "#{params[:deploy_to]}/releases"
  directory "#{params[:deploy_to]}/shared"
  directory "#{params[:deploy_to]}/shared/system"
end
```

In your recipes you can use the definition name instead of putting all the three `directory` resources. Inside the block you use dynamically generated methods to fill each parameter with its value:

```
capistrano_deploy_dirs do
  deploy_to "/srv"
end
```

There's more...

Be aware that definitions are expanded into their containing resources. Definitions are not available during the execution phase. You cannot notify a definition, but only the resources it contains.

You could *not* address the definition:

```
notifies :delete, 'capsitrano_deploy_dirs', :immediately
```

But you *could* address the individual resources inside the definition:

```
notifies :delete, 'directory[/srv/releases], :immediately
```

See also

 ▸ Read more about definitions at: `http://docs.opscode.com/essentials_cookbook_definitions.html`

Creating your own Light Weight Resource Providers (LWRP)

Chef offers the opportunity to extend the list of available resources by creating a custom **Light Weight Resource Provider** (**LWRP**). By creating your own custom resources, you can simplify writing cookbooks because your own custom resources enrich the Chef DSL and make your recipe code more expressive.

Many of the custom resources in Opscode's community cookbooks (and elsewhere) are implemented as LWRPs. So there are many working examples in the real world such as `iptables_rule` or `apt_repository`, and many more.

In this section, we will create a very simple LWRP to demonstrate the basic mechanics.

Getting ready

Make sure you've a cookbook named `greeting` and the `run_list` of your node includes `greeting` in the *Creating and using cookbooks* section in *Chapter 1, Chef Infrastructure*.

How to do it...

Let's see how to build a very simple LWRP to create a text file on your node:

1. Create your custom resource in your `greeting` cookbook:

   ```
   mma@laptop:~/chef-repo $ subl cookbooks/greeting/resources/
   default.rb
   ```

   ```
   actions :create, :remove

   attribute :title, kind_of: String, default: "World"
   attribute :path, kind_of: String, default: "/tmp/greeting.txt"
   ```

2. Create the provider for your resource in your `greeting` cookbook:

   ```
   mma@laptop:~/chef-repo $ subl cookbooks/greeting/providers/
   default.rb
   ```

   ```
   action :create do
     log "Adding '#{new_resource.name}' greeting as #{new_resource.
   path}"
       file new_resource.path do
         content "#{new_resource.name}, #{new_resource.title}!"
         action :create
       end
   end

   action :remove do
     Chef::Log.info "Removing '#{new_resource.name}' greeting #{new_
   resource.path}"
       file new_resource.path do
         action :delete
       end
   end
   ```

3. Use your new resource by editing your `greeting` cookbook's default recipe:

   ```
   mma@laptop:~/chef-repo $ subl cookbooks/greeting/recipes/default.
   rb
   ```

   ```
   greeting "Ohai" do
     title "Chef"
     action :create
   end
   ```

4. Upload the modified cookbook to the Chef Server:

   ```
   mma@laptop:~/chef-repo $ knife cookbook upload greeting
   ```

   ```
   Uploading greeting      [0.1.0]
   ```

5. Run Chef Client on your node:

```
user@server:~$ sudo chef-client

...TRUNCATED OUTPUT...
2013-06-28T21:32:54+00:00] INFO: Processing greeting[Ohai] action
create (greeting::default line 9)
[2013-06-28T21:32:54+00:00] INFO: Adding 'Ohai' greeting as /tmp/
greeting.txt
[2013-06-28T21:32:54+00:00] INFO: Processing file[/tmp/greeting.
txt] action create (/srv/chef/file_store/cookbooks/greeting/
providers/default.rb line 7)
[2013-06-28T21:32:54+00:00] INFO: entered create
[2013-06-28T21:32:54+00:00] INFO: file[/tmp/greeting.txt] created
file /tmp/greeting.txt
...TRUNCATED OUTPUT...
```

6. Validate the content of the generated file:

```
user@server:~$ cat /tmp/greeting.txt

Ohai, Chef!
```

How it works...

LWRPs live in cookbooks. A custom resource, which you define in a file called `default.rb` in the `resources` directory of your cookbook, will be available under the cookbook name.

We create `greeting/resources/default.rb` and use it in our default recipe as follows:

```
greeting "..." do
end
```

Let's see how the resource definition in `greeting/resources/default.rb` looks like.

First, we define the actions, which our resource should support:

```
actions :create, :remove
```

Then, we define attributes you can pass to the resource when using it in your cookbook. In our case, we define two string attributes with their default values:

```
attribute :title, kind_of: String, default: "World"
attribute :path, kind_of: String, default: "/tmp/greeting.txt"
```

Now, we can use those actions and attributes in our recipe:

```
greeting "Ohai" do
  title "Chef"
  action :create
end
```

We've defined the resource, now it's time to make it do something. The implementation of a resource lives in one or many providers. You might find multiple providers for the same resource for different operating systems. But we keep it simple here and create only one provider in `greeting/providers/default.rb`.

The provider has to implement each action defined in the resource in our case we need to implement two actions: `create` and `remove`.

```
action :create do
  ...
end
action :remove do
  ...
end
```

Now, you can use pure Ruby and existing Chef resources to make your provider do something. First, we create a log statement and then we use the existing `file` resource to create a text file containing the greeting:

```
log "Adding '#{new_resource.name}' greeting as #{new_resource.path}"
file new_resource.path do
  ...
end
```

`new_resource` is a Ruby variable containing the resource definition from the recipe using the resource. In our case, `new_resource.name` evaluates to "Ohai" and `new_resource.path` evaluates to the attribute's default value (because we did not use that attribute when using the `greeting` resource in our cookbook).

Inside the `file` resource, we use our resource's title (`new_resource.title`) attribute to fill the text file:

```
file new_resource.path do
  content "#{new_resource.name}, #{new_resource.title}!"
  action :create
end
```

The `remove` action works similar to the `create` action, but calling the `file` resource's `delete` action instead.

There's more...

To simplify the usage of your custom resource, you can define a default action. You declare it using the `default_action` call:

```
default_action :create
```

Now you can use your new resource like this:

```
greeting "Ohai" do
  title "Chef"
end
```

 If you're using plain Ruby code in your providers, you need to make sure that your code is idempotent. This means that it only runs if it has to modify something. You should be able to run your code multiple times on the same machine, without executing unnecessary actions on each run.

If you want your resource to support the `why-run`, you need to add the following to it:

```
def whyrun_supported?
  true
end
```

Then, you can wrap your code with a `converge_by` block. This will produce the message it displays in `why-run` mode instead of executing the code inside.

```
converge_by("Doing something with #{ @new_resource }") do
  ...
end
```

See also

▶ Read more about what LWRPs are at `http://docs.opscode.com/lwrp.html`

▶ You find a more detailed explanation about how to create LWRPs at `http://docs.opscode.com/lwrp_custom.html`

▶ The *Using why-run mode to find out what a recipe might do section*, in *Chapter 2, Evaluating and Troubleshooting Cookbooks and Chef Runs*

Extending community cookbooks by using application wrapper cookbooks

Using community cookbooks is great. But sometimes they do not exactly match your use case. You need to modify them. If you don't want to use Git vendor branches generated by `knife cookbook site install`, you need to use the *library* versus *application* cookbook approach.

In this approach, you don't touch the community (*library*) cookbook. Instead, you include it in your own application cookbook and modify resources from the library cookbook.

Let's see how to extend a community cookbook within your own application cookbook.

Getting ready

We'll use the `ntp` cookbook as a library cookbook and will change the `ntpdate` configuration it installs.

1. Install the `ntp` cookbook:

    ```
    mma@laptop:~/chef-repo $ knife cookbook site install ntp
    ```

    ```
    Installing ntp to /Users/mma/work/chef-repo/cookbooks
    ...TRUNCATED OUTPUT...
    Cookbook ntp version 1.3.2 successfully installed
    ```

2. Upload the `ntp` cookbook to the Chef Server:

    ```
    mma@laptop:~/chef-repo $ knife cookbook upload ntp
    ```

    ```
    Uploading ntp      [1.3.2]
    ```

3. Create your own application cookbook:

    ```
    mma@laptop:~/chef-repo $ knife cookbook create my-ntp
    ```

    ```
    ** Creating cookbook my-ntp
    ** Creating README for cookbook: my-ntp
    ** Creating CHANGELOG for cookbook: my-ntp
    ** Creating metadata for cookbook: my-ntp
    ```

4. Add the new `my-ntp` cookbook to the run list of your node:

    ```
    mma@laptop:~/chef-repo $ knife node edit server
    ```

    ```
    "run_list": [
      "recipe[my-ntp]"
    ]
    ```

 You could use Berkshelf as described in the *Managing cookbook dependencies with Berkshelf* section in *Chapter 1, Creating and Using Cookbooks*, to manage the dependency on the `ntp` cookbook within your `my-ntp` cookbook

How to do it...

Let's see how we can change the `ntp` cookbook's behavior from our own cookbook:

1. Add the dependency on the `ntp` cookbook to the `my-ntp` metadata:

   mma@laptop:~/chef-repo $ subl cookbooks/my-ntp/metadata.rb

   ```
   version            '0.1.0'
   ...
   depends 'ntp'
   ```

2. Change the `ntpdate` recipe from the `ntp` cookbook to load the template for `/etc/default/ntpdate` from your own cookbook instead of using the one provided by the `ntp` cookbook:

   mma@laptop:~/chef-repo $ subl cookbooks/my-ntp/recipes/default.rb

   ```
   ...
   include_recipe 'ntp::ntpdate'
   resources("template[/etc/default/ntpdate]").cookbook "my-ntp"
   ```

3. Add our own version of the `ntpdate` template to your cookbook:

   mma@laptop:~/chef-repo $ subl cookbooks/my-ntp/templates/default/ntpdate.erb

   ```
   <% if @disable %>exit 0<% end %>
   ...
   NTPOPTIONS="-v"
   ```

4. Upload your cookbook to the Chef Server:

   mma@laptop:~/chef-repo $ knife cookbook upload my-ntp

   ```
   Uploading my-ntp      [0.1.0]
   ```

5. Run Chef Client on your node:

   user@server $ sudo chef-client

   ```
   ...TRUNCATED OUTPUT...
   [2013-01-19T22:14:31+00:00] INFO: Processing template[/etc/
   default/ntpdate] action create (ntp::ntpdate line 28)
   [2013-01-19T22:14:32+00:00] INFO: template[/etc/default/ntpdate]
   updated content
   [2013-01-19T22:14:32+00:00] INFO: template[/etc/default/ntpdate]
   owner changed to 0
   [2013-01-19T22:14:32+00:00] INFO: template[/etc/default/ntpdate]
   group changed to 0
   [2013-01-19T22:14:32+00:00] INFO: template[/etc/default/ntpdate]
   mode changed to 644
   [2013-01-19T22:14:32+00:00] INFO: Chef Run complete in 2.251344614
   seconds
   ...TRUNCATED OUTPUT...
   ```

6. Validate that your own version of /etc/default/ntpdate has been installed (with NTPOPTIONS="-v" instead of NTPOPTIONS=""):

user@server $ cat /etc/default/ntpdate

```
...TRUNCATED OUTPUT...
# Additional options to pass to ntpdate
NTPOPTIONS="-v"
```

How it works...

We retrieve and modify the template resource for the /etc/default/ntpdate file from the ntp cookbook. First, we need to include the recipe, which defines the resource we want to modify. This is necessary so that Chef creates the resource during the compile phase of the Chef run.

```
include_recipe 'ntp::ntpdate'
```

The resources method retrieves the given resource. We can then call all the methods on it, which we could call while defining it in a recipe. In our example, we want to tell the template resource that it can find the ERB template in our cookbook instead of the original ntp cookbook.

```
resources("template[/etc/default/ntpdate]").cookbook "my-ntp"
```

This modification of the resource happens during the compile phase. Only after Chef has evaluated the whole recipe will it execute all resources it built during the compile phase.

There's more...

If you're using any cookbook dependency management solution such as libarian-chef or berkshelf, or you're not using Git, this is currently the only way to modify parts of recipes, which are not meant to be configured via attributes.

I don't like this approach too much. It is the exact same thing as monkey-patching any Ruby class by reopening it in your own source files. This usually leads to brittle code as your code now depends on implementation details of another piece of code instead of depending on its public interface (in Chef recipes the public interface is its attributes).

You should be aware of the fact that what you're doing is dangerous. Keep such cookbook modifications in a separate place so that you can easily find out what you did later. If you bury your modifications deep inside your complicated cookbooks, you might experience very bad debug issues later.

- The *Downloading and integrating cookbooks as vendor branches into your Git repository* section in *Chapter 1, Creating and Using Cookbooks*
- The *Using templates* section

Creating custom Ohai plugins

Ohai is the tool used by Chef Client to find out everything about the node's environment. During a Chef Client run, it populates the node object with all the information it found out about the node such as its operating system, hardware, and so on.

It is possible to write custom Ohai plugins to query additional properties about a node's environment.

In this example, we will see how to query the currently active firewall rules using **iptables** and make them available as node attributes.

Getting ready

Make sure you have iptables installed on your node. See the *Managing firewalls with iptables* section in *Chapter 7, Servers and Cloud Infrastructure*.

Make sure you have the `chef-client` cookbook available:

1. Install the `chef-client` cookbook:

   ```
   mma@laptop:~/chef-repo $ knife cookbook site install chef-client

   Installing chef-client to /Users/mma/work/chef-repo/cookbooks
   ```

2. Upload the `chef-client` cookbook to your Chef Server:

   ```
   mma@laptop:~/chef-repo $ knife cookbook upload chef-client

   Uploading chef-client    [3.0.4]
   ```

3. Add the `chef-client` cookbook to your node's run list:

   ```
   mma@laptop:~/chef-repo $ knife node run_list add server 'chef-client::config'

   server:
     run_list:
       recipe[chef-client::config]
   ```

How to do it...

Let's write a simple Ohai plugin, which lists all currently active iptables rules:

1. Install the ohai cookbook:

   ```
   mma@laptop:~/chef-repo $ knife cookbook site install ohai

   Installing ohai to /Users/mma/work/chef-repo/cookbooks
   ```

2. Add your plugin to the `ohai` cookbook:

   ```
   mma@laptop:~/chef-repo $ subl cookbooks/ohai/files/default/
   plugins/iptables.rb

   provides "iptables"

   iptables Mash.new

   `iptables -S`.each_line.with_index do |line,i|
     iptables[i] = line
   end
   ```

3. Upload the modified `ohai` cookbook to the Chef Server:

   ```
   mma@laptop:~/chef-repo $ knife cookbook upload ohai

   Uploading ohai      [1.1.8]
   ```

4. Add the `ohai` cookbook to the run list of your node:

   ```
   mma@laptop:~/chef-repo $ knife node run_list add server ohai

   server:
     run_list:
       recipe[chef-client::config]
       recipe[ohai]
   ```

5. Run Chef Client on your node:

   ```
   user@server:~$ sudo chef-client

   ...TRUNCATED OUTPUT...
   Recipe: ohai::default
     * ohai[custom_plugins] action reload
       - re-run ohai and merge results into node attributes
   ...TRUNCATED OUTPUT...
   ```

6. Validate that the iptables rules show up as node attributes, for example, by navigating to your Chef Server's management console. The iptables rules should show up among the other node attributes:

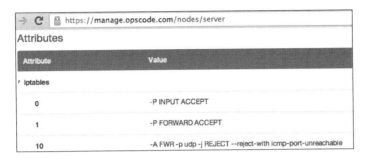

How it works...

The `chef-client` cookbook configures Chef Client to look for additional Ohai plugins in the directory `/etc/chef/ohai_plugins` by adding this line to `/etc/chef/client.rb`:

```
Ohai::Config[:plugin_path] << "/etc/chef/ohai_plugins"
```

You can simply install the `ohai` cookbook and add your Ohai plugins to the `cookbooks/ohai/files/default/plugins` directory. The `ohai` cookbook will then upload your plugins to your node.

A custom Ohai plugin has only a few basic parts:

```
provides "iptables"
```

The preceding code tells Ohai that the node attributes you fill will be available under the `iptables` key.

You collect the node attributes in a Mash—an extended version of a Hash.

```
iptables Mash.new
```

The preceding line of code creates an empty node attribute.

Then we run `iptables -S` to list all currently loaded firewall rules and loop through the lines. Each line gets added to the Mash with its line number as the key:

```
`sudo iptables -S`.each_line.with_index do |line,i|
  iptables[i] = line
end
```

Ohai will add the contents of that Mash as node attributes during a Chef Client run. We can now use the new `iptables` node attribute in our recipes:

```
node['iptables']
```

There's more...

You can use your Ohai plugin as a library. This enables you to use the functionality of your Ohai plugins in arbitrary Ruby scripts. Fire up IRB in the `/etc/chef/ohai_plugins` directory and run the following commands:

```
user@server:/etc/chef/ohai_plugins$ /opt/chef/embedded/bin/irb
>> require 'ohai'
>> Ohai::Config[:plugin_path] << '.'
>> o = Ohai::System.new
>> o.all_plugins
>> o.iptables
=> {0=>"-P INPUT ACCEPT\n", 1=>"-P FORWARD ACCEPT\n", 2=>"-P OUTPUT
ACCEPT\n", 3=>"-N FWR\n", 4=>"-A INPUT -j FWR\n", 5=>"-A FWR -i lo
-j ACCEPT\n", 6=>"-A FWR -m state --state RELATED,ESTABLISHED -j
ACCEPT\n", 7=>"-A FWR -p icmp -j ACCEPT\n", 8=>"-A FWR -p tcp -m
tcp --dport 22 -j ACCEPT\n", 9=>"-A FWR -p tcp -m tcp --tcp-flags
SYN,RST,ACK SYN -j REJECT --reject-with icmp-port-unreachable\n",
10=>"-A FWR -p udp -j REJECT --reject-with icmp-port-unreachable\n"}
```

See also

▸ Read more about Ohai at: `http://docs.opscode.com/ohai.html`

▸ Read more about how to distribute Ohai plugins here: `http://docs.opscode.com/ohai.html#use-the-ohai-cookbook`

▸ Find the source code of the Ohai cookbook here: `https://github.com/opscode-cookbooks/ohai`

Creating custom Knife plugins

Knife, the command-line client for the Chef Server, has a plugin system. This plugin system enables us to extend the functionality of Knife in any way we need it. The `knife-ec2` plugin is a common example: it adds commands such as `ec2 server create` to Knife.

In this section, we will create a very basic custom Knife plugin to learn about all the required building blocks of Knife plugins. As Knife plugins are pure Ruby programs, which can use any external libraries, there are no limits for what you can make Knife do. This freedom enables you to build your whole DevOps workflow on Knife, if you want to.

Now, let's teach Knife to tweet in your name!

Getting ready

Make sure you have a Twitter user account and you have created an application with Twitter (`https://dev.twitter.com/apps/new`).

While creating your Twitter application, you should set the **OAuth** access level to "Read and write" to enable your application to post in your name.

Create an access token by connecting the application to your Twitter account. This will enable your Twitter application (and therefore your Knife plugin) to tweet as your Twitter user.

Make sure you have the `twitter` gem installed. It will enable you to interact with Twitter from within your Knife plugin:

1. Add the `twitter` gem to your `Gemfile`:

   mma@laptop:~/chef-repo $ subl Gemfile

   ```
   source 'https://rubygems.org'

   gem 'twitter'
   ```

2. Run Bundler to install the `twitter` gem:

   mma@laptop:~/chef-repo $ bundle install

   ```
   Fetching gem metadata from https://rubygems.org/
   ...TRUNCATED OUTPUT...
   Installing twitter (4.8.1)
   ```

How to do it...

Let's create a Knife plugin so that we can tweet using Knife using the following command:

$ knife tweet "having fun building knife plugins"

1. Create a directory for your Knife plugin inside your Chef repository:

   mma@laptop:~/chef-repo $ mkdir -p .chef/plugins/knife

2. Create your Knife plugin:

   mma@laptop:~/chef-repo $ subl .chef/plugins/knife/knife_twitter.rb

   ```
   require 'chef/knife'
   module KnifePlugins
     class Tweet < Chef::Knife
       deps do
         require 'twitter'
       end

       banner "knife tweet MESSAGE"
   ```

```
      def run
        Twitter.configure do |config|
          config.consumer_key = "Your Twitter app consumer key"
          config.consumer_secret = "Your Twitter app consumer
secret"
          config.oauth_token = "Your OAuth token for your Twitter
app"
          config.oauth_token_secret = "Your OAuth token secret for
your Twitter app"
        end
        Twitter.update("#{name_args.first} #opschef")
      end
    end
end
```

3. Send your first tweet:

   ```
   mma@laptop:~/chef-repo $ knife tweet "having fun with building
   knife plugins"
   ```

4. Validate whether the tweet went live:

How it works...

There are three ways to make your Knife plugins available: in your home directory under `~/.chef/plugins/knife` (so that you can use them for all your Chef repositories), in your Chef repository under `.chef/plugins/knife` (so that every co-worker using that repository can use them), or as a Ruby gem (so that everyone in the Chef community can use them).

We chose the second way so that everyone working on our Chef repository can download and use our Twitter Knife plugin.

First, we need to include Chef's Knife library into our Ruby file in order to be able to create a Knife plugin:

```
require 'chef/knife'
```

Then, we define our plugin as follows:

```
module KnifePlugins
  class Tweet < Chef::Knife
    ...
  end
end
```

The preceding code creates the new Knife command `tweet`. The command is derived from the class name we give our plugin. Each Knife plugin needs to extend `Chef::Knife`.

The next step is to load all required dependencies. Instead of simply putting multiple `require` calls at the beginning of our Ruby file, Knife provides the `deps` method (which we can override) to load dependencies lazily on demand:

```
deps do
  require 'twitter'
end
```

Putting `require 'twitter'` inside the `deps` method makes sure that the `twitter` gem only gets loaded if our plugin gets run. Not doing so would mean that the `twitter` gem would get loaded on each Knife run, no matter whether it would be used or not.

After defining the dependencies, we need to tell the users of our plugin what it does and how to use it. `Chef::Knife` provides the `banner` method for defining the message users see when they call our plugin with the `--help` parameter:

```
banner "knife tweet MESSAGE"
```

Let's see how this works:

```
mma@laptop:~/chef-repo $ knife tweet --help

  knife tweet MESSAGE
```

Finally, we need to actually do something. The `run` method is the place to put the code we want to execute. In our case, we connect to our Twitter application by calling `configure` on the `Twitter` class, passing our authentication credentials. Then we send our tweet:

```
Twitter.update("#{name_args.first} #opschef")
```

The `name_args` variable contains the command-line arguments. We take the first one as the message we send to Twitter and add the `#opschef` hash tag to every message we send.

There's more...

You can add simple error handling to make sure that the user doesn't send empty tweets by adding this block right at the beginning of the run method:

```
run
  unless name_args.size == 1
    ui.fatal "You need to say something!"
    show_usage
    exit 1
  end
  ...
end
```

This piece of code gets executed if there isn't exactly one command-line argument available to the `knife tweet` call. In that case it will print the error message, and the user would get same message when using the `--help` parameter. Then, this block will exit with the error code `1` without doing anything else.

See also

▸ Read more about how to write custom Knife plugins at: `http://docs.opscode.com/plugin_knife_custom.html`

▸ Find the `twitter` gem at: `https://github.com/sferik/twitter`

4
Writing Better Cookbooks

"When you know better, you do better"

- Maya Angelou

In this chapter, we will cover the following:

- ▶ Setting environment variables
- ▶ Passing arguments to shell commands
- ▶ Overriding attributes
- ▶ Using search to find nodes
- ▶ Using data bags
- ▶ Using search to find data bag items
- ▶ Using encrypted data bag items
- ▶ Accessing data bag values from external scripts
- ▶ Getting information about the environment
- ▶ Writing cross-platform cookbooks
- ▶ Finding the complete list of operating systems you can use in cookbooks
- ▶ Making recipes idempotent by using conditional execution

Introduction

In this chapter, we'll see some of the more advanced topics in action. You'll see how to make your recipes more flexible using search and data bags and how to make sure your cookbooks run on different operating systems. You'll gain critical knowledge to create extensible and maintainable cookbooks for your infrastructure.

Setting environment variables

You might have experienced this: you try out a command on your node's shell and it works perfectly. Now, you try to execute the very same command from within your Chef recipe but it fails. One reason might be that there are certain environment variables set in your shell, which are unset during the Chef run. You might have set them manually or you might have set them in your shell startup scripts—it does not really matter. You'll need to set them again in your recipe.

 In this section, you will see how to set environment variables needed during a Chef run.

Getting ready

Make sure you have a cookbook called `my_cookbook`, and the `run_list` of your node includes `my_cookbook` as described in the *Creating and using cookbooks* section in *Chapter 1, Chef Infrastructure*.

How to do it...

Let's see how we can set environment variables from within Chef recipes:

1. Set an environment variable to be used during the Chef Client run:

    ```
    mma@laptop:~/chef-repo $ subl
      cookbooks/my_cookbook/recipes/default.rb

    ENV['MESSAGE'] = 'Hello from Chef'

    execute 'print value of environment variable $MESSAGE' do
      command 'echo $MESSAGE > /tmp/message'
    end
    ```

2. Upload the modified cookbook to the Chef Server:

    ```
    mma@laptop:~/chef-repo $ knife cookbook upload my_cookbook

    Uploading my_cookbook      [0.1.0]
    ```

3. Run Chef Client to create the `tmp` file:

`user@server:~$ sudo chef-client`

```
...TRUNCATED OUTPUT...
[2013-01-25T15:01:57+00:00] INFO: Processing execute[print
  value of environment variable $MESSAGE] action run
  (my_cookbook::default line 11)
[2013-01-25T15:01:57+00:00] INFO: execute[print value of
  environment variable $MESSAGE] ran successfully
...TRUNCATED OUTPUT...
```

4. Validate that it worked:

`user@server:~$ cat /tmp/message`

```
Hello from Chef
```

How it works...

Ruby exposes the current environment via ENV—a hash to read or modify environment variables. We are using ENV to set our environment variable. It is valid for the Ruby process in which Chef Client runs as well as all child processes.

The execute resource is spawning a child process of the Ruby process running Chef Client. Because it is a child process, the environment variable we set in the recipe is available to the script code the execute resource runs.

We simply access the environment variable by $MESSAGE as we would do on the command line as well.

There's more...

The execute resource offers a way to pass environment variables to the command it executes.

1. Change the my_cookbook default recipe:

`mma@laptop:~/chef-repo $ subl`
`  cookbooks/my_cookbook/recipes/default.rb`

```
execute 'print value of environment variable $MESSAGE' do
  command 'echo $MESSAGE > /tmp/message'
  environment 'MESSAGE' => 'Hello from the execute resource'
end
```

2. Upload the modified cookbook to your Chef Server and run Chef Client as shown in the *How to do it...* section.

3. Validate the contents of the `tmp` file:

```
user@server:~$ cat /tmp/message
```

```
Hello from the execute resource
```

> Setting an environment variable using `ENV` will make that variable available during the whole Chef run. In contrast, passing it to the execute resource will only make it available for that one command executed by the resource.

See also

▶ Read more about handling Unix environment variables in Chef at:

```
http://docs.opscode.com/essentials_environment_variables.html
```

Passing arguments to shell commands

Chef Client enables you to run shell commands by using the `execute` resource. But how can you pass arguments to such shell commands? Let's assume you want to calculate a value you need to pass to the shell command in your recipe. How can you do that? Let's find out...

Getting ready

Make sure you have a cookbook called `my_cookbook` and the `run_list` of your node includes `my_cookbook` as described in the *Creating and using cookbooks* section in *Chapter 1, Chef Infrastructure*.

How to do it...

Let's see how we can pass Ruby variables into shell commands:

1. Edit your default recipe. You'll pass an argument to a shell command using an `execute` resource:

```
mma@laptop:~/chef-repo $ subl
  cookbooks/my_cookbook/recipes/default.rb
```

```
max_mem = node['memory']['total'].to_i * 0.8

execute 'echo max memory value into tmp file' do
  command "echo #{max_mem} > /tmp/max_mem"
end
```

2. Upload the modified cookbook to the Chef Server:

   mma@laptop:~/chef-repo $ knife cookbook upload my_cookbook

   ```
   Uploading my_cookbook    [0.1.0]
   ```

3. Run Chef Client on your node to create the `tmp` file:

   user@server:~$ sudo chef-client

   ```
   ...TRUNCATED OUTPUT...
   [2013-01-25T15:01:57+00:00] INFO: Processing execute[echo max
   memory value into tmp file] action run (my_cookbook::default line
   11)
   [2013-01-25T15:01:57+00:00] INFO: execute[echo max memory value
   into tmp file] ran successfully
   ...TRUNCATED OUTPUT...
   ```

4. Validate that it worked:

   user@server:~$ cat /tmp/max_mem

   ```
   299523.2
   ```

How it works...

We calculate a value, which we want to pass to the command we want to execute. The `node['memory']['total']` call returns a string. We need to convert it to integer by calling `to_i` on the returned string to be able to multiply it with `0.8`.

As recipes are Ruby files, you can use string expansion if you need it. One way to pass arguments to shell commands defined by `execute` resources is to use string expansion in the `command` parameter:

```
command "echo #{max_mem} > /tmp/max_mem"
```

In the preceding line, Ruby will replace `#{max_mem}` with the value of the `max_mem` variable just defined. The string, which we pass as a command to the `execute` resource could look like this (assuming that `node['memory']['total']` returns `1000`):

```
command "echo 800 > /tmp/max_mem"
```

 Be careful! You need to use double quotes if you want Ruby to expand your string.

There's more...

String expansion works in multiline strings as well. You can define them like this:

```
command <<EOC
echo #{message} > /tmp/message
EOC
```

 EOC is the string delimiter. You're free to use whatever you want here. It can be EOF, EOH, STRING, FOO, or whatever you want it to be. Just make sure to use the same delimiter at the beginning and the end of your multiline string.

We've seen another way to pass arguments to shell commands by using environment variables in the previous section.

See also

▶ The *Mixing plain Ruby with Chef DSL* section in *Chapter 3, Chef Language and Style*
▶ The *Setting environment variables* section

Overriding attributes

You can set attribute values in attribute files. Usually, cookbooks come with reasonable default values for attributes. But the default values might not suit your needs. If they don't fit, you can override attribute values.

In this section, we'll look at how to override attributes from within recipes and roles.

Getting ready

Make sure you have a cookbook called `my_cookbook` and the `run_list` of your node includes `my_cookbook` as described in the *Creating and using cookbooks* section in *Chapter 1, Chef Infrastructure*.

How to do it...

Let's see how we can override attribute values:

1. Edit the default attributes file to add an attribute:

```
mma@laptop:~/chef-repo $ subl
  cookbooks/my_cookbook/attributes/default.rb
```

```
default['my_cookbook']['version'] = '1.2.6'
```

2. Edit your default recipe. You'll override the value of the `version` attribute and print it to the console:

```
mma@laptop:~/chef-repo $ subl
  cookbooks/my_cookbook/recipes/default.rb

node.override['my_cookbook']['version'] = '1.5'
execute 'echo the path attribute' do
  command "echo #{node['my_cookbook']['version']}"
end
```

3. Upload the modified cookbook to the Chef Server:

```
mma@laptop:~/chef-repo $ knife cookbook upload my_cookbook

Uploading my_cookbook      [0.1.0]
```

4. Run Chef Client on your node to create the `tmp` file:

```
user@server:~$ sudo chef-client

...TRUNCATED OUTPUT...
  * execute[echo the path attribute into a temp file]
    action run[2013-02-08T11:27:19+00:00] INFO: Processing
    execute[echo the path attribute into a temp file]
    action run (my_cookbook::default line 9)
1.5
[2013-02-08T11:27:19+00:00] INFO: execute[echo the path
  attribute into a temp file] ran successfully

    - execute echo 1.5
```

How it works...

You set a default value for the `version` attribute in your cookbook's default attributes file. Chef evaluates the attributes file early in the Chef run and makes all defined attributes available via the `node` object. Your recipes can use the `node` object to access the values of the attributes.

The Chef DSL provides various ways to modify attributes once they are set. In our example, we used the `override` method to change the value of the attribute inside our recipe. After that call, the node will carry the newly set value for the attribute instead of the old value set via the attributes file.

There's more...

You can override attributes from within roles and environments as well. In the following example, we set the `version` attribute to `2.0.0` (instead of keeping the default value of `1.2.6`).

1. Edit the default attributes file to add an attribute:

    **mma@laptop:~/chef-repo $ subl
      cookbooks/my_cookbook/attributes/default.rb**

    ```
    default['my_cookbook']['version'] = '1.2.6'
    ```

2. Use the attribute in your default recipe:

    **mma@laptop:~/chef-repo $ subl
      cookbooks/my_cookbook/recipes/default.rb**

    ```
    execute 'echo the path attribute' do
      command "echo #{node['my_cookbook']['version']}"
    end
    ```

3. Create a role named `upgraded_hosts` by creating a file called `roles/upgraded_hosts.rb`:

    mma@laptop:~/chef-repo $ subl roles/upgraded_hosts.rb

    ```
    name "upgraded_hosts"

    run_list "recipe[my_cookbook]"
    default_attributes 'my_cookbook' => { 'version' => '2.0.0' }
    ```

4. Upload the role to the Chef Server:

    **mma@laptop:~/chef-repo $ knife role from file
      upgraded_hosts.rb**

    ```
    Updated Role upgraded_hosts!
    ```

5. Change the `run_list` of your node

    mma@laptop:~/chef-repo $ knife node edit server

    ```
    "run_list": [
       "role[upgraded_hosts]"
     ]
    Saving updated run_list on node server
    ```

6. Run Chef Client on your node:

```
user@server:~$ sudo chef-client

...TRUNCATED OUTPUT...
Recipe: my_cookbook::default
  * execute[echo the path attribute into a temp file]
    action run[2013-02-08T10:23:48+00:00] INFO: Processing
    execute[echo the path attribute into a temp file]
    action run (my_cookbook::default line 9)
/opt/my_cookbook-2.0.0
[2013-02-08T10:23:48+00:00] INFO: execute[echo the path
  attribute into a temp file] ran successfully

    - execute echo /opt/my_cookbook-2.0.0

[2013-02-08T10:23:49+00:00] INFO: Chef Run complete in
  2.483312728 seconds
```

See also

▸ Learn more about roles at:

http://docs.opscode.com/essentials_roles.html

▸ Read more about attribute files and attribute precedence at:

http://docs.opscode.com/essentials_cookbook_attribute_files.html

Using search to find nodes

If you are running your infrastructure in any type of virtualized environment like a public or private cloud, the server instances you use change frequently. Instead of having a well-known set of servers, you destroy and create virtual servers regularly.

In this situation, your cookbooks cannot rely on hard coded server names when you need a list of available servers. You might need such a list to add them to monitoring or building firewall rules for your nodes.

Chef provides a way to find nodes by their attributes, for example, their roles. In this section, we'll see how you can retrieve a set of nodes to use them in your recipes.

Getting ready

Make sure you have a cookbook called my_cookbook as described in the *Creating and using cookbooks* section in *Chapter 1, Chef Infrastructure*.

How to do it...

Let's see how we can find all nodes having a certain role:

1. Create a role called web having my_cookbook in its run list:

   mma@laptop:~/chef-repo $ knife role create web

   ```
     "run_list": [
       "recipe[my_cookbook]"
     ],
   Created role[web]
   ```

2. Create at least one node having the new role in its run list:

   mma@laptop:~/chef-repo $ knife node create webserver

   ```
     "run_list": [
       "role[web]"
     ],
   Created node[webserver]
   ```

3. Edit your default recipe to search for all nodes having the web role:

   mma@laptop:~/chef-repo $ subl
   ** cookbooks/my_cookbook/recipes/default.rb**

   ```
   servers = search(:node, "role:web")

   servers.each do |srv|
     log srv.name
   end
   ```

4. Upload your modified cookbook:

   mma@laptop:~/chef-repo $ knife cookbook upload my_cookbook

   ```
   Uploading my_cookbook    [0.1.0]
   ```

5. Run Chef Client on one of your nodes:

   user@server:~$ sudo chef-client

   ```
   ...TRUNCATED OUTPUT...
   [2013-02-19T21:32:00+00:00] INFO: webserver
   ...TRUNCATED OUTPUT...
   ```

How it works...

The Chef Server stores all nodes with their attributes. The attributes are partly auto-detected using ohai (such as name, IP address, CPUs, and so on) and partly configured by you (such as run_list). The Chef DSL offers the search method to look up nodes based on your search criteria. In the preceding example, we simply used a role as the search criteria. But, you can use any combination of available node attributes to construct your search.

The search method returns a list of node objects, which you can use in your recipe. In the preceding example, we looped through the list of nodes using the standard Ruby each iterator. The current element is available as the variable you declare between the | after the do. In our case, it is a full-blown node object and you can use it to retrieve its attributes or even modify it.

There's more...

Search is a very powerful tool for dynamically identifying nodes. You cannot only search for roles but for all node attributes, you can use Boolean operators to craft more complex queries and you can use search in your cookbooks as well as with Knife. Let's see how you take search a bit further:

Using Knife to search for nodes

Knife offers the very same search syntax as the search method within your recipes. It lets you search for nodes via the command line:

```
mma@laptop:~/chef-repo $ knife search node "role:web"

    3 items found
    Node Name:    web
    ...TRUNCATED OUTPUT...
    Node Name:    web1
    ...TRUNCATED OUTPUT...
    Node Name:    web2
    ...TRUNCATED OUTPUT...
```

Searching for arbitrary node attributes

In addition to searching for roles, you can search for any attribute of a node. Let's see how you can search for a node having ubuntu as its platform using knife:

```
mma@laptop:~/chef-repo $ knife search node "platform:ubuntu"

    3 items found
    Node Name:    web
    ...TRUNCATED OUTPUT...
    Node Name:    vagrant
```

```
...TRUNCATED OUTPUT...
Node Name:    db
...TRUNCATED OUTPUT...
```

Using Boolean operators in search

If you want to combine multiple attributes in your search query, you can use Boolean operators such as NOT, AND, and OR:

```
mma@laptop:~/chef-repo $ knife search node 'platform:ubuntu AND
  name:v*'

    1 items found
    Node Name:    vagrant
    ...TRUNCATED OUTPUT...
```

See also

▶ Read more about search at:

`http://docs.opscode.com/essentials_search.html`

▶ Read more about how to use search from within a recipe here:

`http://docs.opscode.com/dsl_recipe_method_search.html`

Using data bags

There are situations where you have data, which you do neither want to hard code in your recipes nor store as attributes in your cookbooks. Users, external servers, or database connections are examples of such data. Chef offers the so called **data bags** to manage arbitrary collections of data, which you can use with your cookbooks.

Let's see how we can create and use a data bag and its data bag items.

Getting ready

In the following example, we want to send HTTP requests. To be able to follow along with the example, you'll need an HTTP end point.

One way to establish an HTTP end point is to just run `nc -l 80` on any server accessible by your node and use its IP address below.

Another way to establish an HTTP end point, which shows us the requests we make, is a free service called RequestBin. To use it, follow these steps:

1. Open `http://requestb.in` in your browser and create a new RequestBin.

2. Note the URL for your new RequestBin. We'll call it from within our recipe below:

How to do it...

Let's create a data bag holding our HTTP end point URL and use it from within our recipe:

1. Create a directory for your data bag:

   ```
   mma@laptop:~/chef-repo $ mkdir data_bags/hooks
   ```

2. Create a data bag item for RequestBin. Make sure to use your own RequestBin URL you noted in the *Getting ready* section:

   ```
   mma@laptop:~/chef-repo $ subl data_bags/hooks/request_bin.json

   {
     "id": "request_bin",
     "url": "http://requestb.in/1abd0kf1"
   }
   ```

3. Create the data bag on the Chef Server:

   ```
   mma@laptop:~/chef-repo $ knife data bag create hooks

   Created data_bag[hooks]
   ```

4. Upload your data bag item to the Chef Server:

   ```
   mma@laptop:~/chef-repo $ knife data bag from file hooks
     requestbin.json

   Updated data_bag_item[hooks::RequestBin]
   ```

5. Edit the default recipe of `my_cookbook` to retrieve the RequestBin URL from your data bag:

```
mma@laptop:~/chef-repo $ subl
  cookbooks/my_cookbook/recipes/default.rb

hook = data_bag_item('hooks', 'request_bin')
http_request 'callback' do
  url hook['url']
end
```

6. Upload your modified cookbook to the Chef Server:

```
mma@laptop:~/chef-repo $ knife cookbook upload my_cookbook

Uploading my_cookbook    [0.1.0]
```

7. Run Chef Client on your node to test whether the HTTP request to your RequestBin gets executed:

```
user@server:~$ sudo chef-client

...TRUNCATED OUTPUT...
[2013-02-22T20:37:35+00:00] INFO: http_request[callback]
  GET to http://requestb.in/1abd0kf1 successful
...TRUNCATED OUTPUT...
```

8. Check your RequestBin. The request should show up there:

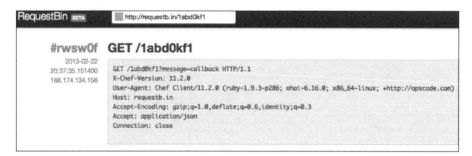

How it works...

A data bag is a named collection of structured data entries. You define each data entry, called a data bag item, in a **JSON** file. You can search for data bag items from within your recipes to use the data stored in the data bag.

In our example, we created a data bag called `hooks`. A data bag is a directory within your Chef repository, and you can use `knife` to create it on the Chef Server.

Then, we created a data bag item with the name `request_bin` in a file called `request_bin.json` inside the data bag's directory and uploaded it to the Chef Server as well.

Our recipe retrieves the data bag item using the `data_bag_item` method, taking the data bag name as first parameter and the item name as second parameter.

Then, we create an `http_request` resource passing it the `url` attribute of the data bag item. You can retrieve any attribute from a data bag item using the Hash notation `hook['url']`.

See also

▸   Read more about data bags at:

    http://docs.opscode.com/essentials_data_bags.html

Using search to find data bag items

You might want to execute code in your recipe multiple times—once for every data bag item like for each user or each HTTP end point.

You can use search to find certain data bag items and loop through search results to execute code multiple times.

Let's see how we can make our recipes more dynamic by searching for data bag items.

Getting ready

Follow the *Getting ready* and *How to do it...* (steps 1–4) sections, in the *Using data bags* section.

How to do it...

Let's create a recipe searching for data bag items and calling the `http_request` resource for everyone:

1.   Edit the default recipe of `my_cookbook` to retrieve all HTTP hooks, which should be called by our recipe from your data bag:

```
mma@laptop:~/chef-repo $ subl
  cookbooks/my_cookbook/recipes/default.rb

search(:hooks, '*:*').each do |hook|
  http_request 'callback' do
    url hook['url']
  end
end
```

2. Upload your modified recipe to the Chef Server, run Chef Client on your node, and verify that your HTTP end point received the HTTP request as described in steps 6-8 in the preceding *Using data bags* section.

How it works...

Our recipe is using the `search` method to retrieve all items from the data bag called `hooks`. The first parameter to the `search` method is the name of the data bag (as Ruby symbol). The second parameter is the search query—in our case we're looking for all data bag items by using `*:*`. Using the `each` iterator, we loop through all found data bag items. Inside the Ruby block, which gets executed for each item, we can access the item using the variable `hook`.

We create an `http_request` resource for each data bag item, passing the URL stored in the item as the `url` parameter to the resource. You can access arbitrary attributes of your data bag item using a Hash-like notation.

There's more...

You can use various search patterns to find certain data bag items, for example:

```
search(:hooks, "id:request_bin")
```

or

```
search(:hooks, "url:*request*")
```

See also

- ▸ The *Using data bags* section
- ▸ The *Using search to find nodes* section
- ▸ Find out what else is possible with data bag search at:

  ```
  http://docs.opscode.com/chef/essentials_data_bags.html
  #using-search
  ```

Using encrypted data bag items

Data bags are a great way to store user and application-specific data. Before long you'll want to store passwords and private keys in data bags as well. But, you might (and should) be worried about uploading confidential data to a Chef Server.

Chef offers encrypted data bag items to enable you to put confidential data into data bags, reducing the implied security risk.

Getting ready

Make sure you have a Chef repository and can access your Chef Server.

How to do it...

Let's create and encrypt a data bag item and see how we can use it:

1. Create a directory for your encrypted data bag:

   ```
   mma@laptop:~/chef-repo $ mkdir data_bags/accounts
   ```

2. Create a data bag item for a Google account:

   ```
   mma@laptop:~/chef-repo $ subl data_bags/accounts/google.json

   {
     "id": "google",
     "email": "some.one@gmail.com",
     "password": "Oh! So secret?"
   }
   ```

3. Create the data bag on the Chef Server:

   ```
   mma@laptop:~/chef-repo $ knife data bag create accounts

   Created data_bag[accounts]
   ```

4. Upload your data bag item to the Chef Server, encrypting it on the fly:

    Be careful! Using the `--secret` command line switch is dangerous, because it will show up in your shell history and in log files. Have a look at the following *There's more...* section to find out how to use a private key instead of a plain text secret.

   ```
   mma@laptop:~/chef-repo $ knife data bag from file accounts
     google.json --secret 'Open sesame!'

   Updated data_bag_item[accounts::google]
   ```

5. Verify that your data bag item is encrypted:

   ```
   mma@laptop:~/chef-repo $ knife data bag show accounts google

   email:
     cipher:
       aes-256-cbc
     encrypted_data:
       DqYu8DnI8E1XQ5I/
       jNyaFZ7LVXIzRUzuFjDHJGHymgxd9cbUJQ48nYJ3QHxi
   ```

```
3xyE

iv:                    B+eQ1hD35PfadjUwe+e18g==

version:          1
id:         google
password:
  cipher:             aes-256-cbc
  encrypted_data:
    m3bGPmp6cObnmHQpGipZYHNAcxJYkIfx4udsM8GPt7cT1ec0w+
    IuLZk0Q9F8
  2pX0

  iv:                  Bp5jEZG/cPYMRWiUX1UPQA==

  version:          1
```

6. Now, let's have a look at the decrypted data bag by providing the secret:

```
mma@laptop:~/chef-repo $ knife data bag show accounts google
  --secret 'Open sesame!'
```

```
email:    some.one@gmail.com
id:       google
password: Oh! So secret?
```

How it works...

Passing `--secret` to the `knife` command creating the data bag item encrypts the contents of the data bag.

 The ID of the data bag item will not be encrypted, because the Chef Server needs it to work with the data bag item.

Chef uses a shared secret to encrypt and decrypt data bag items. Everyone having access to the shared secret will be able to decrypt the contents of the encrypted data bag item.

There's more...

Accessing encrypted data bag items from the command line with `knife` is usually not what you want. Let's have a look at how to use encrypted data bag items in real life.

Accessing encrypted data bag items from within recipes

To use encrypted data bag items in your recipe, use a code similar to the following:

```
google_account = Chef::EncryptedDataBagItem.load("accounts",
  "google", "Open sesame!")
google_account["password"] # will give you the decrypted password
```

Using a private key file

Instead of passing the shared secret via the command line or hard coding it into your recipe (which is a really bad idea anyways), you can create an **openssl** format private key and pass its file location to the `knife` command:

 You can create an openssl format private key like this:

```
$ openssl genrsa -out data_bag_secret_key.pem 1024
```

```
mma@laptop:~/chef-repo $ knife data bag from file accounts
  google.json --secret-file .chef/data_bag_secret_key.pem
```

The preceding command assumes that you have a file called `data_bag_secret_key.pem` in the `.chef` directory.

To enable your node to decrypt the data bag item, you need to `scp` your secret key file to your node and put it in the `/etc/chef/` directory.

 The initial bootstrap procedure for a node will put the key in the right place on the node, if one already exists in your Chef repository.

Make sure that `/etc/chef/client.rb` points to your `data_bag_secret_key.pem` file:

```
encrypted_data_bag_secret "/etc/chef/data_bag_secret_key.pem"
```

Now, you can access the decrypted contents of your data bag items in your recipes without passing the secret to the `load` call:

```
google_account = Chef::EncryptedDataBagItem.load("accounts",
  "google")
```

Chef will look for the file configured in `client.rb` and use the secret given there to decrypt the data bag item.

See also

▸ The *Using data bags* section
▸ Learn more about encrypted data bag items at:

    http://docs.opscode.com/essentials_data_bags_encrypt.html

Accessing data bag values from external scripts

Sometimes you cannot put a server under full Chef control (yet). In such cases, you might want to be able to access values managed in Chef data bags from scripts, which are not maintained by Chef. The easiest way to do this is to dump the data bag values (or any node values for that matter) into a **JSON** file and let your external script read them from there.

Getting ready

Make sure you have a cookbook called `my_cookbook` and the `run_list` of your node includes `my_cookbook` as described in the *Creating and using cookbooks* section in *Chapter 1, Chef Infrastructure*.

Create a data bag so that we can use its values later:

1. Create the data bag:

   ```
   mma@laptop:~/chef-repo $ mkdir data_bags/servers
   mma@laptop:~/chef-repo $ knife data bag create servers

   Created data_bag[servers]
   ```

2. Create the first data bag item:

   ```
   mma@laptop:~/chef-repo $ subl data_bags/servers/backup.json

   {
     "id": "backup",
     "host": "10.0.0.12"
   }

   mma@laptop:~/chef-repo $ knife data bag from file servers
     backup.json

   Updated data_bag_item[servers::backup]
   ```

How to do it...

Let's create a JSON file containing data bag values using our cookbook so that external scripts can access those values:

1. Edit your cookbook's default recipe:

   ```
   mma@laptop:~/chef-repo $ subl
     cookbooks/my_cookbook/recipes/default.rb

   file "/etc/backup_config.json" do
   ```

```
  owner "root"
  group "root"
  mode 0644
  content data_bag_item('servers', 'backup')['host'].to_json
end
```

2. Upload the modified cookbook to the Chef Server:

    mma@laptop:~/chef-repo $ knife cookbook upload my_cookbook

    Uploading my_cookbook   [0.1.0]

3. Run Chef Client on your node:

    user@server:~$ sudo chef-client

    ```
    ...TRUNCATED OUTPUT...
    [2013-03-14T20:30:33+00:00] INFO: Processing
      file[/etc/backup_config.json] action create
      (my_cookbook::default line 9)
    [2013-03-14T20:30:34+00:00] INFO: entered create
    [2013-03-14T20:30:34+00:00] INFO:
      file[/etc/backup_config.json] owner changed to 0
    [2013-03-14T20:30:34+00:00] INFO:
      file[/etc/backup_config.json] group changed to 0
    [2013-03-14T20:30:34+00:00] INFO:
      file[/etc/backup_config.json] mode changed to 644
    [2013-03-14T20:30:34+00:00] INFO:
      file[/etc/backup_config.json] created file
      /etc/backup_config.json
    ...TRUNCATED OUTPUT...
    ```

4. Validate the content of the generated file:

    user@server:~$ cat /etc/backup_config.json

    "10.0.0.12"

5. Now, you can access the `backup_config.json` file from within your external scripts, which are not managed by Chef.

How it works...

The file resource creates a JSON file in the `/etc` directory. It gets the file's content directly from the data bag by using the `data_bag_item` method. This method expects the name of the data bag as first argument and the name of the data bag item as second argument. We then access the host value from the data bag item and convert it to JSON.

The file resource uses this JSON-converted value as its content and writes it to disk.

Now any external script can read the value from that file.

There's more...

If you are sure that your data bag values don't get modified by the Chef Client run on the node, you could use the Chef API directly from your script.

See also

▶ Read more about how to do this at:

http://stackoverflow.com/questions/10318919/how-to-access-current-values-from-a-chef-data-bag

▶ The *Using data bags* section

Getting information about the environment

Sometimes your recipes need to know details about the environment they are modifying. I'm not talking about Chef environments but about things like Linux kernel versions, existing users, or network interfaces.

Chef provides all this information via the `node` object. Let's have a look how to retrieve it.

Getting ready

Log in to any of your Chef-managed nodes and start the Chef Shell:

```
user@server:~$ sudo chef-shell --client

chef >
```

How to do it...

Let's play around with the node object and have a look at which information it stores:

1. List which information is available. The example shows the keys available on a Vagrant VM. Depending on what kind of server you work, you'll find different data.

   ```
   chef > node.keys.sort

   => ["block_device", "chef_packages", "command", "counters",
   "cpu", "current_user", "dmi", "domain", "etc", "filesystem",
   "fqdn", "hostname", "idletime", "idletime_seconds", "ip6address",
   "ipaddress", "kernel", "keys", "languages", "lsb", "macaddress",
   "memory", "network", "ntp", "ohai_time", "os", "os_version",
   "platform", "platform_family", "platform_version", "recipes",
   "roles", "root_group", "tags", "uptime", "uptime_seconds",
   "virtualization"]
   ```

2. Get a list of available network interfaces:

```
chef > node['network']['interfaces'].keys.sort
```

```
=> ["lo", "eth0"]
```

3. List all existing user accounts:

```
chef > node['etc']['passwd'].keys.sort
```

```
=> ["backup", "bin", "daemon", "games", "gnats", "irc", "libuuid",
"list", "lp", "mail", "man", "messagebus", "news", "nobody",
"ntp", "proxy", "root", "sshd", "sync", "sys", "syslog", "uucp",
"vagrant", "vboxadd", "www-data"]
```

4. Get the details of the root user:

```
chef > node['etc']['passwd']['root']
```

```
=> {"dir"=>"/root", "gid"=>0, "uid"=>0, "shell"=>"/bin/bash",
"gecos"=>"root"}
```

5. Get the code name of the installed Ubuntu distribution:

```
chef > node['lsb']['codename']
```

```
=> "precise"
```

6. Find out which kernel modules are available:

```
chef > node['kernel']['modules'].keys.sort
```

```
=> ["dm_crypt", "drm", "e1000", "ext2", "i2c_piix4", "lp", "mac_
hid", "microcode", "parport", "parport_pc", "ppdev", "psmouse",
"serio_raw", "vboxguest", "vboxsf", "vboxvideo", "vesafb"]
```

How it works...

Chef uses Ohai to retrieve a node's environment. It stores the data found by Ohai with the node object in a Hash-like structure called a **Mash**. In addition to providing key-value pairs, it adds methods to the node object to query the keys directly.

Instead of using node['lsb']['codename'] you could use node.lsb.codename as well.

There's more...

You can use the exact same calls we used in Chef Shell inside your recipes.

See also

Ohai is responsible for filling the node with all that information. Read more about Ohai at:

```
http://docs.opscode.com/ohai.html
```

Writing cross-platform cookbooks

Imagine you have written a great cookbook for your Ubuntu node and now you need to run it on that CentOS server. Ouch. It will most probably fail miserably. Package names might be different, you need to use **YUM** instead of **APT**, and configuration files are in different places. Things get even worse if you want to run your cookbook on a Windows box.

Luckily, Chef provides you with a host of features to write cross-platform cookbooks. With just a few simple commands, you can make sure that your cookbook adapts to the platform your node is running on. Let's have a look how to do this.

Getting ready

Make sure you have a cookbook called `my_cookbook` and the `run_list` of your node includes `my_cookbook` as described in the *Creating and using cookbooks* section in *Chapter 1, Chef Infrastructure*.

How to do it...

Retrieve the node's platform and execute conditional logic in your cookbook depending on the platform:

1. Log a message only if your node is on `ubuntu`:

    ```
    mma@laptop:~/chef-repo $ subl
       cookbooks/my_cookbook/recipes/default.rb

    Log.info("Running on ubuntu") if node.platform['ubuntu']
    ```

2. Upload the modified cookbook to your Chef Server:

    ```
    mma@laptop:~/chef-repo $ subl
       cookbooks/my_cookbook/recipes/default.rb

    Uploading my_cookbook      [0.1.0]
    Uploaded 1 cookbook.
    ```

3. Log in to your node and run Chef Client to see whether it works:

    ```
    user@server:~$ sudo chef-client

    ...TRUNCATED OUTPUT...
    [2013-03-03T20:07:39+00:00] INFO: Running on Ubuntu
    ...TRUNCATED OUTPUT...
    ```

Alternatively, if you are not interested in the specific platform but you only need to know whether you run on a Debian derivative, you can put the following line into your default recipe:

```
Log.info("Running on a debian derivative") if
  platform_family?('debian')
```

Upload, the modified cookbook and running Chef Client on a Ubuntu node would show:

```
[2013-03-03T20:16:14+00:00] INFO: Running on a debian
  derivative
```

How it works...

Ohai discovers the current node's operating system and stores it as platform attribute with the node object. You can access it like any other attribute using either Hash syntax:

```
node['platform']
```

or you can use method style syntax:

```
node.platform
```

Chef knows which operating systems belong together. You can use this knowledge by using the `platform_family` method from the Chef DSL.

You can then use basic Ruby conditionals, such as `if`, `unless`, or even `case` to make your cookbook do platform specific things.

There's more...

Let's have a closer look at what else is possible.

Avoiding case statements to set values based on platform

The Chef DSL offers the convenience methods `value_for_platform` and `value_for_platform_family`. You can use them to avoid complex case statements and use a simple Hash instead. The `runit` cookbook, for example, uses `value_for_platform` to pass the start command for the `runit` service to the `execute` resource:

```
execute "start-runsvdir" do
  command value_for_platform(
    "debian" => { "default" => "runsvdir-start" },
    "ubuntu" => { "default" => "start runsvdir" },
    "gentoo" => { "default" => "/etc/init.d/runit-start start" }
  )
  action :nothing
end
```

The command will be `runsvdir-start` on Debian, `start runsvdir` on Ubuntu, and will use an `init.d` script on Gentoo.

> Some of the built-in resources have platform-specific providers. For example, the `group` resource uses one of the following providers depending on the platform:
>
> `Chef::Provider::Group::Dscl` on Mac OS X
>
> `Chef::Provider::Group::Pw` on FreeBSD
>
> `Chef::Provider::Group::Usermod` on Solaris

Declaring support for specific operating systems in your cookbook's metadata

If your cookbook is written for a well-defined set of operating systems, you should list the supported platforms in your cookbook's metadata:

```
mma@laptop:~/chef-repo $ subl
  cookbooks/my_cookbook/recipes/metadata.rb

    supports 'ubuntu'
```

If your cookbook supports multiple platforms, you can use a nice Ruby shortcut to list all the platforms as a Ruby array of strings (using the `%w` shortcut) and loop through that array to call `supports` for each platform:

```
%w(debian ubuntu redhat centos fedora scientific amazon oracle).each
do |os|
  supports os
end
```

See also

▶ The *Mixing plain Ruby with Chef DSL* section in *Chapter 3, Chef Language and Style*

▶ Find the `runit` cookbook at:

   https://github.com/opscode-cookbooks/runit/blob/master/recipes/
   default.rb

Finding the complete list of operating systems you can use in cookbooks

You want to write cookbooks, which work on different operating systems such as Ubuntu, RedHat, Debian, or Windows.

Inside your cookbooks, you need to distinguish between those different platforms. And you need to tell your cookbook which platforms it supports. But, you don't know which platform values you can use inside your metadata.rb or your recipes.

In this section, we'll look at a very simple way to ask Chef which values for platform it defines.

How to do it...

Let's use plain Ruby to find out all possible values for platform and use a subset of those in our metadata.rb:

1. Print a list of supported platforms by querying the Chef::Platform class:

   ```
   mma@laptop:~/chef-repo/cookbooks $ ruby -rubygems -rchef -e
     'puts Chef::Platform.platforms.keys.sort.join(", ")'
   ```

   ```
   aix, amazon, arch, centos, debian, default, fedora,
   ...TRUNCATED OUTPUT...
   ubuntu, windows, xenserver
   ```

2. Tell the users of your cookbook which platforms it supports:

   ```
   mma@laptop:~/chef-repo/cookbooks $ subl
     my_cookbook/metadata.rb
   ```

   ```
   . . .

   %w(debian ubuntu mac_os_x).each do |os|
     supports os
   end
   ```

How it works...

Chef maintains a set of supported operating system platforms it runs on in the Chef::Platform class. To query this class for the list of platforms, we use the Ruby command line.

We need to require rubygems and the chef by adding two -r parameters to the ruby call.

The -e parameter contains the Ruby code we want to execute. In our case, we use puts to print the result of our query to your console.

The `Chef::Platform` class holds a collection called **platforms**. We get its keys, sort them, and join the contents of the resulting Ruby array to a comma-separated string:

```
Chef::Platform.platforms.keys.sort.join(", ")
```

There's more...

Each platform in the `Chef::Platforms` collection has not only the platform name as key (this is what we used to display all supported platforms in the preceding example) but also a set of default providers.

Providers contain the platform-specific implementation details for resources. For example, the package resource has providers to use Apt on Ubuntu, but Yum on RedHat.

> Instead of using the Ruby command line, we can use the Chef classes in the **Interactive Ruby shell** (**IRB**) as well.

mma@laptop:~/chef_helpster $ irb

```
1.9.3p194 :001 > require 'chef'
 => true
1.9.3p194 :002 > Chef::Platform.platforms[:ubuntu]
 => {:default=>{:package=>Chef::Provider::Package::Apt,
    :service=>Chef::Provider::Service::Debian,
    :cron=>Chef::Provider::Cron,  :mdadm=>Chef::Provider::Mdadm}}
```

You can change how your recipe works depending on the platform it runs on (example taken from Opscode's `apache` cookbook):

```
service "apache2" do
  case node[:platform]
  when "centos","redhat","fedora","suse"
    service_name "httpd"
  ...TRUNCATED OUTPUT...
when "arch"
    service_name "httpd"
  end
  supports value_for_platform(
    "debian" => { ... },
    "ubuntu" => { ... },
    ...TRUNCATED OUTPUT...
"default" => { ... }
  )
  action :enable
end
```

This version of the `apache` cookbook sets up the `apache` service with different names and commands depending on the platform and tells Chef which actions may be called to manage the `apache` service.

Chef sets the node attribute `:platform` according to the underlying operating system. You can use this node attribute to tailor your recipe code for each platform you need to.

See also

▶ To see some examples on how to use the platform values go to:

```
http://docs.opscode.com/dsl_recipe.html
```

Making recipes idempotent by using conditional execution

Chef manages the configuration of your nodes. It is not simply an installer for new software but you will run Chef Client on existing nodes as well as new nodes.

If you run Chef Client on an existing node, you have to make sure that your recipes do not try to re-execute resources that have already reached the desired state.

Running resources repeatedly will be a performance issue at best and will break your servers at worst. Chef offers a way to tell resources to not run or only if a certain condition is met. Let's have a look how conditional execution of resources works.

Getting ready

Make sure you have a cookbook called `my_cookbook` and the `run_list` of your node includes `my_cookbook` as described in the *Creating and using cookbooks* section in *Chapter 1, Chef Infrastructure*.

How to do it...

Let's see how to use conditional execution in our cookbooks:

1. Edit your default recipe to trigger a callback only if the node knows about the callback URL:

```
mma@laptop:~/chef-repo $ subl
  cookbooks/my_cookbook/recipes/default.rb

http_request 'callback' do
  url node['my_cookbook']['callback']['url']
  only_if { node['my_cookbook']['callback']['enabled'] }
end
```

2. Add the attributes to your cookbook:

```
mma@laptop:~/chef-repo $ subl
  cookbooks/my_cookbook/attributes/default.rb
```

```
default['my_cookbook']['callback']['url'] =
  'http://www.opscode.com'
default['my_cookbook']['callback']['enabled'] = true
```

3. Upload your modified cookbook to the Chef Server:

```
mma@laptop:~/chef-repo $ knife cookbook upload my_cookbook
```

```
Uploading my_cookbook      [0.1.0]
```

4. Run Chef Client on your node to test whether the HTTP request gets executed:

```
user@server:~$ sudo chef-client
```

```
...TRUNCATED OUTPUT...
[2013-03-04T20:28:01+00:00] INFO: Processing http_
request[callback] action get (my_cookbook::default line 9)
[2013-03-04T20:28:02+00:00] INFO: http_request[callback] GET to
http://www.opscode.com successful
...TRUNCATED OUTPUT...
```

How it works...

You can use `only_if` and `not_if` with every resource. In our example we passed it a Ruby block. The Ruby block simply queried a node attribute. Because we set the `enabled` attribute to `true`, the Ruby block evaluates to `true`. And, because we used `only_if`, the resource executes.

You can use the full power of Ruby to find out whether the resource should run or not. Instead of using the curly braces, you can use `do ... end` to surround a multiline Ruby block.

There's more...

Instead of passing a Ruby block, you can pass a shell command as well:

```
http_request 'callback' do
  url node['my_cookbook']['callback']['url']
  only_if "test -f /etc/passwd"
end
```

In this example, Chef will execute the `test` command in a shell. If the shell command returns the exit code `0`, the resource will run.

See also

▶ The *Using attributes* section in *Chapter 3, Chef Language and Style*

▶ Learn more about conditional execution at:

```
http://docs.opscode.com/resource_common_conditionals.html
```

5
Working with Files and Packages

"The file is a gzipped tar file. Your browser is playing tricks with you and trying to be smart."

– Rasmus Lerdorf

In this chapter, we will cover the following:

- ▸ Creating configuration files using templates
- ▸ Using pure Ruby in templates for conditionals and iterations
- ▸ Installing packages from a third-party repository
- ▸ Installing software from source
- ▸ Running a command when a file is updated
- ▸ Distributing directory trees
- ▸ Cleaning up old files
- ▸ Distributing different files based on the target platform

Introduction

Moving files around and installing software are the most common tasks when setting up your nodes. In this chapter, we'll have a look at the various ways Chef supports you in dealing with files and software packages.

Creating configuration files using templates

The term **Configuration Management** already says it loud and clear: your recipes manage the configuration of your nodes. This means managing configuration files in most cases. Chef uses templates to dynamically create configuration files from given values. It takes such values from data bags or attributes, or even calculates them on the fly before passing them into the template.

Let's see how we can create configuration files using templates.

Getting ready

Make sure you have a cookbook named `my_cookbook` and the `run_list` of your node includes `my_cookbook` as described in the *Creating and using cookbooks* section in *Chapter 1, Chef Infrastructure*.

How to do it...

Let's use a `template` resource to create a configuration file:

1. Edit your cookbook's default recipe:

   mma@laptop:~/chef-repo $ subl cookbooks/my_cookbook/recipes/ default.rb

   ```
   template "/etc/logrotate.conf" do
     source "logrotate.conf.erb"
     variables(
       how_often: "daily",
       keep: "31"
     )
   end
   ```

2. Add an **Embedded Ruby** (**ERB**) template file to your recipe in its `default` folder:

   mma@laptop:~/chef-repo $ subl cookbooks/my_cookbook/templates/ default/logrotate.conf.erb

   ```
   <%= @how_often -%>
   rotate <%= @keep -%>
   create
   ```

3. Upload the modified cookbook to the Chef Server:

   mma@laptop:~/chef-repo $ knife cookbook upload my_cookbook

   ```
   Uploading my_cookbook    [0.1.0]
   ```

4. Run Chef Client on your node:

```
user@server:~$ sudo chef-client

...TRUNCATED OUTPUT...
[2013-03-05T21:40:58+00:00] INFO: Processing template[/etc/
logrotate.conf] action create (my_cookbook::default line 9)
[2013-03-05T21:41:04+00:00] INFO: template[/etc/logrotate.
conf] backed up to /srv/chef/cache/etc/logrotate.conf.chef-
20130305214104
[2013-03-05T21:41:04+00:00] INFO: template[/etc/logrotate.conf]
updated content
...TRUNCATED OUTPUT...
```

5. Validate the content of the generated file:

```
user@server:~$ cat /etc/logrotate.conf

daily
rotate 31
create
```

How it works...

If you want to manage any configuration file with Chef, you have to follow the given steps:

1. Copy the desired configuration file from your node to your cookbook's `default` directory under the `templates` folder.

2. Add the extension `.erb` to that copy.

3. Replace any configuration value you want to manage with your cookbook, with an ERB statement printing out a variable. Chef will create variables for every parameter you define in the `variables` call in your template resource:

```
<%= @variable_name -%>
```

4. Create a `template` resource in your recipe using the newly created template as `source`, and pass all the variables you had introduced in your ERB file to it.

5. Running your recipe on the node will now back up the original configuration file and replace it with the dynamically generated version.

 Whenever possible, try using attributes instead of hardcoding values in your recipes.

There's more...

Be careful when a package update makes changes to default configuration files. You need to be aware of those changes and merge them manually into your hand-crafted configuration file template.

Otherwise, you'll lose all the configuration settings you did using Chef.

 It's usually a good idea to add a comment at the top of your configuration file, saying it is managed by Chef, to avoid accidental changes.

See also

▶ Read everything about templates at `http://docs.opscode.com/essentials_cookbook_templates.html`

▶ The *Using templates* section in *Chapter 3, Chef Language and Style*

Using pure Ruby in templates for conditionals and iterations

Switching options on and off in a configuration file is a pretty common thing. Since Chef is using ERB as its template language, you can use pure Ruby to control the flow in your templates. You can use conditionals or even loops in your templates.

Getting ready

Make sure you have a cookbook called `my_cookbook` and the `run_list` of your node includes `my_cookbook` as described in the *Creating and using cookbooks* section in *Chapter 1, Chef Infrastructure*.

How to do it...

Let's create a hypothetical configuration file listing the IP addresses of a given set of backend servers. We only want to print that list if the flag called `enabled` is set to `true`:

1. Edit your cookbook's default recipe:

   ```
   mma@laptop:~/chef-repo $ subl cookbooks/my_cookbook/recipes/
   default.rb
   
   template "/tmp/backends.conf" do
   ```

```
    mode "0444"
    owner "root"
    group "root"
    variables({
      :enabled => true,
      :backends => ["10.0.0.10", "10.0.0.11", "10.0.0.12"]
    })
  end
```

2. Create your template:

   **mma@laptop:~/chef-repo $ subl cookbooks/my_cookbook/templates/
   default/backends.conf.erb**

```
<%- if @enabled %>
  <%- @backends.each do |backend| %>
    <%= backend %>
  <%- end %>
<%- else %>
  No backends defined!
<%- end %>
```

3. Upload the modified cookbook to the Chef Server:

   mma@laptop:~/chef-repo $ knife cookbook upload my_cookbook

```
Uploading my_cookbook      [0.1.0]
```

4. Run Chef Client on your node:

   user@server:~$ sudo chef-client

```
...TRUNCATED OUTPUT...
[2013-03-18T20:40:43+00:00] INFO: Processing template[/tmp/
backends.conf] action create (my_cookbook::default line 9)
[2013-03-18T20:40:44+00:00] INFO: template[/tmp/backends.conf]
updated content
[2013-03-18T20:40:44+00:00] INFO: template[/tmp/backends.conf]
owner changed to 0
[2013-03-18T20:40:44+00:00] INFO: template[/tmp/backends.conf]
group changed to 0
[2013-03-18T20:40:44+00:00] INFO: template[/tmp/backends.conf]
mode changed to 444
...TRUNCATED OUTPUT...
```

5. Validate the content of the generated file:

   user@server:~$ cat /tmp/backends.conf

```
    10.0.0.10
    10.0.0.11
    10.0.0.12
```

How it works...

You can use plain Ruby in your templates. We mix two concepts in our example. First, we use an if-else block to decide whether we should print a list of IP addresses or just a message. Second, if we are going to print the list of IP addresses, we will use a loop to go through all of them.

Let's have a look at the conditional:

```
<%- if @enabled %>
...
<%- else %>
  No backends defined!
<%- end %>
```

We pass either `true` or `false` as the value of the variable called `enabled`. You can access the given variables directly in your template. If we pass `true`, the first block of Ruby code will be executed while rendering the template. If we pass `false`, Chef will render the string `No backends defined!` as the content of the file.

 You use `<%- %>` if you want to embed Ruby logic into your template file.

Now, let's see how we loop through the list of IPs:

```
<%- @backends.each do |backend| %>
  <%= backend %>
<%- end %>
```

We pass an array of strings as the value of the `backend` variable. In the template, we use the `each` iterator to loop through the array. While looping, Ruby assigns each value to the variable we define as the looping variable between the | characters. Inside the loop, we simply print the value of each array element.

While it is possible to use the full power of Ruby inside your templates, it is a good idea to keep them as simple as possible. It is better to put more involved logic into your recipes and pass pre-calculated values to the templates. You should limit yourself to simple conditionals and loops to keep templates simple.

There's more...

You can use conditionals to print strings such as in the following example:

```
<%= "Hello world!" if @enabled -%>
```

If you use this in your template, the string `Hello world!` will be printed only if the variable `enabled` is set to `true`.

See also

▶ The *Using templates* section in *Chapter 3, Chef Language and Style*

▶ Find more explanations and examples at `http://docs.opscode.com/` `essentials_cookbook_templates.html`

Installing packages from a third-party repository

Even though the Ubuntu package repository contains many up-to-date packages, you might bump into situations where either the package you need is missing or is outdated. In such cases, you can either use third-party repositories or your own (containing self-made packages). Chef makes it simple to use additional package repositories with the `apt` cookbook,if you're on Debian or Ubuntu.

Chef provides a `yum` resource, if you're on RedHat/CentOS/ Fedora/Scientific

Getting ready

Make sure you've a cookbook called `my_cookbook` and the `run_list` of your node includes `my_cookbook` as described in the *Creating and using cookbooks* section in *Chapter 1, Chef Infrastructure*.

Retrieve the `apt` cookbook:

```
mma@laptop:~/chef-repo $ knife cookbook site install apt

    ...TRUNCATED OUTPUT...
    Cookbook apt version 1.9.0 successfully installed
```

How to do it...

Let's have a look at how you can install the `s3cmd` tool from the repository at `s3tools.org`:

1. Edit your cookbook's default recipe:

   ```
   mma@laptop:~/chef-repo $ subl cookbooks/my_cookbook/recipes/
   default.rb

   include_recipe "apt"
   apt_repository "s3tools" do
     uri "http://s3tools.org/repo/deb-all"
     components ["stable/"]
   ```

```
  key "http://s3tools.org/repo/deb-all/stable/s3tools.key"
  action :add
end
package "s3cmd"
```

2. Edit your cookbook's metadata to add a dependency on the `apt` cookbook:

    mma@laptop:~/chef-repo $ subl cookbooks/my_cookbook/metadata.rb

    ```
    ...
    depends "apt"
    ```

3. Upload the `apt` cookbook to the Chef Server:

    mma@laptop:~/chef-repo $ knife cookbook upload apt

    ```
    Uploading apt              [1.9.0]
    Uploaded 1 cookbook.
    ```

4. Upload the modified `my_cookbook` to the Chef Server:

    mma@laptop:~/chef-repo $ knife cookbook upload my_cookbook

    ```
    Uploading my_cookbook      [0.1.0]
    ```

5. Validate that the `s3cmd` package is not yet installed:

    user@server:~$ dpkg -l s3cmd

    ```
    No packages found matching s3cmd.
    ```

6. Validate that the default repository would install an older version of `s3cmd` (`1.0.0-1`):

    user@server:~$ apt-cache showpkg s3cmd

    ```
    Package: s3cmd
    Versions:
    1.0.0-1 (/var/lib/apt/lists/us.archive.ubuntu.com_ubuntu_dists_
    precise_universe_binary-amd64_Packages)
    ```

7. Run Chef Client on your node:

    user@server:~$ sudo chef-client

    ```
    ...TRUNCATED OUTPUT...
    [2013-03-18T21:07:14+00:00] INFO: Processing apt_
    repository[s3tools] action add (my_cookbook::default line 11)
    [2013-03-18T21:07:14+00:00] INFO: Processing remote_file[/srv/
    chef/file_store/s3tools.key] action create (/srv/chef/file_store/
    cookbooks/apt/providers/repository.rb line 53)
    ...TRUNCATED OUTPUT...
    [2013-03-18T21:07:19+00:00] INFO: execute[apt-get update] ran
    successfully
    [2013-03-18T21:07:19+00:00] INFO: Processing package[s3cmd] action
    ```

```
install (my_cookbook::default line 18)
...TRUNCATED OUTPUT...
```

8. Validate that the s3tools repository will install a newer version (1.0.0-4 instead of 1.0.0-1):

user@server:~$ apt-cache showpkg s3cmd

```
Package: s3cmd
Versions:
1.0.0-4 (/var/lib/apt/lists/s3tools.org_repo_deb-all_stable_
Packages) (/var/lib/dpkg/status)
```

9. Validate that the s3cmd package is installed:

user@server:~$ dpkg -l

```
...TRUNCATED OUTPUT...
ii  s3cmd 1.0.0-4  The ultimate Amazon S3 and CloudFront command
line client
```

How it works...

The apt cookbook provides an easy way to deal with additional APT repositories. We install it from the community cookbook site using Knife before getting started.

 You could use Berkshelf as described in the *Managing cookbook dependencies with Berkshelf* section in *Chapter 1, Chef Infrastructure* instead of using knife cookbook site install.

We need to tell Chef that we want to use it by adding the depends call to our cookbook's metadata.rb file.

The apt cookbook defines the apt_repository resource. To be able to use it, we need to include the apt recipe in our default recipe:

```
include_recipe "apt"
```

As soon as we've the apt cookbook available, we can add the third-party repository using the apt_repository resource:

```
apt_repository "s3tools" do
  uri "http://s3tools.org/repo/deb-all"
  components ["stable/"]
  key "http://s3tools.org/repo/deb-all/stable/s3tools.key"
  action :add
end
```

In our case, we choose to add the stable branch only.

After adding the third-party repository, we can install the desired package:

```
package "s3cmd"
```

See also

▶ Find more on the `s3cmd` package at `http://s3tools.org/debian-ubuntu-repository-for-s3cmd`

Installing software from source

If you need to install a piece of software that is not available as a package for your platform, you will need to compile it yourself.

In Chef, you can easily do this by using a `script` resource. What is more challenging is to make such a script resource idempotent.

In the following section, we will see how to do both.

Getting ready

Make sure you have a cookbook called `my_cookbook` and the `run_list` of your node includes `my_cookbook` as described in the *Creating and using cookbooks* section in *Chapter 1, Chef Infrastructure*.

How to do it...

Let's take **nginx** as a well-known example for installing it from source:

 The `nginx` community cookbook has a recipe for installing nginx from source. The following example is only to illustrate how you can install any software from source.

1. Edit your cookbook's default recipe:

   mma@laptop:~/chef-repo $ subl cookbooks/my_cookbook/recipes/default.rb

   ```
   version = "1.3.9"
   bash "install_nginx_from_source" do
     cwd Chef::Config['file_cache_path']
     code <<-EOH
       wget http://nginx.org/download/nginx-#{version}.tar.gz
       tar zxf nginx-#{version}.tar.gz &&
       cd nginx-#{version} &&
   ```

```
    ./configure && make && make install
  EOH
  not_if "test -f /usr/local/nginx/sbin/nginx"
end
```

2. Upload the modified cookbook to the Chef Server:

mma@laptop:~/chef-repo $ knife cookbook upload my_cookbook

```
Uploading my_cookbook    [0.1.0]
```

3. Run Chef Client on your node:

user@server:~$ sudo chef-client

```
...TRUNCATED OUTPUT...
[2013-03-19T21:21:18+00:00] INFO: Processing bash[compile_nginx_
source] action run (my_cookbook::default line 15)
[2013-03-19T21:21:44+00:00] INFO: bash[compile_nginx_source] ran
successfully
...TRUNCATED OUTPUT...
```

4. Validate that nginx is installed:

user@server:~$ /usr/local/nginx/sbin/nginx -v

```
nginx version: nginx/1.3.9
```

How it works...

The `bash` resource executes only if the `nginx` executable is not found in the `/usr/local/nginx/sbin` directory. Our `not_if` block tests for this.

Before it runs the script given as `code`, it changes into the working directory given as `cdw`. We use Chef's file cache directory instead of `/tmp` because `/tmp` might get deleted between reboots. To avoid downloading the source tarball again, we want to keep it at a permanent location.

Usually, you would retrieve the value for the version variable from an attribute defined in `my_cookbook/attributes/default.rb`.

The script itself simply unpacks the tarball, configures, prepares, and installs nginx. We chain the commands using `&&` to avoid running all the later commands if an earlier one fails.

```
<<-EOH
...
EOH
```

The preceding code is a Ruby construct for denoting multiline strings.

There's more...

Right now, the recipe will download the source tarball repeatedly even if it is already there (at least as long as the nginx binary is not found). You can use the `remote_file` resource instead of calling `wget` in your bash script. `remote_file` is idempotent—it will only download the file if it needs to.

Change your default recipe in the following way to use the `remote_file` resource:

```
version = "1.3.9"

remote_file "fetch_nginx_source" do
  source "http://nginx.org/download/nginx-#{version}.tar.gz"
  path "#{Chef::Config['file_cache_path']}/nginx-#{version}.tar.gz"
end

bash "install_nginx_from_source" do
  cwd Chef::Config['file_cache_path']
  code <<-EOH
    tar zxf nginx-#{version}.tar.gz &&
    cd nginx-#{version} &&
    ./configure --without-http_rewrite_module &&
    make && make install
  EOH
  not_if "test -f /usr/local/nginx/sbin/nginx"
end
```

See also

▶ Find the full `nginx::source` recipe on GitHub at `https://github.com/opscode-cookbooks/nginx/blob/master/recipes/source.rb`

▶ Read more about this at `http://stackoverflow.com/questions/8530593/chef-install-and-update-programs-from-source`

Running a command when a file is updated

If your node is not under complete Chef control, it might be necessary to trigger commands when Chef changes a file. For example, you might want to restart a service that is not managed by Chef, when its configuration file (which is managed by Chef) changes. Let's see how you can achieve this with Chef.

Getting ready

Make sure you have a cookbook called `my_cookbook` and the `run_list` of your node includes `my_cookbook` as described in the *Creating and using cookbooks* section in *Chapter 1, Chef Infrastructure*.

How to do it...

Let's create an empty file as trigger and run a bash command, if that file changes:

1. Edit your cookbook's default recipe:

   ```
   mma@laptop:~/chef-repo $ subl cookbooks/my_cookbook/recipes/
   default.rb

   template "/tmp/trigger" do
     notifies :run, "bash[run_on_trigger]", :immediately
   end

   bash "run_on_trigger" do
     user "root"
     cwd "/tmp"
     code "echo 'Triggered'"
     action :nothing
   end
   ```

2. Create an empty template:

   ```
   mma@laptop:~/chef-repo $ touch cookbooks/my_cookbook/templates/
   default/trigger.erb
   ```

3. Upload the modified cookbook to the Chef Server:

   ```
   mma@laptop:~/chef-repo $ knife cookbook upload my_cookbook

   Uploading my_cookbook    [0.1.0]
   ```

4. Run Chef Client on your node:

   ```
   user@server:~$ sudo chef-client

   ...TRUNCATED OUTPUT...
   ```

```
[2013-03-20T20:29:32+00:00] INFO: Processing template[/tmp/
trigger] action create (my_cookbook::default line 9)
[2013-03-20T20:29:33+00:00] INFO: template[/tmp/trigger] updated
content
[2013-03-20T20:29:33+00:00] INFO: template[/tmp/trigger] sending
run action to bash[run_on_trigger] (immediate)
[2013-03-20T20:29:33+00:00] INFO: Processing bash[run_on_trigger]
 action run (my_cookbook::default line 13)
[2013-03-20T20:29:33+00:00] INFO: bash[run_on_trigger] ran
successfully
...TRUNCATED OUTPUT...
```

5. Run Chef Client again to verify that the `run_on_trigger` script does not get executed again:

    user@server:~$ sudo chef-client

    ```
    ...TRUNCATED OUTPUT...
    [2013-03-20T20:29:58+00:00] INFO: Processing template[/tmp/
    trigger] action create (my_cookbook::default line 9)
    [2013-03-20T20:29:58+00:00] INFO: Processing bash[run_on_trigger]
    action nothing (my_cookbook::default line 13)
    ...TRUNCATED OUTPUT...
    ```

How it works...

We define a `template` resource and tell it to notify our `bash` resource immediately. Chef will notify the `bash` resource only if the `template` resource changed the file. To make sure that the bash script runs only when notified, we define its action as `nothing`.

We see in the output of the first Chef Client run (which created the trigger file) that the bash script was executed:

```
bash[run_on_trigger] ran successfully
```

We see in the output of the second Chef Client run that in the preceding message is missing. Chef did not execute the script because it did not modify the trigger file.

There's more...

Instead of a template, you can let a file or `remote_file` resource trigger a bash script. When compiling programs from source, you will download the source tarball using a `remote_file` resource. This resource will trigger a `bash` resource, which will then extract, compile, and install the program.

See also

▶ The *Installing software from source* section

Distributing directory trees

You need to upload a complete directory structure to your nodes. It might be a static website or some backup data, which is needed on your nodes. You want Chef to make sure that all the files and directories are there on your nodes. Chef offers the `remote_directory` resource to handle this case. Let's see how you can use it.

Getting ready

Make sure you have a cookbook called `my_cookbook` and the `run_list` of your node includes `my_cookbook` as described in the *Creating and using cookbooks* section in *Chapter 1, Chef Infrastructure*.

How to do it...

Let's upload a directory with some files to our node:

1. Edit your cookbook's default recipe:

   ```
   mma@laptop:~/chef-repo $ subl cookbooks/my_cookbook/recipes/
   default.rb
   ```

   ```
   remote_directory "/tmp/chef.github.com" do
     files_backup 10
     files_owner "root"
     files_group "root"
     files_mode 00644
     owner "root"
     group "root"
     mode 00755
   end
   ```

2. Create a directory structure with files to upload to your node. In this example, I use a plain GitHub pages directory:

   ```
   mma@laptop:~/chef-repo $ mv chef.github.com cookbooks/my_cookbook/
   files/default
   ```

3. Upload the modified cookbook to the Chef Server:

   ```
   mma@laptop:~/chef-repo $ knife cookbook upload my_cookbook
   ```

   ```
   Uploading my_cookbook    [0.1.0]
   ```

4. Run Chef Client on your node:

```
user@server:~$ sudo chef-client

...TRUNCATED OUTPUT...
[2013-03-22T08:36:45+00:00] INFO: Processing remote_directory[/
tmp/chef.github.com] action create (my_cookbook::default line 9)
[2013-03-22T08:36:45+00:00] INFO: remote_directory[/tmp/chef.
github.com] created directory /tmp/chef.github.com
[2013-03-22T08:36:45+00:00] INFO: remote_directory[/tmp/chef.
github.com] owner changed to 0
[2013-03-22T08:36:45+00:00] INFO: remote_directory[/tmp/chef.
github.com] group changed to 0
[2013-03-22T08:36:45+00:00] INFO: remote_directory[/tmp/chef.
github.com] mode changed to 755
...TRUNCATED OUTPUT...
[2013-03-22T08:36:46+00:00] INFO: Processing cookbook_file[/tmp/
chef.github.com/images/body-bg.png] action create (dynamically
defined)
[2013-03-22T08:36:46+00:00] INFO: cookbook_file[/tmp/chef.github.
com/images/body-bg.png] owner changed to 0
[2013-03-22T08:36:46+00:00] INFO: cookbook_file[/tmp/chef.github.
com/images/body-bg.png] group changed to 0
[2013-03-22T08:36:46+00:00] INFO: cookbook_file[/tmp/chef.github.
com/images/body-bg.png] mode changed to 644
[2013-03-22T08:36:46+00:00] INFO: cookbook_file[/tmp/chef.github.
com/images/body-bg.png] created file /tmp/chef.github.com/images/
body-bg.png

...TRUNCATED OUTPUT...
```

5. Validate that the directory and its files are there on the node:

```
user@server:~$ ls -l /tmp/chef.github.com

total 16
4 drwxr-xr-x 2 root root 4096 Mar 22 08:36 images
4 -rw-r--r-- 1 root root 3383 Mar 22 08:36 index.html
4 drwxr-xr-x 2 root root 4096 Mar 22 08:36 javascripts
4 drwxr-xr-x 2 root root 4096 Mar 22 08:36 stylesheets
```

How it works...

You need to put the directory that you want to distribute to your nodes into your cookbook under the `default` of your cookbook's `files` directory. The `remote_directory` resource picks it up from there and uploads it to your nodes. By default, the name of the resource (in our example `/tmp/chef.github.com`) will act as the target directory.

Be careful not to put very heavy directory structures into your cookbooks. You will not only need to distribute them to every node but also to your Chef Server.

There's more...

While you could use the `remote_directory` resource for deploying your applications, there are better ways to do the same. Either you could use any of Chef's application cookbooks that are available, for example, for Ruby or PHP applications, or you use tools such as Capistrano or Mina for deployment.

See also

- ▸ The *Distributing different files based on target platform* section
- ▸ Find out more about GitHub pages at `http://pages.github.com/`
- ▸ The documentation for the `remote_directory` resource can be found at `http://docs.opscode.com/chef/resources.html#remote-directory`
- ▸ Find out more about Capistrano at `http://www.capistranorb.com/`
- ▸ Find out more about Mina at `http://nadarei.co/mina/`

Cleaning up old files

What happens if you want to remove a software package from your node? You have to be aware of the fact that Chef is not automatically removing stuff from your nodes. Removing a resource from your cookbook does not mean that Chef will remove the resource from your nodes. You need to do this by yourself.

Getting ready

Make sure you have a cookbook called `my_cookbook` and the `run_list` of your node includes `my_cookbook` as described in the *Creating and using cookbooks* section in *Chapter 1, Chef Infrastructure*.

Make sure you have a `remote_directory` resource in `my_cookbook` as described in the *Distributing directory trees* section.

How to do it...

Let's remove the `remote_directory` resource from `my_cookbook` and see what happens:

1. Edit your cookbook's default recipe and remove the `remote_directory` resource:

    **mma@laptop:~/chef-repo $ subl cookbooks/my_cookbook/recipes/
    default.rb**

    ```
    # there used to be the remote_directory resource
    ```

2. Upload the modified cookbook to the Chef Server:

    mma@laptop:~/chef-repo $ knife cookbook upload my_cookbook

    ```
    Uploading my_cookbook      [0.1.0]
    ```

3. Run Chef Client on your node:

    user@server:~$ sudo chef-client

    ```
    ...TRUNCATED OUTPUT...


    ...TRUNCATED OUTPUT...
    ```

4. Validate that the directory and its files are still there on the node:

    user@server:~$ ls -l /tmp/chef.github.com

    ```
    total 16
    4 drwxr-xr-x 2 root root 4096 Mar 22 08:36 images
    4 -rw-r--r-- 1 root root 3383 Mar 22 08:36 index.html
    4 drwxr-xr-x 2 root root 4096 Mar 22 08:36 javascripts
    4 drwxr-xr-x 2 root root 4096 Mar 22 08:36 stylesheets
    ```

Now, let's explicitly remove the directory structure:

1. Edit your cookbook's default recipe:

    **mma@laptop:~/chef-repo $ subl cookbooks/my_cookbook/recipes/
    default.rb**

    ```
    directory "/tmp/chef.github.com" do
      action :delete
      recursive true
    end
    ```

2. Upload the modified cookbook on the Chef Server:

    mma@laptop:~/chef-repo $ knife cookbook upload my_cookbook

    ```
    Uploading my_cookbook      [0.1.0]
    ```

3. Run Chef Client on your node:

```
user@server:~$ sudo chef-client

...TRUNCATED OUTPUT...
2013-03-25T21:05:20+00:00] INFO: Removing cookbooks/my_cookbook/
files/default/chef.github.com/javascripts/main.js from the cache;
it is no longer needed by chef-client.
  [2013-03-25T21:05:20+00:00] INFO: Removing cookbooks/my_cookbook/
files/default/chef.github.com/stylesheets/print.css from the
cache; it is no longer needed by chef-client.
...TRUNCATED OUTPUT...
```

4. Validate that the directory and its files are gone from the node:

```
user@server:~$ ls -l /tmp/chef.github.com

ls: cannot access /tmp/chef.github.com: No such file or directory
```

How it works...

Removing a resource from your cookbook will lead to Chef not knowing anything about it anymore. Chef does not touch the things that are not defined in cookbooks, even if Chef created them once.

To clean up stuff you created using Chef, you need to put the reverse actions into your cookbooks. If you created a directory using Chef, you need to explicitly delete it by using the `directory` resource with `action :delete` in your cookbook.

The directory resource is idempotent. Even if the directory is already deleted, it will run fine and simply do nothing.

There's more...

If you upload a directory structure using the `remote_directory` resource, you can use the `purge` parameter to delete files within that directory structure, if they are no longer in your cookbook. In this case, you do not need to delete each file by using a file resource with the `delete` action:

```
remote_directory "/tmp/chef.github.com" do
  ...
  purge true
end
```

See also

▸ The *Distributing directory trees* section

▸ Learn more about the `directory` resource at `http://docs.opscode.com/resource_directory.html`

▸ Learn more about the `remote_directory` resource at `http://docs.opscode.com/chef/resources.html#remote-directory`

Distributing different files based on the target platform

If you have nodes with different operating systems such as Ubuntu and CentOS, you might want to deliver different files to each of them. There might be differences in the necessary configuration options and the like. Chef offers a way for files and templates to differentiate which version to use based on a node's platform.

Getting ready

Make sure you have a cookbook called `my_cookbook` and the `run_list` of your node includes `my_cookbook` as described in the *Creating and using cookbooks* section in *Chapter 1, Chef Infrastructure*.

How to do it...

Let's add two templates to our cookbook and see which one gets used:

1. Edit your cookbook's default recipe:

   ```
   mma@laptop:~/chef-repo $ subl cookbooks/my_cookbook/recipes/default.rb
   ```

   ```
   template "/tmp/message" do
     source "message.erb"
   end
   ```

2. Create a template as default:

   ```
   mma@laptop:~/chef-repo $ subl cookbooks/my_cookbook/templates/default/message.erb
   ```

   ```
   Hello from default template!
   ```

3. Create a template only for Ubuntu 12.04 nodes:

   ```
   mma@laptop:~/chef-repo $ subl cookbooks/my_cookbook/templates/ubuntu-12.04/message.erb
   ```

   ```
   Hello from Ubuntu 12.04!
   ```

4. Upload the modified cookbook to the Chef Server:

```
mma@laptop:~/chef-repo $ knife cookbook upload my_cookbook

Uploading my_cookbook    [0.1.0]
```

5. Run Chef Client on your node:

```
user@server:~$ sudo chef-client

...TRUNCATED OUTPUT...
[2013-03-25T21:31:02+00:00] INFO: template[/tmp/message] updated
content
...TRUNCATED OUTPUT...
```

6. Validate that Chef uses the platform specific template:

```
user@server:~$ sudo cat /tmp/message

Hello from Ubuntu 12.04!
```

How it works...

Chef tries to use the most specific template for a given platform by looking for templates in the following order, if the given platform would be Ubuntu 12.04:

```
my_cookbook/templates/my_node.example.com/message.erb
my_cookbook/templates/ubuntu-12.04/message.erb
my_cookbook/templates/ubuntu-12/message.erb
my_cookbook/templates/ubuntu/message.erb
my_cookbook/templates/default/message.erb
```

Chef takes the first hit. If there is a file in a directory with the same name as the **fully qualified domain name** (**FQDN**) of the node, it will take that one.

If not, it will look through the other directories (if existing) like `ubuntu` or `ubuntu-12.04`, and so on.

The only directory that is mandatory, is the `default` directory.

See also

▶ The *Using templates* section in *Chapter 4, Writing Better Cookbooks*

▶ Find more details about file specificity at `http://docs.opscode.com/resource_template.html#file-specificity`

6

Users and Applications

"The system should treat all user input as sacred."

– Jef Raskin

In this chapter, we will cover the following:

- ▸ Creating users from data bags
- ▸ Securing the Secure Shell Daemon (SSHD)
- ▸ Enabling passwordless sudo
- ▸ Managing NTP
- ▸ Managing nginx
- ▸ Creating nginx sites
- ▸ Creating MySQL databases and users
- ▸ Managing WordPress sites
- ▸ Managing Ruby on Rails applications
- ▸ Managing Varnish
- ▸ Managing your local workstation

Introduction

In this chapter, we'll see how to manage the user accounts on your nodes with Chef. This is one of the fundamental things you can start your infrastructure automation efforts with.

After dealing with users, we'll have a look at how to install and manage more advanced applications. Our examples are mainly covering a web application stack using nginx as a web server, MySQL as the database, and WordPress or Ruby on Rails for the web application.

We'll close the chapter with showing you how to manage your local workstation with Chef.

Creating users from data bags

When managing a set of servers it's important to make sure that the right people (and only them) have access to them. You definitely don't want a shared account whose password is known by everyone. You don't want to hardcode any users into your recipes either because you want to separate logic and data.

Chef helps you to manage users on your nodes using data bags for your users and to let a recipe create and remove the users accordingly.

Let's have a look at how you can do that.

Getting ready

Make sure you've a cookbook named `my_cookbook` and the `run_list` of your node includes `my_cookbook` as described in the *Creating and using cookbooks* section in *Chapter 1, Chef Infrastructure*.

Make sure you've the `berkshelf` gem installed as described in the *Managing cookbook dependencies with Berkshelf* section in *Chapter 1, Chef Infrastructure*.

Create your `Berksfile` in your Chef repository including `my_cookbook`:

```
mma@laptop:~/chef-repo $ subl Berksfile

  cookbook 'my_cookbook', path: './cookbooks/my_cookbook'
```

Make sure you've a public SSH key available for your user by following the instructions at: `http://git-scm.com/book/en/Git-on-the-Server-Generating-Your-SSH-Public-Key`

How to do it...

First, we need to set up the data bag and at least one data bag item for our first user:

1. Create a data bag for your users:

   ```
   mma@laptop:~/chef-repo $ knife data bag create users

   Created data_bag[users]
   ```

2. Create a directory for your data bag item's JSON files:

   ```
   mma@laptop:~/chef-repo $ mkdir data_bags/users
   ```

3. Create a data bag item for your first user. Use the username as filename (here: mma):

   ```
   mma@laptop:~/chef-repo $ subl data_bags/users/mma.json
   ```

```
{
  "id": "mma",
  "ssh_keys": [
    "ssh-rsa AAA345...bla== mma@laptop"
  ],
  "groups": [ "staff"],
  "shell": "\/bin\/bash"
}
```

4. Upload the data bag item to the Chef Server:

    mma@laptop:~/chef-repo $ knife data bag from file users mma.json

    Updated data_bag_item[users::mma]

Now it's time to set up the recipe to manage our users:

 Because the Chef Server indexes data bags, it can take a few minutes until a new data bag is available for use. If you encounter an error, please wait a few minutes and then try again.

1. Edit your cookbook's metadata.rb to include the dependency on the users cookbook:

    mma@laptop:~/chef-repo $ subl cookbooks/my_cookbook/metadata.rb

    depends "users"

2. Install your cookbooks dependencies:

    mma@laptop:~/chef-repo $ berks install

    Using my_cookbook (0.1.0) at './cookbooks/my_cookbook'
    ...TRUNCATED OUTPUT...

3. Edit your cookbook's default recipe:

    mma@laptop:~/chef-repo $ subl cookbooks/my_cookbook/recipes/ default.rb

    include_recipe "users"

    users_manage "staff" do
      group_id 50
      action [:remove, :create]

4. Upload the modified cookbook to the Chef Server:

    mma@laptop:~/chef-repo $ berks upload

    ...TRUNCATED OUTPUT...

```
Uploading my_cookbook (0.1.0) to: 'https://api.opscode.com:443/
organizations/agilewebops'
...TRUNCATED OUTPUT...
```

5. Run Chef Client on your node:

```
user@server:~$ sudo chef-client

...TRUNCATED OUTPUT...
- create user user[mma]
...TRUNCATED OUTPUT...
- alter group group[staff]
- replace group members with new list of members
...TRUNCATED OUTPUT...
```

6. Validate that the user mma exists:

```
user@server:~$ fgrep mma /etc/passwd

mma:x:1000:1001::/home/mma:/bin/bash
```

7. Validate that the user mma belongs to group staff now:

```
user@server:~$ fgrep staff /etc/group

staff:x:50:mma
```

How it works...

The users cookbook requires that you create a users data bag and one data bag item for each user. In that data bag item, you define the attributes of the user: groups, shell, and so on. You even can include an "action" attribute, which defaults to "create" but could be "remove" as well.

To be able to manage users, you need to include it as a dependency in your cookbook's metadata. In your recipe you include the users cookbook default recipe to be able to use the manage_users **Light Weight Resource Provider** (**LWRP**) provided by the users cookbook.

The manage_users LWRP takes its name attribute "staff" as the group name it should manage. It searches for data bag items having that group in their groups entry and uses every entry found to create those users and groups.

 The manage_users LWRP replaces group members—existing (non-Chef managed) users will get thrown out of the given group (bad, if you manage the sudo group on Vagrant).

By passing both actions :create and :remove into the LWRP, we make sure that it searches for both: users to remove and users to add.

There's more...

Let's have a look at how you can remove a user:

1. Edit the data bag item for your first user, setting the `action` to `remove`:

    mma@laptop:~/chef-repo $ subl data_bags/users/mma.json

    ```
    {
      "id": "mma",
      "ssh_keys": [
        "ssh-rsa AAA345...bla== mma@laptop"
      ],
      "groups": [ "staff"],
      "shell": "\/bin\/bash",
      "action": "remove"
    }
    ```

2. Upload the data bag item to the Chef Server:

    mma@laptop:~/chef-repo $ knife data bag from file users mma.json

    ```
    Updated data_bag_item[users::mma]
    ```

3. Run Chef Client on your node:

    user@server:~$ sudo chef-client

    ```
    ...TRUNCATED OUTPUT...
    - remove user user[mma]
    ...TRUNCATED OUTPUT...
    - alter group group[staff]
    - replace group members with new list of members
    ...TRUNCATED OUTPUT...
    ```

4. Validate that the user mma does not exist anymore:

    user@server:~$ fgrep mma /etc/passwd

    ```
    ...NO OUTPUT...
    ```

     If the user you want to remove is currently logged in, you will get an error. This happens because the underlying operating system command userdel cannot remove the user (and exits with return code 8):

    ```
    Chef::Exceptions::Exec
    ----------------------
    userdel mma returned 8, expected 0
    ```

See also

▸ Find the `users` cookbook on GitHub: `https://github.com/opscode-cookbooks/users`

▸ The *Using data bags* section in *Chapter 4, Writing Better Cookbooks*

Securing the Secure Shell Daemon (SSHD)

Depending on your Linux flavor, the `ssh` daemon might listen on all network interfaces on the default port and allow root and password logins.

This default configuration is not very safe. Automated scripts can try to guess the root password. You're at the mercy of the strength of your root passwords.

It's a good idea to make things stricter. Let's see how you can do this.

Getting ready

Create a user who can log in using his `ssh` key instead of a password. Doing this with Chef is described in the *Creating users from data bags* section.

Make sure you have a cookbook named `my_cookbook` and the `run_list` of your node includes `my_cookbook` as described in the *Creating and using cookbooks section* in *Chapter 1, Chef Infrastructure*.

Make sure you've the `berkshelf` gem installed as described in the *Managing cookbook dependencies with Berkshelf section* in *Chapter 1, Chef Infrastructure*.

Create your `Berksfile` in your Chef repository including `my_cookbook`:

```
mma@laptop:~/chef-repo $ subl Berksfile
```

```
cookbook 'my_cookbook', path: './cookbooks/my_cookbook'
```

 Attention: Configuring `sshd` might lock you out of your system. Make sure you've an open `ssh` connection with root access to fix what an error in your cookbook might have broken!

How to do it...

We'll secure `sshd` by disabling root login (you should use `sudo` instead) and by disabling password logins. Users should only be able to log in using their `ssh` key.

1. Edit your cookbook's `metadata.rb` and add a dependency on the `openssh` cookbook:

   `mma@laptop:~/chef-repo $ subl cookbooks/my_cookbook/metadata.rb`

   ```
   ...
   depends "openssh"
   ```

2. Install your cookbook's dependencies:

   `mma@laptop:~/chef-repo $ berks install`

   ```
   Using my_cookbook (0.1.0) at './cookbooks/my_cookbook'
   ...TRUNCATED OUTPUT...
   ```

3. Edit your cookbook's default recipe:

   `mma@laptop:~/chef-repo $ subl cookbooks/my_cookbook/recipes/default.rb`

   ```
   node.default['openssh']['server']['permit_root_login'] = "no"
   node.default['openssh']['server']['password_authentication'] =
   "no"

   include_recipe 'openssh'
   ```

4. Upload the modified cookbook to the Chef Server:

   `mma@laptop:~/chef-repo $ berks upload`

   ```
   ...TRUNCATED OUTPUT...
   Uploading my_cookbook (0.1.0) to: 'https://api.opscode.com:443/
   organizations/agilewebops'
   ...TRUNCATED OUTPUT...
   ```

5. Run Chef Client on your node:

   `user@server:~$ sudo chef-client`

   ```
   ...TRUNCATED OUTPUT...
     * template[/etc/ssh/sshd_config] action create[2013-03-
   29T19:42:38+00:00] INFO: Processing template[/etc/ssh/sshd_config]
   action create (openssh::default line 66)
   ...TRUNCATED OUTPUT...
    [2013-03-29T19:42:38+00:00] INFO: service[ssh] restarted
   ...TRUNCATED OUTPUT...
   ```

6. Validate the content of the generated file:

```
user@server:~$ cat /etc/ssh/sshd_config

# Generated by Chef for server

AuthorizedKeysFile %h/.ssh/authorized_keys
ChallengeResponseAuthentication no
PermitRootLogin no
PasswordAuthentication no
UsePAM yes
...TRUNCATED OUTPUT...
```

How it works...

The `openssh` cookbook offers attributes for most configuration parameters in `ssh_config` and `sshd_config`. We override the default values in our cookbook and include the `openssh` default recipe.

The order is significant here because this way the `openssh` recipe will use our overridden values instead of its defaults.

The `openssh` cookbook writes the `/etc/ssh/sshd_config` file and restarts the `sshd` service. After running this recipe, you will no longer be able to SSH into the node using a password.

There's more...

If your nodes are connected to a **Virtual Private Network** (**VPN**) by using a second network interface, it's a good idea to bind `sshd` to that secure network only. That way you block anyone from the public Internet trying to hack your `sshd`.

You can override the `listen_address` attribute in your cookbook:

```
node.default['openssh']['server']['listen_address']
```

If your nodes need to be accessible via the Internet, you might want to move `sshd` to a higher port to get rid of the automated attacks:

```
node.default['openssh']['server']['port'] = '6222'
```

In this case, you need to use `-p 6222` with your `ssh` commands to be able to connect to your nodes.

Moving your `sshd` to a non-privileged port is adding one layer of security, but comes at the cost that you move from a privileged port to a non-privileged port on your node. This holds the risk that someone on your box highjacks that port. Read more about the implications at: `http://www.adayinthelifeof.nl/2012/03/12/why-putting-ssh-on-another-port-than-22-is-bad-idea/`

See also

▶ Find the `openssh` cookbook on GitHub: `https://github.com/opscode-cookbooks/openssh`

▶ Find a detailed list of all attributes the `openssh` cookbook offers to configure `sshd`: `https://github.com/opscode-cookbooks/openssh/blob/master/attributes/default.rb`

Enabling passwordless sudo

You've secured your `sshd` so that your users can only log in with their own user accounts instead of root. Additionally, you've made sure that your users do not need a password but are forced to use their private keys for authentication.

But once authenticated, they want to administer the system. That's why it is a good idea to have `sudo` installed on all boxes. Sudo enables non-root users to execute commands as root, if they're allowed to. Sudo will log all such command executions.

To make sure that your users don't need passwords here either you should configure `sudo` for passwordless logins. Let's have a look at how to do that.

Getting ready

Make sure you've a cookbook named `my_cookbook` and the `run_list` of your node includes `my_cookbook` as described in the *Creating and using cookbooks* section in *Chapter 1, Chef Infrastructure*.

Make sure you've the `berkshelf` gem installed as described in the *Managing cookbook dependencies with Berkshelf* section in *Chapter 1, Chef Infrastructure*.

Create your `Berksfile` in your Chef repository including `my_cookbook`:

mma@laptop:~/chef-repo $ subl Berksfile

```
cookbook 'my_cookbook', path: './cookbooks/my_cookbook'
```

How to do it...

Let's make Chef modify the `sudo` configuration to enable passwordless `sudo` for the staff group:

1. Edit your cookbook's `metadata.rb` and add the dependency on the `sudo` cookbook:

   mma@laptop:~/chef-repo $ subl cookbooks/my_cookbook/metadata.rb

   ```
   ...
   depends "sudo"
   ```

2. Install your cookbook's dependencies:

`mma@laptop:~/chef-repo $ berks install`

```
Using my_cookbook (0.1.0) at './cookbooks/my_cookbook'
...TRUNCATED OUTPUT...
```

3. Edit your cookbook's default recipe:

 Vagrant users: If you are working with a Vagrant-managed VM, make sure to include the `vagrant` group in the `sudo` configuration. Otherwise, your `vagrant` user will not be able to `sudo` anymore.

`mma@laptop:~/chef-repo $ subl cookbooks/my_cookbook/recipes/`
`default.rb`

```
node.default['authorization']['sudo']['passwordless'] = true
node.default['authorization']['sudo']['groups'] = ['staff',
'vagrant']

include_recipe 'sudo'
```

4. Upload the modified cookbook to the Chef Server:

`mma@laptop:~/chef-repo $ berks upload`

```
...TRUNCATED OUTPUT...
Uploading my_cookbook (0.1.0) to: 'https://api.opscode.com:443/
organizations/agilewebops'
...TRUNCATED OUTPUT...
```

5. Run Chef Client on your node:

`user@server:~$ sudo chef-client`

```
...TRUNCATED OUTPUT...
[2013-04-12T19:48:51+00:00] INFO: Processing template[/etc/
sudoers] action create (sudo::default line 41)
[2013-04-12T19:48:51+00:00] INFO: template[/etc/sudoers] backed up
to /srv/chef/cache/etc/sudoers.chef-20130412194851
[2013-04-12T19:48:51+00:00] INFO: template[/etc/sudoers] updated
content
[2013-04-12T19:48:51+00:00] INFO: template[/etc/sudoers] owner
changed to 0
[2013-04-12T19:48:51+00:00] INFO: template[/etc/sudoers] group
changed to 0
[2013-04-12T19:48:51+00:00] INFO: template[/etc/sudoers] mode
changed to 440
...TRUNCATED OUTPUT...
```

6. Validate the content of the generated `sudoers` file:

```
user@server:~$ sudo cat /etc/sudoers

. . .
# Members of the group 'staff' may gain root privileges
%staff ALL=(ALL) NOPASSWD:ALL
# Members of the group 'vagrant' may gain root privileges
%vagrant ALL=(ALL) NOPASSWD:ALL
```

How it works...

The `sudo` cookbook rewrites the `/etc/sudoers` file using the attribute values we set in the node. In our case, we set:

```
node.default['authorization']['sudo']['passwordless'] = true
```

This will tell the `sudo` cookbook that we want to enable our users to `sudo` without any password.

Then, we tell the `sudo` cookbook which groups should have passwordless `sudo` rights:

```
node.default['authorization']['sudo']['groups'] = ['staff', 'vagrant']
```

The last step is to include the `sudo` cookbook's default recipe to let it install and configure `sudo` on your nodes:

```
include_recipe 'sudo'
```

There's more...

By using the LWRP from the `sudo` cookbook, you can manage each group or user individually. The LWRP will place configuration fragments inside `/etc/sudoers.d`. You can use this to use your own template for the `sudo` configuration:

```
sudo 'mma' do
  template    'staff_member.erb' # local cookbook template
  variables   :cmds => ['/etc/init.d/ssh restart']
end
```

This snippet assumes that you have `my_cookbook/templates/default/staff_member.erb` in place.

See also

▶ The *Creating users from a data bags* section

▶ Find the `sudo` cookbook at GitHub: `https://github.com/opscode-cookbooks/sudo`

Managing NTP

Your nodes should always have synchronized clocks, if nothing else because Chef Server requires clients' clocks to be synchronized with it. This is required because the authentication of clients is based on a time window to prevent man-in-the-middle attacks.

NTP is there to synchronize your nodes' clocks with its upstream peers. It usually uses a set of trusted upstream peers so that it gets a reliable timing signal.

It's a good idea to put the installation of NTP into a role, which you assign to every node. Bugs caused by clocks running are not nice to track down. Better avoid them in the first place by using NTP on every node.

Getting ready

Make sure you've the `berkshelf` gem installed as described in the *Managing cookbook dependencies with Berkshelf* section in *Chapter 1, Chef Infrastructure*.

Create your `Berksfile` in your Chef repository including the `ntp` cookbook:

```
mma@laptop:~/chef-repo $ subl Berksfile

    cookbook 'ntp'
```

Install the `ntp` cookbook:

```
mma@laptop:~/chef-repo $ berks install --path cookbooks/

    Using ntp (1.3.2)
    ...TRUNCATED OUTPUT...
```

Upload the `ntp` cookbook to the Chef Server:

```
mma@laptop:~/chef-repo $ berks upload

    ...TRUNCATED OUTPUT...
    Uploading ntp (1.3.2) to: 'https://api.opscode.com:443/organizations/
    agilewebops'
    ...TRUNCATED OUTPUT...
```

How to do it...

Let's create a role called "base", which ensures that your nodes will synchronize their clocks using NTP:

1. Create a `base.rb` file for your role:

    ```
    mma@laptop:~/chef-repo $ subl roles/base.rb
    ```

```
name "base"

run_list "recipe[ntp]"

default_attributes ("ntp" => {
  "servers" => ["0.pool.ntp.org", "1.pool.ntp.org", "2.pool.ntp.
org"]
})
```

2. Upload the new role to the Chef Server:

   mma@laptop:~/chef-repo $ knife role from file base.rb

   ```
   Updated Role base!
   ```

3. Add the base role to your node's run list:

   mma@laptop:~/chef-repo $ knife node edit server

   ```
   ...
     "run_list": [
       "role[base]"
     ]
   ...
   ```

4. Run Chef Client on your node:

   user@server:~$ sudo chef-client

   ```
   ...TRUNCATED OUTPUT...
   [2013-04-16T18:22:36+00:00] INFO: service[ntp] restarted
   ...TRUNCATED OUTPUT...
   ```

5. Validate that ntp is installed correctly:

   user@server:~$ /etc/init.d/ntp status

   ```
   * NTP server is running
   ```

How it works...

The ntp cookbook installs the required packages for your node's platform and writes a configuration file. You can influence the configuration by setting default attributes in the ntp namespace. In our preceding example, we configured the upstream NTP servers for our node to query.

 If you're on Debian or Ubuntu, the ntp cookbook installs ntpdate as well. ntpdate is there to quickly synchronize and set a node's date and time.

There's more...

The `ntp` cookbook contains an `ntp::disable` recipe and an `ntp::undo` recipe as well. You can disable the NTP service by adding `ntp::disable` to your node's run list, and you can completely remove NTP from your node by adding `ntp::undo` to your node's run list.

See also

- ► You find the `ntp` cookbook on GitHub at: `https://github.com/opscode-cookbooks/ntp`

- ► The *Overriding attributes* section in *Chapter 4, Writing Better Cookbooks*

Managing nginx

Suppose you need to set up a website that handles a lot of traffic simultaneously. nginx is a web server designed to handle high loads and is used by a lot of big web companies such as Facebook, Dropbox, and WordPress.

You'll find nginx packages in most major distributions, but if you want to extend nginx using modules, you'll need to compile nginx from source.

In this section, we'll configure the `nginx` community cookbook to just do that.

Getting ready

Make sure you've the `berkshelf` gem installed as described in the *Managing cookbook dependencies with Berkshelf section* in *Chapter 1, Chef Infrastructure*.

Create your `Berksfile` in your Chef repository including the `nginx` cookbook:

```
mma@laptop:~/chef-repo $ subl Berksfile

    cookbook 'nginx'
```

Install the `nginx` cookbook:

```
mma@laptop:~/chef-repo $ berks install --path cookbooks/

    Using nginx (1.7.0)
    ...TRUNCATED OUTPUT...
```

Upload the `nginx` cookbook to your Chef Server:

```
mma@laptop:~/chef-repo $ berks upload

    Using nginx (1.7.0)
```

```
...TRUNCATED OUTPUT...
Uploading nginx (1.7.0) to: 'https://api.opscode.com:443/
organizations/agilewebops'
...TRUNCATED OUTPUT...
```

How to do it...

Let's set up a role and configure how we want to build nginx:

1. Create a new role called `web_server` with the following contents:

    mma@laptop:~/chef-repo $ subl roles/web_server.rb

    ```
    name "web_server"
    run_list "recipe[nginx::source]"

    default_attributes ("nginx" => {
      "init_style" => "init",
      "enable_default_site" => false,
      "upload_progress" => {
        "url" => "https://github.com/masterzen/nginx-upload-progress-
    module/tarball/v0.9.0"
      },
      "source" => {
        "modules" => ["upload_progress_module"]
      }
    })
    ```

2. Upload the role to the Chef Server:

    mma@laptop:~/chef-repo $ knife role from file web_server.rb

    ```
    Updated Role web_server!
    ```

3. Add the `web_server` role to your node's run list:

    mma@laptop:~/chef-repo $ knife node edit server

    ```
    ...
      "run_list": [
        "role[web_server]"
      ]
    ...
    ```

4. Run Chef Client on your node:

    user@server:~$ sudo chef-client

    ```
    ...TRUNCATED OUTPUT...
    [2013-04-19T07:40:35+00:00] INFO: Loading cookbooks [apt, build-
    ```

```
essential, nginx, ohai, yum]
...TRUNCATED OUTPUT...
[2013-04-19T07:41:47+00:00] INFO: service[nginx] restarted
...TRUNCATED OUTPUT...
```

5. Validate that nginx is installed with the `upload_progress_module`:

user@server:~$ sudo nginx -V

```
nginx version: nginx/1.2.6
built by gcc 4.6.3 (Ubuntu/Linaro 4.6.3-1ubuntu5)
TLS SNI support enabled
configure arguments: --prefix=/opt/nginx-1.2.6 --conf-path=/etc/
nginx/nginx.conf --with-http_ssl_module --with-http_gzip_static_
module --add-module=/srv/chef/file_store/nginx_upload_progress/7b3
f81d30cd3e8af2c343b73d8518d2373b95aeb3d0243790991873a3d91d0c5
```

How it works...

We configure how we want to use nginx in our new role, `web_server`. First, we decide that we want to install nginx from source, because we want to add an additional module. We do this by adding the `nginx::source` recipe to the run list:

```
run_list "recipe[nginx::source]"
```

Then, we set the attributes necessary for our source build. They all live in the `nginx` namespace:

```
default_attributes ("nginx" => {
...
})
```

As we want to use the default way of starting the nginx service on Ubuntu, we set the `init_style` to `init`. That will create startup scripts for `init.d`.

```
"init_style" => "init",
```

Other options would have been to use `runit` or `bluepill` among others.

Then, we have to tell the `nginx` recipe where to find the source code for the `upload_progress` module:

```
"upload_progress" => {
    "url" => "https://github.com/masterzen/nginx-upload-progress-
module/tarball/v0.9.0"
  },
```

Finally, we've to instruct the `nginx` recipe to compile nginx with the `upload_progress_module` enabled:

```
"source" => {
    "modules" => ["upload_progress_module"]
}
```

After defining the role, we have to upload it to the Chef Server and to add it to the node's run list. Running Chef Client on the node will now create all necessary directories, download all required sources, and build nginx with the module enabled.

The `nginx` cookbook will create a default site by default. You can check its configuration here:

```
user@server:~$ sudo nginx -V
```

There's more...

If you only want to use your distribution's default nginx package, you can use the `nginx` default recipe instead of `nginx::source` in your role's run list:

```
run_list "recipe[nginx]"
```

If you want to disable the default site, you need to set the attribute accordingly:

```
"default_site_enabled" => false
```

You'll find all tunable configuration parameters in the `nginx` cookbook's attributes file. You can modify them according to preceding examples.

 The `nginx` cookbook sets up handling of sites and its configuration similar to Debian's way of configuring Apache2. You can use `nxdissite` and `nxensite` to disable and enable your sites, which you find under `/etc/nginx/sites-available` and `/etc/nginx/sites-enabled` respectively.

You can set up nginx as reverse proxy using the `application_nginx` cookbook.

See also

▶ Find the `nginx` cookbook on GitHub at: `https://github.com/opscode-cookbooks/nginx`
▶ Find the `application_nginx` cookbook on GitHub at: `https://github.com/opscode-cookbooks/application_nginx`
▶ Find the HTTP Upload Progress Module at: `http://wiki.nginx.org/HttpUploadProgressModule`
▶ The *Overriding attributes* section in *Chapter 4, Writing Better Cookbooks*

Creating nginx sites

Assuming you've nginx installed, you want to manage your websites with Chef. You need to create an nginx configuration file for your website and upload your HTML file(s). Let's see how to do this.

Getting ready

Make sure you've a cookbook named `my_cookbook` as described in the *Creating and using cookbooks* section in *Chapter 1, Chef Infrastructure*.

Make sure you've the `berkshelf` gem installed as described in the *Managing cookbook dependencies with Berkshelf* section in *Chapter 1, Chef Infrastructure*.

1. Create your `Berksfile` in your Chef repository including `my_cookbook`:

   mma@laptop:~/chef-repo $ subl Berksfile

   ```
   cookbook 'my_cookbook', path: './cookbooks/my_cookbook'
   ```

2. Create or edit a role called `web_server` with the following contents:

   mma@laptop:~/chef-repo $ subl roles/web_server.rb

   ```
   name "web_server"
   run_list "recipe[my_cookbook]"

   default_attributes "nginx" => {
     "init_style" => "init",
     "enable_default_site" => false
   }
   ```

3. Upload the role to the Chef Server:

   mma@laptop:~/chef-repo $ knife role from file web_server.rb

   ```
   Updated Role web_server!
   ```

4. Add the `web_server` role to your node's run list:

   mma@laptop:~/chef-repo $ knife node edit server

   ```
   . . .
     "run_list": [
       "role[web_server]"
     ]
   . . .
   ```

How to do it...

Let's put together all the code to configure your site in nginx and to upload a sample `index.html` file:

1. Edit your cookbook's `metadata.rb` to include the dependency on the `nginx` cookbook:

   mma@laptop:~/chef-repo $ subl cookbooks/my_cookbook/metadata.rb

   ```
   ...
   depends "nginx"
   ```

2. Install your cookbook's dependencies:

   mma@laptop:~/chef-repo $ berks install

   ```
   Using my_cookbook (0.1.0) at './cookbooks/my_cookbook'
   ...TRUNCATED OUTPUT...
   ```

3. Edit your cookbook's default recipe:

   mma@laptop:~/chef-repo $ subl cookbooks/my_cookbook/recipes/ default.rb

   ```
   include_recipe "nginx::source"

   app_name = "my_app"
   app_home = "/srv/#{app_name}"

   template "#{node[:nginx][:dir]}/sites-available/#{app_name}" do
     source "nginx-site-#{app_name}.erb"
     owner  "root"
     group  "root"
     mode   "0644"
     variables :app_home => app_home
     notifies :restart, resources(:service => "nginx")
   end

   directory "#{app_home}/public" do
     recursive true
   end

   file "#{app_home}/public/index.html" do
     content "<h1>Hello World!</h1>"
   end

   nginx_site "#{app_name}"
   ```

4. Create a template for your nginx configuration:

```
mma@laptop:~/chef-repo $ subl cookbooks/my_cookbook/templates/
default/nginx-site-my_app.erb

server {
  listen 80;
  server_name _;
  root <%= @app_home %>/public;
}
```

5. Upload the modified cookbook to the Chef Server:

```
mma@laptop:~/chef-repo $ berks upload

...TRUNCATED OUTPUT...
Uploading my_cookbook (0.1.0) to: 'https://api.opscode.com:443/
organizations/agilewebops'
...TRUNCATED OUTPUT...
```

6. Run Chef Client on your node:

```
user@server:~$ sudo chef-client

...TRUNCATED OUTPUT...
[2013-04-22T20:18:46+00:00] INFO: Processing execute[nxensite my_
app] action run (my_cookbook::default line 23)
...TRUNCATED OUTPUT...
```

7. Validate whether the nginx site is up and running by requesting index.html from the web server:

```
user@server:~$ wget localhost

--2013-04-22 20:18:59--  http://localhost/
Resolving localhost (localhost)... 127.0.0.1
Connecting to localhost (localhost)|127.0.0.1|:80... connected.
HTTP request sent, awaiting response... 200 OK
Length: 21 [text/html]
Saving to: `index.html'

100%[================================================================
================================================================
============>] 21          --.-K/s   in 0s

2013-04-22 20:18:59 (1.47 MB/s) - `index.html' saved [21/21]
```

8. Validate whether the downloaded index.html contains the text we set:

```
user@server:~$ cat index.html

<h1>Hello World!</h1>
```

How it works...

After setting two variables, the recipe installs a template for the nginx configuration file. The template ends up as `/etc/nginx/sites-enabled/my_app`.

Next, we create the directory and the `index.html` file in `/srv/my_app/public`. This is the directory our nginx configuration template uses as its `root` location.

Finally, we enable the site we just created using the `nginx_site` resource, which is defined by the `nginx` cookbook.

The configuration file template `nginx-site-my_app.erb` makes nginx listen on port 80 and defines the root location as `/srv/my_app/public`.

There's more...

If you want to disable your site, you simply replace:

```
nginx_site "#{app_name}"
```

with:

```
nginx_site "#{app_name}"  do
  enable false
end
```

After uploading the modified cookbook and running Chef Client again, you should not be able to retrieve `index.html` anymore:

user@server:~$ wget localhost

```
--2013-04-22 20:50:44--  http://localhost/
Resolving localhost (localhost)... 127.0.0.1
Connecting to localhost (localhost)|127.0.0.1|:80... failed:
Connection refused.
```

See also

▸ The *Managing nginx* section

▸ Read more about the `nginx_site` resource at: `https://github.com/opscode-cookbooks/nginx/blob/master/definitions/nginx_site.rb`

Creating MySQL databases and users

You need to use two different cookbooks for managing MySQL (or any other database) on your nodes: the generic `database` cookbook and the `mysql` cookbook.

The `database` cookbook provides resources for managing databases and database users for MySQL, PostgreSQL, and Microsoft SQL Server. The `mysql` cookbook installs a MySQL Client and server.

Let's see how we can install a MySQL server and create a database and a database user.

Getting ready

Make sure you've a cookbook called `my_cookbook` and the `run_list` of your node includes `my_cookbook` as described in the *Creating and using cookbooks* section in *Chapter 1, Chef Infrastructure*.

Make sure you've the `berkshelf` gem installed as described in the *Managing cookbook dependencies with Berkshelf* section in *Chapter 1, Chef Infrastructure*.

Create your `Berksfile` in your Chef repository including `my_cookbook`:

```
mma@laptop:~/chef-repo $ subl Berksfile

    cookbook 'my_cookbook', path: './cookbooks/my_cookbook'
```

How to do it...

We'll install MySQL server with a database and a user:

1. Edit your cookbook's `metadata.rb` file to include the dependencies on the `database` and the `mysql` cookbooks:

   ```
   mma@laptop:~/chef-repo $ subl cookbooks/my_cookbook/metadata.rb

   ...
   depends "database"
   depends "mysql"
   ```

2. Install your cookbook's dependencies:

   ```
   mma@laptop:~/chef-repo $ berks install

   Using my_cookbook (0.1.0) at './cookbooks/my_cookbook'
   ...TRUNCATED OUTPUT...
   ```

3. Edit your cookbook's default recipe:

   mma@laptop:~/chef-repo $ subl cookbooks/my_cookbook/recipes/
   default.rb

   ```
   include_recipe 'mysql::server'
   include_recipe 'mysql::ruby'

   include_recipe 'database'

   connection_params = {
     :username => 'root',
     :password => node['mysql']['server_root_password']
   }

   mysql_database 'my_db' do
     connection connection_params
     action :create
   end

   mysql_database_user 'me' do
     connection connection_params
     password 'my_password_11'
     privileges [:all]
     action [:create, :grant]
   end
   ```

4. Upload the modified cookbook to the Chef Server:

   mma@laptop:~/chef-repo $ berks upload

   ```
   ...TRUNCATED OUTPUT...
   Uploading my_cookbook (0.1.0) to: 'https://api.opscode.com:443/
   organizations/agilewebops'
   ...TRUNCATED OUTPUT...
   ```

5. Run Chef Client on your node:

   user@server:~$ sudo chef-client

   ```
   ...TRUNCATED OUTPUT...
   [2013-04-23T19:32:07+00:00] INFO: Processing chef_gem[mysql]
   action install (mysql::ruby line 36)
     [2013-04-23T19:32:07+00:00] INFO: Processing mysql_database[my_
   db] action create (my_cookbook::default line 25)
     [2013-04-23T19:32:07+00:00] INFO: Processing mysql_database_
   user[me] action create (my_cookbook::default line 30)
     ...TRUNCATED OUTPUT...
   ```

6. Validate that we can log in to our MySQL server with the user we just created and see the database `my_db`:

```
user@server:~$ mysql -u me -p

mysql> show databases;
+--------------------+
| Database           |
+--------------------+
| information_schema |
| my_db              |
...
```

How it works...

First, we include the `mysql::server` recipe to install MySQL:

```
include_recipe 'mysql::server'
```

Additionally we need the `msql` Ruby gem to create the database and the user:

```
include_recipe 'mysql::ruby'
```

Then it's time to include the `database` recipe to be able to use the `database` and `database_user` resources later in our recipe:

```
include_recipe 'database'
```

As we want to connect to our MySQL server multiple times, we define the connection parameters as a variable called `connection_params` in our recipe:

```
connection_params = {
  :username => 'root',
  :password => node['mysql']['server_root_password']
}
```

The `mysql::server` recipe creates a random root password and stores it in the node under the key `['mysql']['server_root_password']`.

Then we use the `mysql_database` resource from the database cookbook to create a database called `my_db`:

```
mysql_database 'my_db' do
  connection connection_params
  action :create
end
```

And finally, we use the `mysql_database_user` resource to create a user called `me` and grant him all privileges:

```
mysql_database_user 'me' do
  connection connection_params
  password 'my_password_11'
  privileges [:all]
  action [:create, :grant]
end
```

There's more...

It's quite common to have things such as a database name or users with their privileges stored in data bags. You can find out how to do this in the *Using search to find data bag items* section in *Chapter 4, Writing Better Cookbooks*.

See also

▸   The *Using data bags* section in *Chapter 4, Writing Better Cookbooks*

▸   Find the `database` cookbook on GitHub at: `https://github.com/opscode-cookbooks/database`

▸   Find the `mysql` cookbook on GitHub at: `https://github.com/opscode-cookbooks/mysql`

Managing WordPress sites

You need to enable your business users to manage their own website. WordPress has come a long way providing all necessary features. You might have seen it as a simple blogging tool. But, it has grown to a fully featured content management system in recent years. Fortunately, managing WordPress with Chef is pretty straightforward.

Let's have a look how to do it.

Getting ready

Make sure you've a cookbook called `my_cookbook` and the `run_list` of your node includes `my_cookbook` as described in the *Creating and using cookbooks* section in *Chapter 1, Chef Infrastructure*.

Make sure you've the `berkshelf` gem installed as described in the *Managing cookbook dependencies with Berkshelf* section in *Chapter 1, Chef Infrastructure*.

Create your `Berksfile` in your Chef repository including `my_cookbook`:

mma@laptop:~/chef-repo $ subl Berksfile

```
cookbook 'my_cookbook', path: './cookbooks/my_cookbook'
```

How to do it...

We'll install WordPress using the community cookbook:

1. Edit your cookbook's metadata to make sure it depends on all necessary cookbooks:

   mma@laptop:~/chef-repo $ subl cookbooks/my_cookbook/metadata.rb

   ```
   ...
   depends "apt"
   depends "wordpress"
   ```

2. Install your cookbook's dependencies:

   mma@laptop:~/chef-repo $ berks install

   ```
   Using my_cookbook (0.1.0) at './cookbooks/my_cookbook'
   ...TRUNCATED OUTPUT...
   ```

3. Edit your cookbook's default recipe to set some attributes for the `wordpress` cookbook and to include the required cookbooks:

   mma@laptop:~/chef-repo $ subl cookbooks/my_cookbook/recipes/default.rb

   ```
   node.default['wordpress']['db']['database'] = "my_wordpress"
   node.default['wordpress']['db']['user'] = "me"
   node.default['wordpress']['db']['password'] = "my_password_11"

   include_recipe "apt"
   include_recipe 'wordpress'
   ```

4. Upload the modified cookbook to the Chef Server:

   mma@laptop:~/chef-repo $ berks upload

   ```
   ...TRUNCATED OUTPUT...
   Uploading my_cookbook (0.1.0) to: 'https://api.opscode.com:443/
   organizations/agilewebops'
   ...TRUNCATED OUTPUT...
   ```

5. Run Chef Client on your node:

```
user@server:~$ sudo chef-client

...TRUNCATED OUTPUT...
[2013-04-27T19:29:44+00:00] INFO: Navigate to 'http://vagrant.vm/
wp-admin/install.php' to complete wordpress installation
...TRUNCATED OUTPUT...
```

6. Validate whether WordPress is installed on your host by firing up your browser and navigating to the WordPress install page:

How it works...

The `wordpress` cookbook installs a full Apache-MySQL-PHP-stack. That's why when you're installing it into your repository, it will install quite a few supporting cookbooks as well.

To use the `wordpress` cookbook, you simply include it in your own cookbook's recipe:

```
include_recipe 'wordpress'
```

Because the `wordpress` cookbook will install software from your operating system's package repository (using apt in our case on Ubuntu), we include the `apt` cookbook right before including the `wordpress` cookbook. That way we make sure that the package list on your node is up-to-date. If you omit this step, the `wordpress` cookbook might fail because some outdated packages do not fit together.

```
include_recipe 'apt'
include_recipe 'wordpress'
```

And, because we do not like the default values for the database name, database user, and the password for the database user, we override those attributes in the beginning of our default recipe:

```
node.default['wordpress']['db']['database'] = 'my_wordpress'
node.default['wordpress']['db']['user'] = 'me'
node.default['wordpress']['db']['password'] = 'my_password_11'
```

You can look up the default values in `cookbooks/wordpress/attributes/default.rb`.

There's more...

The `wordpress` cookbook installs the complete stack but does not set up your first blog. It asks you to call the WordPress installation page with your browser to set up your first blog.

If you already have a tarball of your blog available, you could deliver it to your node as described in the *Distributing Directory Trees* section in *Chapter 5, Working with Files and Packages*.

See also

▸ You find the `wordpress` cookbook on GitHub at: `https://github.com/opscode-cookbooks/wordpress`

Managing Ruby on Rails applications

Ruby on Rails helps you to quickly get up and running with your web applications. But, deployment is not an issue solved by the framework. In this section, we'll see how to write the simplest possible recipe to deploy a Rails application, using unicorn as the application server and SQLite as the database.

Getting ready

Make sure you've a cookbook called `my_cookbook` and the `run_list` of your node includes `my_cookbook` as described in the *Creating and using cookbooks* section in *Chapter 1, Chef Infrastructure*..

Make sure you've the `berkshelf` gem installed as described in the *Managing cookbook dependencies with Berkshelf* section in *Chapter 1, Chef Infrastructure*.

Create your `Berksfile` in your Chef repository including `my_cookbook`:

mma@laptop:~/chef-repo $ subl Berksfile

```
cookbook 'my_cookbook', path: './cookbooks/my_cookbook'
```

How to do it...

Let's get our Ruby on Rails application up and running on our node:

1. Edit your cookbook's `metadata.rb`, to make it depend on the `application_ruby` cookbook:

   mma@laptop:~/chef-repo $ subl cookbooks/my_cookbook/metadata.rb

   ```
   ...
   depends "application_ruby"
   ```

2. Install your cookbook's dependencies:

   mma@laptop:~/chef-repo $ berks install

   ```
   Using my_cookbook (0.1.0) at './cookbooks/my_cookbook'
   ...TRUNCATED OUTPUT...
   ```

3. Edit your cookbook's default recipe:

   mma@laptop:~/chef-repo $ subl cookbooks/my_cookbook/recipes/default.rb

   ```
   application "rails-app" do
     packages %w[ruby1.9.3 runit git sqlite3 libsqlite3-dev]

     path "/usr/local/www/rails-app"
     owner "www-data"
     group "www-data"

     environment_name "development"

     repository "https://github.com/mmarschall/rails-app.git"

     rails do
       gems %w[bundler]

       database_template "sqlite3_database.yml.erb"

       database do
         adapter "sqlite3"
         database "db/rails-app.sqlite3"
       end
     end

     unicorn do
     end
   end
   ```

4. Add your own template file for your `database.yml`:

```
mma@laptop:~/chef-repo $ subl cookbooks/my_cookbook/templates/
default/sqlite3_database.yml.erb
```

```
<%= @rails_env %>:
  adapter: <%= @database['adapter'] %>
  host: <%= @host %>
  database: <%= @database['database'] %>
  pool: 5
  timeout: 5000
```

5. Upload the modified cookbook to the Chef Server:

```
mma@laptop:~/chef-repo $ berks upload
```

```
...TRUNCATED OUTPUT...
Uploading my_cookbook (0.1.0) to: 'https://api.opscode.com:443/
organizations/agilewebops'
...TRUNCATED OUTPUT...
```

6. Run Chef Client on your node:

```
user@server:~$ sudo chef-client
```

```
...TRUNCATED OUTPUT...
[2013-05-09T20:36:40+00:00] INFO: execute[/etc/init.d/rails-app
hup] ran successfully
...TRUNCATED OUTPUT...
```

7. Validate whether your Rails application is up and running by hitting your node at port 8080:

```
user@server:~$ wget localhost:8080
```

```
2013-05-10 20:08:41 (16.4 MB/s) - `index.html' saved [14900]
```

8. Then, you can have a look at the downloaded file to verify whether the **Welcome page** of your Rails app shows up:

```
user@server:~$ cat index.html
```

```
<!DOCTYPE html>
<html>
  <head>
    <title>Ruby on Rails: Welcome aboard</title>
  ...
```

How it works...

Opscode provides the abstract `application` cookbook for deploying web applications. We call our application "rails-app":

```
application "rails-app" do
...
end
```

Inside the application block, we define the details of our web app. First, we need to install a few operating system packages. In our case, we assume an empty node, not even having Ruby installed.

```
packages %w[ruby1.9.3 runit git sqlite3 libsqlite3-dev]
```

`ruby1.9.3` will make sure that we have a Ruby runtime installed. If you installed your Chef Client using the Omnibus installer, it comes with an embedded Ruby, which you might not want to use for running your Rails application.

As we're going to use unicorn to run our Rails application, we need to install `runit`, because that's the way unicorn is installed at the writing of this book.

Git is required to be able to checkout our repository from `github.com`.

Finally, we're using SQLite for our Rails application and need to install it first.

The next step is to configure the deployment details. Where should our app go (`path`)? Which user and group should own the application (`owner`, `group`), and where do we find the source code of our app (`repository`)?

```
path "/usr/local/www/rails-app"
  owner "www-data"
  group "www-data"
...
repository "https://github.com/mmarschall/rails-app.git"
```

 Make sure you've enabled `therubyracer` and the `unicorn` gems in your Rails application's `Gemfile`:

```
gem 'therubyracer', platforms: :ruby
gem 'unicorn'
```

If you don't want to run your application in a production environment, you can specify the desired `environment_name` in your cookbook, like we do:

```
environment_name "development"
```

Your application will be fetched from github.com and the cookbook will install it in a directory structure you are familiar with from using **Capistrano**. It will put the current revision of your app into the releases directory and create a **symlink** to it as current.

Now, it's time to define the Rails-specific things. First of all, we want to install the bundler gem because our Rails application is using a Gemfile for its dependencies:

```
rails do
    gems %w[bundler]
    ...
end
```

The %w[] syntax creates an array of strings. You could write ["bundler"] instead. It doesn't make any difference for one element, but when putting multiple elements into your array, you save a lot of double quotes and commas with the %w syntax.

As our Rails application uses SQLite as its persistence store, we need to use our own template for the database.yml file.

```
database_template "sqlite3_database.yml.erb"
```

Then, we can use a database block to populate it with the values we need:

```
database do
  adapter "sqlite3"
  database "db/rails-app.sqlite3"
end
```

We're telling our Rails application that we're using an SQLite database and want it to store its data in a file called db/rails-app.sqlite3.

Finally, we need to tell our cookbook that we want to run our Rails application using unicorn. An empty block will suffice as long as we don't want to change any default attributes like port or number of workers.

```
unicorn do
end
```

There's more...

Usually, the application cookbook's deploy resource will only deploy new revisions of your Rails app. If you want to ensure that it grabs the same revision again and again, you need to call the force_deploy action on your application resource:

```
application "rails-app" do
  ...
  action :force_deploy
end
```

If you want to use a new or existing MySQL server, you can assign it a role, for example, `rails_database_master` and pass that role name to the `application` resource. It will then search for the node and use its IP address in the `database.yml`:

```
application "rails-app" do
  ...
  database_master_role " rails_database_master"
end
```

In this case, you don't need to use your own `database.yml` template.

If you want to run a cluster of nodes, each one installed with your Rails application, you can use the `application_nginx` cookbook to install an nginx load balancer in front of your application server cluster.

See also

▶ Find the `application` cookbook on GitHub at: `https://github.com/opscode-cookbooks/application`

▶ Find the `application_ruby` cookbook on GitHub at: `https://github.com/opscode-cookbooks/application_ruby`

▶ The *Using search to find nodes* section in *Chapter 4, Writing Better Cookbooks*

Managing Varnish

`Varnish` is a web application accelerator. You install it in front of your web application to cache generated HTML files and serve them faster. It will take a lot of burden from your web application and can even provide you with extended uptime—covering up for application failures through its cache while you are fixing your application.

Let's see how to install `Varnish`.

Getting ready

You need a web server running on your node at port `8080`. We'll set up `Varnish` to use `localhost:8080` as its backend host and port. You can achieve this by installing a Ruby on Rails application on your node as described in the *Managing Ruby on Rails applications* section.

Make sure you've a cookbook called `my_cookbook` and the `run_list` of your node includes `my_cookbook` as described in the *Creating and using cookbooks* section in *Chapter 1, Chef Infrastructure*.

Make sure you've the `berkshelf` gem installed as described in the *Managing cookbook dependencies with Berkshelf* section in *Chapter 1, Chef Infrastructure*.

Create your `Berksfile` in your Chef repository including `my_cookbook`:

mma@laptop:~/chef-repo $ subl Berksfile

```
cookbook 'my_cookbook', path: './cookbooks/my_cookbook'
```

How to do it...

Let's install `Varnish` with its default parameters. We will use the `Varnish` provided apt repository to have access to the latest versions of `Varnish`:

> If you don't have the `apt` cookbook in your node's run list (which you should have), you need to add `depends "apt"` to your cookbook's metadata and `include_recipe "apt"` in your cookbook's default recipe.

1. Edit your cookbook's metadata to add the dependency on the `varnish` cookbook:

   mma@laptop:~/chef-repo $ subl cookbooks/my_cookbook/metadata.rb

   ```
   ...
   depends "varnish"
   ```

2. Install your cookbook's dependencies:

   mma@laptop:~/chef-repo $ berks install

   ```
   Using my_cookbook (0.1.0) at './cookbooks/my_cookbook'
   ...TRUNCATED OUTPUT...
   ```

3. Edit your cookbook's default recipe:

   mma@laptop:~/chef-repo $ subl cookbooks/my_cookbook/recipes/ default.rb

   ```
   include_recipe "varnish::apt_repo"

   node.set['varnish']['storage_file'] = '/var/lib/varnish/vagrant/ varnish_storage.bin'
   include_recipe "varnish"
   ```

4. Upload the modified cookbook to the Chef Server:

   mma@laptop:~/chef-repo $ berks upload

   ```
   ...TRUNCATED OUTPUT...
   Uploading my_cookbook (0.1.0) to: 'https://api.opscode.com:443/ organizations/agilewebops'
   ...TRUNCATED OUTPUT...
   ```

5. Run Chef Client on your node:

```
user@server:~$ sudo chef-client

...TRUNCATED OUTPUT...
[2013-05-11T19:23:37+00:00] INFO: service[varnish] restarted
...TRUNCATED OUTPUT...
```

6. Validate whether your `Varnish` cache is up and running by hitting your node at port `6081`:

```
user@server:~$ wget localhost:6081

2013-05-10 20:08:41 (16.4 MB/s) - `index.html' saved [14900]
```

How it works...

As we want to use the latest Version of `varnish` (and not the usually outdated one from the default Ubuntu package repository), we set up the `varnish` apt repository first:

```
include_recipe "varnish::apt_repo"
```

By default, the `varnish` cookbook uses `"/var/lib/varnish/$INSTANCE/varnish_storage.bin"` as its file storage location. This does not work on a Vagrant box. That's why we override the default attribute and set our own path:

```
node.set['varnish']['storage_file'] = '/var/lib/varnish/vagrant/varnish_storage.bin'
```

Finally, we include the `Varnish` recipe itself to install, configure, and start the `Varnish` server listening to its default port `6081`:

```
include_recipe "varnish"
```

There's more...

You can connect to the `Varnish` admin interface by logging in to your node and running telnet:

```
user@server:~$ sudo telnet localhost 6082
```

See also

- ▶ Find out more about `Varnish` at: `https://www.varnish-cache.org/`
- ▶ You find the `varnish` cookbook on GitHub at: `https://github.com/opscode-cookbooks/varnish`
- ▶ The *Managing Ruby on Rails applications* section

Managing your workstation

You know the drill. You get a brand new MacBook and need to set up all your software—again. Chef can help here, too.

We will have a look at how to install applications and tweak settings on your local development box with Chef.

 This example is based on recipes for OS X only, but you can tweak it to run on Windows or Linux, too.

Getting ready

Follow the instructions given in the *Installing Chef on your workstation* section in *Chapter 1, Chef Infrastructure*, to get the basic Chef environment working on your box.

First, we need to prepare our own repository for our individual setup:

1. Fork the `github.com/mmarschall/osx-workstation` repository:

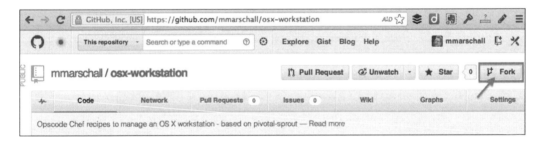

2. Clone it to your local development box, replacing `<YOUR GITHUB USER>` with the name of your GitHub account:

   ```
   mma@laptop:~/ $ git clone https://github.com/<YOUR GITHUB USER>/
   osx-workstation.git
   ```

3. Go into your clone of the `osx-workstation` repository:

   ```
   mma@laptop:~/ $ cd osx-workstation
   ```

4. Make sure you've the `soloist` gem installed by running:

   ```
   mma@laptop:~/osx-workstation $ bundle install

   ...TRUNCATED OUTPUT...
   Installing soloist (1.0.1)
   ...TRUNCATED OUTPUT...
   ```

How to do it...

Let's set up Soloist to use a few readymade recipes provided by the folks at PivotalLabs:

1. Create a `Cheffile` in your local repository:

   mma@laptop:~/osx-workstation $ subl Cheffile

   ```
   site 'http://community.opscode.com/api/v1'

   cookbook 'pivotal_workstation',
     :git => 'git://github.com/pivotal-sprout/sprout.git',
     :path => 'pivotal_workstation'

   cookbook 'sprout-osx-apps',
     :git => 'git://github.com/pivotal-sprout/sprout.git',
     :path => 'sprout-osx-apps'

   cookbook 'sprout-osx-settings',
     :git => 'git://github.com/pivotal-sprout/sprout.git',
     :path => 'sprout-osx-settings'

   cookbook 'osx',
     :git => 'git://github.com/pivotal-sprout/sprout.git',
     :path => 'osx'
   ```

2. Create a configuration for Soloist telling it, what to install on your box:

   mma@laptop:~/osx-workstation $ subl soloistrc

   ```
   recipes:
   - sprout-osx-apps::freeruler
   - sprout-osx-settings::dock_preferences

   node_attributes:
     dock_preferences:
       orientation: left
   ```

3. Run Soloist on your development box:

   mma@laptop:~/osx-workstation $ sudo soloist

   ```
   Installing dmg (1.1.0)
   Installing osx (0.1.0)
   Installing sprout-osx-apps (0.1.0)
   Installing sprout-osx-settings (0.1.0)
   Installing pivotal_workstation (1.0.0)
   Starting Chef Client, version 11.4.4
   ```

```
...TRUNCATED OUTPUT...
Recipe: sprout-osx-apps::freeruler
...TRUNCATED OUTPUT...
Chef Client finished, 3 resources updated
```

4. Now your dock should be located at the left-hand side of the screen and the application **Free Ruler** should show up in your `Applications` folder.

How it works...

Soloist is a quick and easy way to configure Chef Solo on your box. It uses **Librarian** to manage cookbook dependencies. You define which cookbooks to use by including them into your `Cheffile`:

```
cookbook 'sprout-osx-apps',
  :git => 'git://github.com/pivotal-sprout/sprout.git',
  :path => 'sprout-osx-apps'
```

You define the cookbook name, tell Librarian in which Git repository this cookbook lives, and tell it a pathname, where to install it locally. Librarian will install all cookbooks defined in the `Cheffile` to the local cookbook's directory.

The other part we need to configure is what Soloist should run. We do this in the `soloistrc` file. First, we tell Soloist, which recipes it should converge on our local development box:

```
recipes:
- sprout-osx-apps::freeruler
- sprout-osx-settings::dock_preferences
```

Then, we set some attributes, further finetuning the setup on our box:

```
node_attributes:
  dock_preferences:
    orientation: left
```

Here we set the attribute `node['dock_preferences']['orientation'] = 'left'`. This attribute is used by the `sprout-osx-settings::dock_preferences` cookbook.

Soloist will use Librarian to install all cookbooks defined in the `Cheffile` and then converge all recipes listed in the `soloistrc` file. Before converging, it will set all given node attributes to be used by the recipes.

The sprout repository holds a huge amount of cookbooks to install OS X apps and configure settings.

The sprout `osx` cookbook provides us with the `osx_defaults` provider used by the `sprout-osx-settings` cookbook. To install applications, the `sprout-osx-applications` cookbook uses either the standard Chef `dmg_package` resource or a mixture of `remote_file` and `execute` blocks to install a tarball.

There's more...

If you want to create your own cookbooks to be used by Soloist, just create a directory in your `osx-workstation` repository:

```
mma@laptop:~/osx-workstation $ mkdir site-cookbooks
```

And add that new cookbook path to your `Cheffile` for Librarian to find your new cookbooks:

```
cookbook 'meta',
    :path => 'site-cookbooks/meta'
```

Now you can use your own cookbooks in your `soloistrc` file.

Instead of using `dmg_package` and `osx_default` resources for OS X, you can use the default package providers for your own operating system. You might want to create your own provider for settings specific to your platform, if not available already in Chef.

See also

▸ Find Soloist at: `https://github.com/mkocher/soloist`

▸ Find sprout at: `https://github.com/pivotal-sprout/sprout`

▸ Look at the Free Ruler recipe at: `https://github.com/pivotal-sprout/sprout/blob/master/sprout-osx-apps/recipes/freeruler.rb`

▸ You find the `dock_preferences` recipe here: `https://github.com/pivotal-sprout/sprout/blob/master/sprout-osx-settings/recipes/dock_preferences.rb`

▸ Librarian lives here: `https://github.com/applicationsonline/librarian`

7
Servers and Cloud Infrastructure

"The interesting thing about cloud computing is that we've redefined cloud computing to include everything that we already do."

– Richard Stallman

In this chapter, we will cover the following:

- ► Creating cookbooks from a running system with Blueprint
- ► Running the same command on many machines at once
- ► Setting up SNMP for external monitoring services
- ► Deploying a Nagios monitoring server
- ► Building high-availability services using Heartbeat
- ► Using HAProxy to load-balance multiple web servers
- ► Using custom bootstrap scripts
- ► Managing firewalls with iptables
- ► Managing fail2ban to ban malicious IP addresses
- ► Managing Amazon EC2 instances
- ► Loading your Chef infrastructure from a file with Spiceweasel and Knife

Introduction

In the preceding chapters, we mostly looked at individual nodes. Now, it's time to consider your infrastructure as a whole. We'll see how to manage services spanning multiple machines like load balancers and how to manage the networking aspects of your infrastructure.

Creating cookbooks from a running system with Blueprint

Everyone has it: that one server in the corner of the data center that no one dares to touch anymore. It's like a precious snowflake: unique and infinitely fragile. How do you get such a server under configuration management?

Blueprint is a tool to find out and record exactly what's on your server. It records all directories, packages, configuration files, and so on.

Blueprint can spit out that information about your server in various formats; one of them is a Chef recipe. You can use such a generated Chef recipe as a basis to rebuild that one unique snowflake server.

Let's see how to do that.

Getting ready

Make sure you've Python and Git installed on the node you want to run Blueprint on:

```
user@server:~$ sudo apt-get install git python
```

How to do it...

Let's see how to install Blueprint and create a Chef cookbook for our node:

1. Install Blueprint using the following command line:

    ```
    user@server:~$ pip install blueprint
    ```

2. Create Blueprint. Replace `my-server` with any name you want to use for your Blueprint. This name will become the name of the cookbook in the following step:

    ```
    user@server:~$ sudo blueprint create my-server

    # [blueprint] using cached blueprintignore(5) rules
    # [blueprint] searching for Python packages
    # [blueprint] searching for PEAR/PECL packages
    # [blueprint] searching for Yum packages
    # [blueprint] searching for Ruby gems
    ```

```
# [blueprint] searching for npm packages
# [blueprint] searching for software built from source
# [blueprint] searching for configuration files
# [blueprint] /etc/ssl/certs/AC_Ra\xc3\xadz_Certic\xc3\
xa1mara_S.A..pem not UTF-8 - skipping it
# [blueprint] /etc/ssl/certs/NetLock_Arany_=Class_Gold=_F\xc5\
x91tan\xc3\xbas\xc3\xadtv\xc3\xa1ny.pem not UTF-8 - skipping it
# [blueprint] /etc/ssl/certs/EBG_Elektronik_Sertifika_Hizmet_Sa\
xc4\x9flay\xc4\xb1c\xc4\xb1s\xc4\xb1.pem not UTF-8 - skipping it
# [blueprint] /etc/ssl/certs/Certinomis_-_Autorit\xc3\xa9_Racine.
pem not UTF-8 - skipping it
# [blueprint] /etc/ssl/certs/T\xc3\x9cB\xc4\xb0TAK_UEKAE_K\xc3\
xb6k_Sertifika_Hizmet_Sa\xc4\x9flay\xc4\xb1c\xc4\xb1s\xc4\xb1_-_S\
xc3\xbcr\xc3\xbcm_3.pem not UTF-8 - skipping it
# [blueprint] searching for APT packages
# [blueprint] searching for service dependencies
```

3. Create a Chef cookbook from your blueprint:

   user@server:~$ blueprint show -C my-server

   my-server/recipes/default.rb

4. Validate the content of the generated file:

   user@server:~$ cat my-server/recipes/default.rb

```
#
# Automatically generated by blueprint(7).  Edit at your own risk.
#
cookbook_file('/tmp/96468fd1cc36927a027045b223c61065de6bc575.tar')
do
  backup false
  group 'root'
  mode '0644'
  owner 'root'
  source 'tmp/96468fd1cc36927a027045b223c61065de6bc575.tar'
end
execute('/tmp/96468fd1cc36927a027045b223c61065de6bc575.tar') do
  command 'tar xf "/tmp/96468fd1cc36927a027045b223c61065de6bc575.
tar"'
  cwd '/usr/local'
end
directory('/etc/apt/apt.conf.d') do
...TRUNCATED OUTPUT...
service('ssh') do
  action [:enable, :start]
  subscribes :restart, resources('cookbook_file[/etc/default/
keyboard]', 'cookbook_file[/etc/default/console-setup]',
'cookbook_file[/etc/default/ntfs-3g]', 'package[openssh-server]',
'execute[96468fd1cc36927a027045b223c61065de6bc575.tar]')
end
```

How it works...

Blueprint is a Python package that finds out all the relevant configuration data of your node and stores it in a Git repository. Each Blueprint has its own name.

You can ask Blueprint to show the contents of its Git repository in various formats. Using the `-C` flag to the `blueprint show` command creates a Chef cookbook containing everything you need in that cookbook's default recipe. It stores the cookbook in the directory from where you run Blueprint and uses the Blueprint name as the cookbook name as shown in the following code:

```
user@server:~$ ls -l my-server/
```

```
total 8
drwxrwxr-x 3 vagrant vagrant 4096 Jun 28 06:01 files
-rw-rw-r-- 1 vagrant vagrant    0 Jun 28 06:01 metadata.rb
drwxrwxr-x 2 vagrant vagrant 4096 Jun 28 06:01 recipes
```

There's more...

You can inspect your Blueprints using specialized show commands in the following way:

```
user@server:~$ blueprint show-packages my-server
```

```
...TRUNCATED OUTPUT...
apt wireless-regdb 2011.04.28-1ubuntu3
apt zlib1g-dev 1:1.2.3.4.dfsg-3ubuntu4
python2.7 distribute 0.6.45
python2.7 pip 1.3.1
pip blueprint 3.4.2
pip virtualenv 1.9.1
```

The preceding command shows all kinds of installed packages. Other show commands are as follows:

- ▶ `show-files`
- ▶ `show-services`
- ▶ `show-sources`

Blueprint is able to output your server configuration as a **shell script** as shown in the following command line:

```
user@server:~$ blueprint show -S my-server
```

You can use this script as a basis for a `knife bootstrap` as described in the *Using custom bootstrap scripts* section.

▶ Read about all you can do with Blueprint at `http://devstructure.com/blueprint/`

▶ You find the source code of Blueprint at `https://github.com/devstructure/blueprint`

Running the same command on many machines at once

A simple problem with so many self-scripted solutions is logging in to multiple servers in parallel executing the same command on every server at once. No matter whether you want to check the status of a certain service or look at some critical system data on all servers, being able to log in to many servers in parallel can save you a lot of time and hassle (imagine forgetting one of your seven web servers when disabling the basic authentication for your website).

How to do it...

Let's try to execute a few simple commands on multiple servers in parallel:

1. Retrieve the status of the `nginx` processes from all your web servers:

   ```
   mma@laptop:~/chef-repo $ knife ssh 'roles:webserver' 'sudo sv
   status nginx'
   ```

   ```
   www1.prod.example.com run: nginx: (pid 12356) 204667s; run:
   log: (pid 1135) 912026s
   www2.prod.example.com run: nginx: (pid 19155) 199923s; run:
   log: (pid 1138) 834124s
   www.test.example.com  run: nginx: (pid 30299) 1332114s;
   run: log: (pid 30271) 1332117s
   ```

2. Display the uptime of all your nodes in your staging environment running on Amazon EC2:

   ```
   mma@laptop:~/chef-repo $ knife ssh 'chef_environment:staging AND
   ec2:*' uptime
   ```

   ```
   ec2-XXX-XXX-XXX-XXX.eu-west-1.compute.amazonaws.com
   21:58:15 up 23 days, 13:19,  1 user,  load average: 1.32,
   1.88, 2.34
   ec2-XXX-XXX-XXX-XXX.eu-west-1.compute.amazonaws.com
   21:58:15 up 10 days, 13:19,  1 user,  load average: 1.51,
   1.52, 1.54
   ```

How it works...

First, you have to specify a query for finding your nodes. It is usually a good idea to test your queries by running a command such as uptime (instead of dangerous commands like sudo restart now). Your query will obviously use the node index and the complete Knife query syntax is available.

Knife will run the search and connect to each found node executing the given command on every single one. It will collect and display all outputs received by the nodes.

There's more...

You can open terminals to all the nodes identified by your query by using either tmux or screen as commands.

If you don't want to use a search query, you can list the desired nodes using the -m option:

```
mma@laptop:~/chef-repo $ knife ssh 'www1.prod.example.com www2.prod.
example.com' uptime -m

    www1.prod.example.com  22:10:00 up 9 days, 16:00,  1 user,  load
    average: 0.44, 0.40, 0.38
    www2.prod.example.com     22:10:00 up 15 days, 10:28,  1 user,
    load average: 0.02, 0.05, 0.06
```

See also

- ▶ The Knife query syntax is described at the following location: http://docs.opscode.com/knife_search.html.

- ▶ Find more examples at http://docs.opscode.com/knife_ssh.html.

Setting up SNMP for external monitoring services

Simple Network Management Protocol (**SNMP**) is the standard way to monitor all your network devices. You can use Chef to install the SNMP service on your node and configure it to match your needs.

Getting ready

Make sure you've a cookbook named `my_cookbook` and `run_list` of your node includes `my_cookbook` as described in the *Creating and using cookbooks* section in *Chapter 1, Chef Infrastructure*.

Make sure you've the `berkshelf` gem installed as described in the *Managing cookbook dependencies with Berkshelf* section in *Chapter 1, Chef Infrastructure*.

Create your Berksfile in your Chef repository including `my_cookbook`:

mma@laptop:~/chef-repo $ subl Berksfile

```
cookbook 'my_cookbook', path: './cookbooks/my_cookbook'
```

How to do it...

Let's change some attributes and install SNMP on our node:

1. Add the dependency on the `snmp` cookbook to your cookbook's `metadata.rb` file:

   mma@laptop:~/chef-repo $ subl cookbooks/my_cookbook/metadata.rb

   ```
   depends "snmp"
   ```

2. Install the dependent cookbooks:

   mma@laptop:~/chef-repo $ berks install

   ```
   Using my_cookbook (0.1.0) at './cookbooks/my_cookbook'
   ...TRUNCATED OUTPUT...
   ```

3. Edit your cookbook's default recipe:

   mma@laptop:~/chef-repo $ subl cookbooks/my_cookbook/recipes/ default.rb

   ```
   node.default['snmp']['syslocationVirtual'] = "Vagrant VirtualBox"
   node.default['snmp']['syslocationPhysical'] = "My laptop"
   node.default['snmp']['full_systemview'] = true
   include_recipe "snmp"
   ```

4. Upload the modified cookbook to the Chef Server:

   mma@laptop:~/chef-repo $ berks upload

   ```
   ...TRUNCATED OUTPUT...
   Uploading my_cookbook (0.1.0) to:
   'https://api.opscode.com:443/organizations/agilewebops'
   ...TRUNCATED OUTPUT...
   ```

5. Run Chef Client on your node:

```
user@server:~$ sudo chef-client

...TRUNCATED OUTPUT...
   - restart service service[snmpd]
...TRUNCATED OUTPUT...
```

6. Validate whether you can query `snmpd`:

```
user@server:~$ snmpwalk -v 1 localhost -c public
iso.3.6.1.2.1.1.5.0

iso.3.6.1.2.1.1.5.0 = STRING: "vagrant"
```

How it works...

First, we need to tell our cookbook that we want to use the `snmp` cookbook by adding a `depends` call to our metadata file. Then, we modify some of the attributes provided by the `snmp` cookbook. The attributes are used to fill the `/etc/snmp/snmp.conf` file, which is based on the template provided by the `snmp` cookbook.

The last step is to include the `snmp` cookbook's default recipe in our own recipe. This will instruct Chef Client to install `snmpd` as a service on our node.

There's more...

You can override `['snmp']['community']` and `['snmp']['trapcommunity']` as well.

See also

▶ Find the `snmp` cookbook on GitHub at `https://github.com/atomic-penguin/cookbook-snmp`

Deploying a Nagios monitoring server

Nagios is one of the most widely spread monitoring packages available. Opscode provides you with a cookbook for installing a Nagios server as well as Nagios clients. It provides ways to configure service checks, service groups, and so on using data bags instead of manually editing Nagios configuration files.

Getting ready

Make sure you've a cookbook named `my_cookbook` and `run_list` of your node includes `my_cookbook` as described in the *Creating and using cookbooks* section in *Chapter 1, Chef Infrastructure*.

Make sure you've the `berkshelf` gem installed as described in the *Managing cookbook dependencies with Berkshelf section* in *Chapter 1, Chef Infrastructure*.

Create your `Berksfile` in your Chef repository including the `nagios` cookbook:

```
mma@laptop:~/chef-repo $ subl Berksfile

cookbook 'nagios'
```

Install the `nagios` cookbook:

```
mma@laptop:~/chef-repo $ berks install --path cookbooks/

Using nagios (4.1.4)
...TRUNCATED OUTPUT...
```

Upload the `nagios` cookbook to the Chef Server:

```
mma@laptop:~/chef-repo $ berks upload

...TRUNCATED OUTPUT...
Uploading nagios (4.1.4) to: 'https://api.opscode.com:443/
organizations/agilewebops'
...TRUNCATED OUTPUT...
```

How to do it...

Let's create a user for the Nagios web interface and set up a Nagios server with a check for SSH.

1. Create a password hash for your Nagios user:

    You may want to use an online `htpasswd` generator like `http://www.htaccesstools.com/htpasswd-generator/` if you don't have `htpasswd` installed on your system.

   ```
   mma@laptop:~/chef-repo $ htpasswd -n -s mma

   New password:
   Re-type new password:
   mma:{SHA}AcrFI+aFqjxDLBKctCtzW/LkVxg=
   ```

2. Create a data bag for your Nagios user, using the password hash from the preceding step:

mma@laptop:~/chef-repo $ subl data_bags/users/mma.json

```
{
  "id": "mma",
  "htpasswd": "{SHA}AcrFI+aFqjxDLBKctCtzW/LkVxg=",
  "groups": "sysadmin"
}
```

3. Upload the `user` data bag to your Chef Server:

mma@laptop:~/chef-repo $ knife data bag from file users mma.json

```
Updated data_bag_item[users::mma]
```

4. Create a data bag for your service definitions:

mma@laptop:~/chef-repo $ knife data bag create nagios_services

```
Created data_bag_item[nagios_service]
```

5. Create a role for your Nagios server node:

mma@laptop:~/chef-repo $ subl roles/monitoring.rb

```
name "monitoring"
description "Nagios server"
run_list(
  "recipe[apt]",
  "recipe[nagios::server]"
)

default_attributes(
  "nagios" => {
    "server_auth_method" => "htauth"
  }
)
```

6. Upload your monitoring role to your Chef Server:

mma@laptop:~/chef-repo $ knife role from file monitoring.rb

```
Updated Role monitoring!
```

7. Apply the `monitoring` role to your node called `server`:

mma@laptop:~/chef-repo $ knife node edit server

```
...
  "run_list": [
    "role[monitoring]"
  ]
...
saving updated run_list on node server
```

8. Create a data bag item for your first service:

```
mma@laptop:~/chef-repo $ subl data_bags/nagios_service/ssh.json

{
  "id": "ssh",
  "hostgroup_name": "linux",
  "command_line": "$USER1$/check_ssh $HOSTADDRESS$"
}
```

9. Upload your service data bag item:

```
mma@laptop:~/chef-repo $ knife data bag from file nagios_services
ssh.json

Updated data_bag_item[nagios_services::ssh]
```

10. Run Chef Client on your node:

```
user@server:~$ sudo chef-client

...TRUNCATED OUTPUT...
[2013-06-12T20:50:09+00:00] INFO: Processing service[nagios]
action start (nagios::server line 284)
...TRUNCATED OUTPUT...
```

11. Validate the **Nagios** web interface by navigating to your node on `port 80`. Use the user/password combination you set for your user in the `users` data bag:

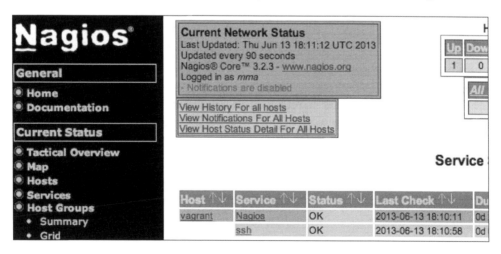

How it works...

First, we set up a user for managing the **Nagios** web interface. We create a data bag called `users` and a data bag item for your user (in the preceding example, the user is called `mma`. You will change that to the usernames you desire).

By default, **Nagios** will set up web access for every user in the `sysadmins` group.

As we want to use HTTP basic authentication for the **Nagios** web interface, we need to create a password hash to put into our `users` data bag.

To make **Nagios** use HTTP basic authentication, we need to set the `server_auth_method` attribute to `htauth` when defining the monitoring role, which we assign to our node.

Then, we configure a service check for SSH using a default template for the Nagios configuration file. To do so we create a data bag and a data bag item for our service.

Finally, we run Chef Client on our node and validate that we can log in with our user/ password to the Nagios web frontend running on our node and make sure that the SSH service check is running.

There's more...

You can change that default group to choose users for the Nagios web interface by modifying the `['nagios']['users_databag_group']` attribute in the role you use to configure your Nagios server.

You can set up your checks using your own templates and you can configure the contact groups and so on.

See also

▶ Find the `nagios` cookbook on GitHub at: `https://github.com/opscode-cookbooks/nagios`.

Building high-availability services using Heartbeat

If you want to offer any IP-based service with automatic failover to provide **high availability** (**HA**), you can use Heartbeat to create an HA cluster.

Heartbeat will run on two or more nodes and ensure that the IP address you chose to make highly available will switch to a working node, if one of them goes down. That way, you have a failover IP address, which is guaranteed to reach a running host as long as there is one left.

Let's have a look at how to install Heartbeat on your nodes and configure it with a failover IP address.

Getting ready

Make sure you've a cookbook called `my_cookbook` and `run_list` of all the nodes you want to add to your HA cluster including `my_cookbook` as described in the *Creating and using cookbooks* section in *Chapter 1, Chef Infrastructure*.

Make sure you've the `berkshelf` gem installed as described in the *Managing cookbook dependencies with Berkshelf* section in *Chapter 1, Chef Infrastructure*.

Create your `Berksfile` in your Chef repository including `my_cookbook`:

mma@laptop:~/chef-repo $ subl Berksfile

```
cookbook 'my_cookbook', path: './cookbooks/my_cookbook'
```

How to do it...

Let's use the community-provided `heartbeat` cookbook and configure it to work with our nodes:

1. Edit your cookbook's `metadata.rb` to add the dependency on the `heartbeat` cookbook:

    mma@laptop:~/chef-repo $ subl cookbooks/my_cookbook/recipes/ default.rb

    ```
    ...
    depends "heartbeat"
    ```

2. Install your cookbooks dependencies:

    mma@laptop:~/chef-repo $ berks install

    ```
    Using my_cookbook (0.1.0) at './cookbooks/my_cookbook'
    ...TRUNCATED OUTPUT...
    ```

3. Edit your cookbook's default recipe, replacing `192.168.0.100` with the IP address that should be highly available (your failover IP address) and `eth1` with the network interface you want to use:

    mma@laptop:~/chef-repo $ subl cookbooks/my_cookbook/recipes/ default.rb

    ```
    include_recipe "heartbeat"

    heartbeat "heartbeat" do
      authkeys "MySecrectAuthPassword"
      autojoin "none"
      warntime 5
      deadtime 15
    ```

```
initdead 60
keepalive 2
logfacility "syslog"
interface "eth1"
mode "bcast"
udpport 694
auto_failback true

resources "192.168.0.100"

search "name:ha*"
end
```

4. Upload the modified cookbook to the Chef Server:

    mma@laptop:~/chef-repo $ berks upload

    ```
    ...TRUNCATED OUTPUT...
    Uploading my_cookbook (0.1.0) to: 'https://api.opscode.com:443/
    organizations/agilewebops'
    ...TRUNCATED OUTPUT...
    ```

5. Run Chef Client on both nodes:

    user@server:~$ sudo chef-client

    ```
    ...TRUNCATED OUTPUT...
    [2013-06-14T20:02:26+00:00] INFO: service[heartbeat] restarted
    ...TRUNCATED OUTPUT...
    ```

6. Validate that your first node holds the failover IP address:

    user@ha1:~$ cl_status rscstatus -m

    ```
    This node is holding all resources.
    ```

7. Validate that your second node does not hold the failover IP address:

    user@ha2:~$ cl_status rscstatus -m

    ```
    This node is holding local resources.
    ```

8. Stop the Heartbeat service on your first node and validate that the failover IP address moves to your second node:

    user@ha1:~$ sudo service hartbeat stop

    user@ha2:~$ cl_status rscstatus -m

    ```
    This node is holding all resources.
    ```

How it works...

The `heartbeat` cookbook installs the Heartbeat service on all your nodes. In this example, we assume that your hostnames are `ha1`, `ha2`, and so on.

Then, we need to configure our HA-cluster. In the preceding example, we do this within our recipe.

First, you need to define a password. The nodes will use this password to authenticate themselves to each other.

Setting `autojoin` to `none` will make it impossible that new nodes get added outside of your Chef Client runs.

Next, we set the timeouts to tell Heartbeat when to act, if something seems wrong. The timeouts are given in seconds.

In the preceding example, we ask Heartbeat to use the broadcast method on the network interface `eth1`.

`resources` is your failover IP address. This IP address will be highly available in your setup.

The `search` call contains the query to find all the nodes to include in the Heartbeat setup. In our example, we search for nodes having their name starting with `ha`.

After uploading all cookbooks and running Chef Client, we can verify our setup by querying the Heartbeat status on both the nodes.

By stopping the Heartbeat service on the node currently having the failover IP address assigned to it, the second node will take over automatically.

There's more...

You can configure the Heartbeat by setting attributes in a role as well. In this case, it would make sense to set the search attribute to find all the nodes having the role.

See also

- ▶ Find the `heartbeat` cookbook on GitHub at `https://github.com/opscode-cookbooks/heartbeat`
- ▶ Read more about how to configure heartbeat at `http://www.linux-ha.org/doc/users-guide/_creating_an_initial_heartbeat_configuration.html`
- ▶ Find the complete reference of the Heartbeat configuration file at `http://linux-ha.org/wiki/Ha.cf`

Using HAProxy to load-balance multiple web servers

You've a successful website and it is time to scale out to multiple web servers to support it. **HAProxy** is a very fast and reliable load-balancer and proxy for TCP and HTTP-based applications.

You can put it in front of your web servers and let it distribute the load. If you configure it on a HA cluster using Heartbeat (see the *Building high-availability services using Heartbeat* section), you have a fully high-availability solution available.

Getting ready

Make sure you've at least one node registered at your Chef Server having the role web_ server in its run list. The following example will set up HAProxy so that it routes all requests to all your nodes having the web_server role.

Make sure you've a cookbook called my_cookbook and run_list of your node includes my_cookbook as described in the *Creating and using cookbooks* section in *Chapter 1, Chef Infrastructure*.

Make sure you've the berkshelf gem installed as described in the *Managing cookbook dependencies with Berkshelf* section in *Chapter 1, Chef Infrastructure*.

Create your Berksfile in your Chef repository including my_cookbook:

```
mma@laptop:~/chef-repo $ subl Berksfile

    cookbook 'my_cookbook', path: './cookbooks/my_cookbook'
```

How to do it...

Let's see how to set up a simple HAProxy balancing to all nodes having the web_server role:

1. Edit your cookbook's metadata.rb:

   ```
   mma@laptop:~/chef-repo $ subl cookbooks/my_cookbook/recipes/
   default.rb

   ...
   depends "haproxy"
   ```

2. Install your cookbooks dependencies:

   ```
   mma@laptop:~/chef-repo $ berks install

   Using my_cookbook (0.1.0) at './cookbooks/my_cookbook'
   ...TRUNCATED OUTPUT...
   ```

3. Edit your cookbook's default recipe:

```
mma@laptop:~/chef-repo $ subl cookbooks/my_cookbook/recipes/
default.rb

node.default['haproxy']['httpchk'] = true
node.default['haproxy']['x_forwarded_for'] = true
node.default['haproxy']['app_server_role'] = "web_server"

include_recipe "haproxy::app_lb"
```

4. Upload the modified cookbook to the Chef Server:

```
mma@laptop:~/chef-repo $ berks upload

...TRUNCATED OUTPUT...
Uploading my_cookbook (0.1.0) to: 'https://api.opscode.com:443/
organizations/agilewebops'
...TRUNCATED OUTPUT...
```

5. Run Chef Client on your node:

```
user@server:~$ sudo chef-client

...TRUNCATED OUTPUT...
[2013-06-16T18:57:07+00:00] INFO: service[haproxy] reloaded
...TRUNCATED OUTPUT...
```

6. Validate that the HAProxy admin interface is running on your node:

HAProxy version 1.4.18, released 2011/09/16

Statistics Report for pid 2050

> General process information

```
pid = 2050 (process #1, nbproc = 1)
uptime = 0d 0h24m06s
system limits: memmax = unlimited; ulimit-n = 8206
maxsock = 8206; maxconn = 4096; maxpipes = 0
current conns = 1; current pipes = 0/0
Running tasks: 1/3
```

	active UP		backup UP
	active UP, going down		backup UP, going down
	active DOWN, going up		backup DOWN, going up
	active or backup DOWN		not checked
	active or backup DOWN for maintenance (MAINT)		

Note: UP with load-balancing disabled is reported as "NOLB".

http

	Queue			Session rate			Sessions					Bytes		Denied		Errors			R
	Cur	Max	Limit	Cur	Max	Limit	Cur	Max	Limit	Total	LbTot	In	Out	Req	Resp	Req	Conn	Resp	
Frontend				0	1	-	0	1	2 000	2		218	424	0		0	0		

servers-http

	Queue			Session rate			Sessions					Bytes		Denied		Errors			Warnings	
	Cur	Max	Limit	Cur	Max	Limit	Cur	Max	Limit	Total	LbTot	In	Out	Req	Resp	Req	Conn	Resp	Retr	Redis
web1	0	0	-	0	0		0	0	100	0		0	0		0		0	0	0	0
web2	0	0	-	0	0		0	0	100	0		0	0		0		0	0	0	0
Backend	0	0		0	1		0	1	0	2	0	218	424	0	0		2	0	0	0

How it works...

First, we download the `haproxy` cookbook provided by Opscode.

Then, we change some of the default values: setting `httpchk` to true makes sure that HAProxy takes backend servers out of the cluster, if they don't respond anymore.

The `x_forwarded_for` attribute tells HAProxy to set the X-Forwarded-For HTTP header. It will contain the client IP address. If you don't set that header, your web servers will only see the IP address of your HAProxy server in their access logs instead of your client's IP addresses. This would make it very difficult to debug problems with your web applications.

The third attribute that we change is `app_server_role`. You can set whatever role your backend application servers have. The `haproxy` cookbook will include every node (using its `ipaddress` node attribute as returned by Ohai) having this role into the cluster.

After overriding those attributes, we run the `app_lb` recipe from the `haproxy` cookbook. The `app_lb` recipe will install HAProxy from a package and run a search for all nodes having the configured role.

After uploading all cookbooks and running Chef Client, you'll find the HAProxy admin interface on your node at `port 22002`. Hitting your HAProxy node at `port 80` will forward your request to one of your web servers.

See also

▶ The *Managing Rails applications* section in *Chapter 6, Users and Applications*

▶ Find HAProxy at `http://haproxy.1wt.eu/`

▶ Find the `haproxy` cookbook on GitHub at `https://github.com/opscode-cookbooks/haproxy`

Using custom bootstrap scripts

While creating a new node, you need to make sure that it has Chef installed on it. Knife offers the bootstrap subcommand to connect to a node via **Secure Shell** (**SSH**) and run a bootstrap script on the node.

The bootstrap script should install Chef Client on your node and register the node with your Chef Server. Opscode comes with a few default bootstrap scripts for various platforms. There are options to install Chef Client using the Opscode Omnibus installer, packages, or Ruby gems.

If you want to modify the way your Chef Client gets installed on your nodes, you can create and use custom bootstrap scripts.

Let's have a look how to do this.

Getting ready

Make sure you've a node ready to become a Chef Client and can SSH into it. In the following example we'll assume that you'll have a username and password to log in to your node.

How to do it...

Let's see how to execute our custom bootstrap script with Knife to install Chef Client on our node:

1. Create your basic bootstrap script from one of the existing Opscode scripts:

   ```
   mma@laptop:~/chef-repo $ curl https://raw.github.com/opscode/chef/
   master/lib/chef/knife/bootstrap/chef-full.erb -o bootstrap/my-
   chef-full.erb

   2013-06-17 13:59:24 (23.4 MB/s) - 'chef-full.erb' saved
   [1495/1495]
   ```

2. Edit your custom bootstrap script:

   ```
   mma@laptop:~/chef-repo $ subl bootstrap/my-chef-full.erb

   ...
   mkdir -p /etc/chef

   cat > /etc/chef/greeting.txt <<'EOS'
   Ohai, Chef!
   EOS
   ...
   ```

3. Bootstrap your node using your modified custom bootstrap script. Replace `192.168.0.100` with the IP address of your node and `user` with your SSH username:

   ```
   mma@laptop:~/chef-repo $ knife bootstrap 192.168.0.100 -x user
   --template-file bootstrap/my-chef-full.erb --sudo

   192.168.0.100 [2013-06-17T11:54:27+00:00] WARN: Node bootstrapped
   has an empty run list.
   ```

4. Validate the content of the generated file:

   ```
   user@server:~$ cat /etc/chef/greeting.txt

   Ohai, Chef!
   ```

How it works...

The `chef-full.erb` bootstrap script uses the Omnibus installer to install Chef Client and all its dependencies on your node. It comes packaged with all dependencies so that you don't need to install a separate Ruby or additional gems on your node.

First, we download the bootstrap script coming as part of Chef. Then, we customize it as we like. Our example of putting an additional text file is trivial, so feel free to change it to whatever you need.

After changing our custom bootstrap script, we're only one command away from a fully bootstrapped Chef node.

> If you want to bootstrap a virtual machine you started with Vagrant for testing your bootstrap script, you might need to use `localhost` as the node's IP address, and add `-p 2222` to your command line to tell knife to connect through the forwarded SSH port of your VM.

There's more...

If you already know the role your node should play or which recipes you want to run on your node, you can add a run list to your bootstrapping call:

```
mma@laptop:~/chef-repo $ knife bootstrap 192.168.0.100 -x user
--template-file bootstrap/my-chef-full.erb --sudo -r 'role[web_server]'
```

Here, we added the role `web_server` to the run list of the node using the `-r` parameter.

See also

▶ Read more about bootstrapping nodes with Knife at: `http://docs.opscode.com/knife_bootstrap.html`

▶ Find the `chef-full` bootstrap script here: `https://github.com/opscode/chef/blob/master/lib/chef/knife/bootstrap/chef-full.erb`

Managing firewalls with iptables

Securing your servers is very important. One basic way of shutting down quite a few attack vectors is running a firewall on your nodes. The firewall will make sure that only those network connections are accepted, which hit the services you decide to allow.

On Ubuntu, iptables is one of the tools available for the job. Let's see how to set it up to make your servers more secure.

Getting ready

Make sure you've a cookbook called `my_cookbook` and `run_list` of your node includes `my_cookbook` as described in the *Creating and using cookbooks* section in *Chapter 1, Chef Infrastructure*.

Make sure you've the `berkshelf` gem installed as described in the *Managing cookbook dependencies with Berkshelf* section in *Chapter 1, Chef Infrastructure*.

Create your `Berksfile` in your Chef repository including `my_cookbook`:

```
mma@laptop:~/chef-repo $ subl Berksfile
```

```
cookbook 'my_cookbook', path: './cookbooks/my_cookbook'
```

How to do it...

Let's set up iptables so that it blocks all network connections to your node and only accepts connections to the SSH and HTTP ports:

1. Edit your cookbook's `metadata.rb`:

   ```
   mma@laptop:~/chef-repo $ subl cookbooks/my_cookbook/recipes/
   default.rb
   ```

   ```
   ...
   depends "iptables"
   ```

2. Install your cookbook's dependencies:

   ```
   mma@laptop:~/chef-repo $ berks install
   ```

   ```
   Using my_cookbook (0.1.0) at './cookbooks/my_cookbook'
   ...TRUNCATED OUTPUT...
   ```

3. Edit your own cookbook's default recipe:

   ```
   mma@laptop:~/chef-repo $ subl cookbooks/my_cookbook/recipes/
   default.rb
   ```

   ```
   include_recipe "iptables"
   iptables_rule "ssh"
   iptables_rule "http"

   execute "ensure iptables is activated" do
     command "/usr/sbin/rebuild-iptables"
     creates "/etc/iptables/general"
     action :run
   end
   ```

4. Create a template for the SSH rule:

```
mma@laptop:~/chef-repo $ subl cookbooks/my_cookbook/templates/
default/ssh.erb
```

```
# Allow ssh access to default port
-A FWR -p tcp -m tcp --dport 22 -j ACCEPT
```

5. Create a template for the HTTP rule:

```
mma@laptop:~/chef-repo $ subl cookbooks/my_cookbook/templates/
default/http.erb
```

```
-A FWR -p tcp -m tcp --dport 80 -j ACCEPT
```

6. Upload the modified cookbook to the Chef Server:

```
mma@laptop:~/chef-repo $ berks upload
```

```
...TRUNCATED OUTPUT...
Uploading my_cookbook (0.1.0) to: 'https://api.opscode.com:443/
organizations/agilewebops'
...TRUNCATED OUTPUT...
```

7. Run Chef Client on your node:

```
user@server:~$ sudo chef-client
```

```
...TRUNCATED OUTPUT...
[2013-06-17T19:26:25+00:00] INFO: execute[rebuild-iptables] ran
successfully
...TRUNCATED OUTPUT...
```

8. Validate that the iptables rules have been loaded:

```
user@server:~$ sudo iptables -L
```

```
Chain FWR (1 references)
target     prot opt source               destination
ACCEPT     all  --  anywhere             anywhere
ACCEPT     all  --  anywhere             anywhere
state RELATED,ESTABLISHED
ACCEPT     icmp --  anywhere             anywhere
ACCEPT     tcp  --  anywhere             anywhere            tcp
dpt:http
ACCEPT     tcp  --  anywhere             anywhere            tcp
dpt:ssh
REJECT     tcp  --  anywhere             anywhere
tcpflags: SYN,RST,ACK/SYN reject-with icmp-port-unreachable
REJECT     udp  --  anywhere             anywhere
reject-with icmp-port-unreachable
```

How it works...

First, we download the `iptables` cookbook from the Opscode community site.

Then, we modify our own cookbook to install iptables. This will set it up in such a way that all network connections get refused by default.

To be able to access the node via SSH afterwards, we need to open up `port 22`. To do so, we create the template `my_cookbook/templates/default/ssh.erb` and include the required iptables rule.

We do the same for `port 80` to accept HTTP traffic to our node.

The `iptables` cookbook will drop off those templates in `/etc/iptables.d` and configure iptables so that it loads all those files on startup. It installs the script `rebuild-iptables` to do that.

Finally, we make sure that iptables has been activated. We add this step because I saw that the `iptables` cookbook ran, but did not load all the rules. That is fatal because you deem your box secured whereas in fact it is wide open.

After doing all our modifications, we upload all cookbooks and run Chef Client on our node.

We can validate whether iptables is running by listing all the active rules using the `-L` parameter to an `iptables` call on our node. You see the `ACCEPT` lines for ports `http` and `ssh`. That's a good sign. The last two lines shut down all other services.

See also

▶ Find the `iptables` cookbook on GitHub at: `https://github.com/opscode-cookbooks/iptables`.

Managing fail2ban to ban malicious IP addresses

Brute-force attacks against any of your password-protected services like SSH or break-in attempts against your web server are happening frequently for every public-facing system.

The fail2ban tool monitors your **logfiles** and acts as soon as it discovers malicious behavior in the way you told it to. One common use case is blocking malicious IP addresses by establishing firewall rules on the fly using iptables.

In this section, we'll have a look at how to set up a basic protection for SSH using fail2ban and iptables.

Getting ready

Make sure you've a cookbook named `my_cookbook` and `run_list` of your node includes `my_cookbook` as described in the *Creating and using cookbooks* section in *Chapter1, Chef Infrastructure*.

Make sure you've the `berkshelf` gem installed as described in the *Managing cookbook dependencies with Berkshelf* section in *Chapter 1, Chef Infrastructure*.

Create your `Berksfile` in your Chef repository including `my_cookbook`:

```
mma@laptop:~/chef-repo $ subl Berksfile

    cookbook 'my_cookbook', path: './cookbooks/my_cookbook'
```

How to do it...

Let's install fail2ban and create a local configuration enabling one additional rule to protect your node against **SSH DDos attacks**. This approach is easily extensible for various additional services.

1. Edit your cookbook's `metadata.rb`:

   ```
   mma@laptop:~/chef-repo $ subl cookbooks/my_cookbook/recipes/
   default.rb


   ...
   depends "iptables"
   depends "fail2ban"
   ```

2. Install your cookbook's dependencies:

   ```
   mma@laptop:~/chef-repo $ berks install

   Using my_cookbook (0.1.0) at './cookbooks/my_cookbook'
   ...TRUNCATED OUTPUT...
   ```

3. Edit your own cookbook's default recipe:

   ```
   mma@laptop:~/chef-repo $ subl cookbooks/my_cookbook/recipes/
   default.rb

   include_recipe "iptables"
   iptables_rule "ssh"

   include_recipe "fail2ban"

   file "/etc/fail2ban/jail.local" do
     content <<-EOS
     [ssh-ddos]
   ```

```
enabled   = true
port      = ssh
filter    = sshd-ddos
logpath   = /var/log/auth.log
maxretry = 6
  EOS
    owner "root"
    group "root"
    mode 0644
    notifies :restart, "service[fail2ban]"
end
```

4. Upload the modified cookbook to the Chef Server:

   mma@laptop:~/chef-repo $ berks upload

   ```
   ...TRUNCATED OUTPUT...
   Uploading my_cookbook (0.1.0) to: 'https://api.opscode.com:443/
   organizations/agilewebops'
   ...TRUNCATED OUTPUT...
   ```

5. Run Chef Client on your node:

   user@server:~$ sudo chef-client

   ```
   ...TRUNCATED OUTPUT...
   [2013-06-19T12:25:40+00:00] INFO: service[fail2ban] started
   ...TRUNCATED OUTPUT...
   ```

6. Validate, that your local fail2ban configuration has been created:

   user@server:~$ cat /etc/fail2ban/jail.local

   ```
   [ssh-ddos]

   enabled   = true
   ...TRUNCATED OUTPUT...
   ```

How it works...

First, we need to install iptables because we want fail2ban to create iptables rules to block malicious IP addresses. Then, we pull the fail2ban cookbook down into our local Chef repository.

In our cookbook's default recipe, we install iptables and fail2ban.

Then, we create a custom configuration for fail2ban to enable the ssh-ddos protection. fail2ban requires you to put your customizations into a file called `/etc/fail2ban/jail.local`.

It first loads `/etc/fail2ban/jail.conf` and then loads `jail.local` overriding the `jail.conf` settings. That way, setting `enabled=true` for the ssh-ddos section in `jail.local` will enable that section after restarting the fail2ban service.

There's more...

If you want to protect more services, just keep copying the desired sections from the `/etc/fail2ban/jail.conf` file into your cookbook, changing `enabled=false` to `enabled=true` on the way and tweaking any other parameters you want to change.

If you've a bigger set of settings, you might want to create a file in `my_cookbook/files/default` and use this instead of adding it to the string in your recipe.

See also

- ▶ The *Managing firewalls with iptables* section
- ▶ Find the `fail2ban` manual at: `http://www.fail2ban.org/wiki/index.php/MANUAL_0_8`
- ▶ Find the `fail2ban` cookbook on GitHub at `https://github.com/opscode-cookbooks/fail2ban`

Managing Amazon EC2 instances

Amazon Web Services (**AWS**) include the **Amazon Elastic Compute Cloud** (**EC2**) where you can start virtual machines running in the cloud. In this section, we will use Chef to start a new EC2 instance and bootstrap Chef Client on it.

Getting ready

Make sure you have an account at AWS.

To be able to manage EC2 instances with Knife, you need security credentials. It's a good idea to create a new user in the **AWS Management Console** using **AWS Identity and Access Management** (**IAM**) by following Amazon's documentation: `http://docs.aws.amazon.com/IAM/latest/UserGuide/Using_SettingUpUser.html`

Note down your new user's **AWS Access Key ID** and **AWS Secret Access Key**.

Additionally, you will need to create an SSH key pair and download the private key to enable Knife to access your node via SSH.

To create a key pair, log in to AWS Console and navigate to **EC2 service** (`https://console.aws.amazon.com/ec2/home`). Then, choose **Key Pairs** under the **Network & Security** section in the navigation. Click on the **Create Key Pair** button and enter something like `aws_knife_key` as the name. Store the downloaded `aws_knife_key.pem` private key in your `~/.ssh` directory.

How to do it...

Let's use the `knife-ec2` plugin to instantiate and bootstrap an EC2 node with Ubuntu 12.04:

1. Install the `knife-ec2` plugin to be able to use the AWS API via Knife:

   ```
   mma@laptop:~/chef-repo $ gem install knife-ec2
   ```

    Use `/opt/chef/embedded/bin/gem install knife-ec2` if you've installed Chef on your local workstation using the Omnibus installer.

2. Create your EC2 instance:

    You need to look up the most current AMI ID for your node at `http://cloud-images.ubuntu.com/locator/ec2/` and use it in your `knife` call instead of `ami-cf5e2ba6`. See the following *How it works...* section for more details about how to identify the correct AMI.

   ```
   mma@laptop:~/chef-repo $ knife ec2 server create -d 'chef-full'
   -r 'recipe[apt]' -S 'aws_knife_key' -x ubuntu -i ~/.ssh/aws_knife_
   key.pem -I 'ami-cf5e2ba6' -f 'm1.small' -A 'Your AWS Access Key
   ID' -K 'Your AWS Secret Access Key'

   Instance ID: i-70165011
   Flavor: m1.small
   Image: ami-cf5e2ba6
   Region: us-east-1
   Availability Zone: us-east-1b
   Security Groups: default
   Tags: {"Name"=>"i-70165011"}
   SSH Key: aws_knife_key

   Waiting for server............................
   Public DNS Name: ec2-54-226-232-107.compute-1.amazonaws.com
   ```

```
Public IP Address: 54.226.232.107
Private DNS Name: ip-10-191-185-138.ec2.internal
Private IP Address: 10.191.185.138

Waiting for sshd...done
Bootstrapping Chef on ec2-54-226-232-107.compute-1.amazonaws.com
...TRUNCATED OUTPUT...
ec2-50-17-112-73.compute-1.amazonaws.com Chef Client finished, 3
resources updated
...TRUNCATED OUTPUT...
```

3. Log in to your new EC2 instance:

   `mma@laptop:~/chef-repo $ ssh -i ~/.ssh/aws_knife_key.pem ubuntu@`
   `ec2-54-226-232-107.compute-1.amazonaws.com`

How it works...

First, we need to install the EC2 plugin for Knife. It comes as a Ruby gem.

Then, we need to make a few decisions on which type of EC2 instance we want to launch and where it should run:

1. Decide on the node size. You'll find a complete list of all available instance types at: `http://aws.amazon.com/ec2/instance-types/`. In this example, we'll just spin up a small instance (`m1.small`).

2. Choose the **Availability Zone** to run your node in. We're using the AWS default zone US East (N. Virginia) in this example. The shorthand name for it is `us-east-1`.

3. Find the correct **Amazon Machine Image** (**AMI**) by navigating to `http://cloud-images.ubuntu.com/locator/ec2/` and selecting the desired one based on the Availability Zone, the Ubuntu version, the CPU architecture, and the desired storage mode. In this example, we'll use the 64-bit version of Ubuntu 12.04 LTS code named precise, using instance-store. At the time of this writing, the most current version was `ami-cf5e2ba6`.

As soon as you know what you want to achieve, it's time to construct the launch command. It consists of the following parts:

The `knife-ec2` plugin adds a few subcommands to Knife. We use the `ec2 server create` subcommand to start a new EC2 instance.

The initial parameters we use are dealing with the desired Chef Client setup:

▶ `-d 'chef-full'` asks Knife to use the bootstrap script for the Omnibus installer. It is described in more detail in the *Using custom bootstrap scripts* section in this chapter.

▶ `-r 'recipe[apt]'` defines the run list in this case we install and run the apt cookbook to automatically update the package cache during the first Chef Client run.

The second group of parameters deals with SSH access to the newly created instance:

- ▶ `-S 'aws_knife_key'` lists the name of the SSH key pair you want to use to access the new node. This is the name you have defined in the AWS console while creating the SSH key pair.

- ▶ `-x ubuntu` is the SSH username. If you are using a default Ubuntu AMI, it is usually `ubuntu`

- ▶ `-i ~/.ssh/aws_knife_key.pem` is your private SSH key, which you downloaded after creating your SSH key pair in the AWS console.

The third set of parameters deals with the AWS API:

- ▶ `-I 'ami-cf5e2ba6'` names the AMI ID. You need to take the latest one as described in the preceding section.

- ▶ `-f 'm1.small'` is the instance type as described in the preceding point.

- ▶ `-A 'Your AWS Access Key ID'` is the ID of your IAM user's AWS Access Key.

- ▶ `-K 'Your AWS Secret Access Key'` is the secret part of your IAM user's AWS Access Key.

> The AWS Access Key ID and AWS Secret Access Key are the security credentials of a user who is allowed to use the AWS API. You create such users in the IAM section of the AWS management console.
>
> The SSH key pair is there for securing the access to your nodes. By defining the name of the key pair in the Knife command, the public key of your SSH key pair will be installed for the SSH user on your new node. You create such SSH key pairs in the EC2 section of the AWS management console.

The command will now start a new EC2 instance via the AWS API using your AWS credentials. Then it will log in using the given SSH user and key and run the given bootstrap script on your new node to make it a working Chef Client and register it with your Chef Server.

There's more...

Instead of adding your AWS credentials to the command line (which is unsafe as they will end up in your shell history), you can put them into your `knife.rb`:

```
knife[:aws_access_key_id]     = "Your AWS Access Key ID"
knife[:aws_secret_access_key] = "Your AWS Secret Access Key"
```

Instead of hard coding it there, you can even use environment variables to configure `knife`:

```
knife[:aws_access_key_id]     = ENV['AWS_ACCESS_KEY_ID']
knife[:aws_secret_access_key] = ENV['AWS_SECRET_ACCESS_KEY']
```

The `knife-ec2` plugin offers additional subcommands. You can list them by just typing the following command line:

```
mma@laptop:~/chef-repo $ knife ec2

   ** EC2 COMMANDS **
   knife ec2 flavor list (options)
   knife ec2 instance data (options)
   knife ec2 server create (options)
   knife ec2 server delete SERVER [SERVER] (options)
   knife ec2 server list (options)
```

See also

▸ The *Using custom Knife plugins* section in *Chapter 1, Chef Infrastructure*

▸ The *Using custom bootstrap scripts* section

▸ Find the `knife-ec2` plugin on GitHub at `https://github.com/opscode/knife-ec2`

Loading your Chef infrastructure from a file with spiceweasel and Knife

Having all your cookbooks, roles, and data bags as code under version control is great, but having your repository alone is not enough to be able to spin up your complete environment from scratch again. Starting from the repository alone, you will need to spin up nodes, upload cookbooks to your Chef Server, and recreate data bags there.

Especially when you are using a cloud provider for spinning up your nodes, it would be great if you could spin up your nodes automatically and hook them up to your freshly created and filled Chef Server.

The Spiceweasel tool lets you define all your cookbooks, data bags, and nodes and generates all necessary knife commands to recreate your complete environment including spinning up nodes and populating your empty Chef Server or organization on Hosted Chef.

Let's see how to dump our current repository and how to recreate our infrastructure with it.

Getting ready

Make sure you are able to spin up Amazon EC2 instances using Knife as described in the *Managing Amazon EC2 instances* section.

How to do it...

Let's use Spiceweasel to dump our current configuration, add some EC2 nodes, and recreate our complete environment:

1. Install the `spiceweasel` Ruby gem:

   ```
   mma@laptop:~/chef-repo $ gem install spiceweasel

   Fetching: ridley-0.12.4.gem (100%)
   Fetching: berkshelf-1.4.6.gem (100%)
   Fetching: spiceweasel-2.4.0.gem (100%)
   Successfully installed ridley-0.12.4
   Successfully installed berkshelf-1.4.6
   Successfully installed spiceweasel-2.4.0
   3 gems installed
   ```

2. Let spiceweasel dump your current repository into an `infrastructure.yml` file:

   ```
   mma@laptop:~/chef-repo $ spiceweasel --extractyaml >
   infrastructure.yml
   ```

3. Look into your new `infrastructure.yml` file (the contents depend on the current state of your Chef repository):

   ```
   mma@laptop:~/chef-repo $ cat infrastructure.yml

   ---
   berksfile:
   cookbooks:
   - my_cookbook:
       version: 0.1.0
   roles:
   - base:
   data bags:
   - users:
       items:
       - mma
   ```

4. Print out all Knife commands, which spiceweasel will run:

   ```
   mma@laptop:~/chef-repo $ spiceweasel infrastructure.yml

   berks upload -b ./Berksfile
   knife cookbook upload my_cookbook
   knife role from file base.rb
   knife data bag create users
   knife data bag from file users mma.json
   ```

5. Let Spiceweasel run the Knife commands as follows:

```
mma@laptop:~/chef-repo $ spiceweasel -e infrastructure.yml
```

```
Uploading my_cookbook      [0.1.0]
Updated Role base!
Data bag users already exists
Updated data_bag_item[users::mma]
```

How it works...

The Spiceweasel scans your local Chef repository and notes down everything as a YAML file.

When reading a given YAML file, it generates Knife commands to make the contents of the Chef repository available on the Chef Server.

There's more...

You can define nodes in your `infrastructure.yml` file: either local nodes, which Spiceweasel will then bootstrap, or nodes for cloud providers. Spiceweasel will then create `knife <provider> server create` commands for each specified node.

Using nodes in your `infrastructure.yml` file enables you to recreate a complete environment including all the necessary VMs using Spiceweasel.

You can use Spiceweasel to delete your setup from your Chef Server by using the `--delete` flag when running Spiceweasel:

```
mma@laptop:~/chef-repo $ spiceweasel --delete infrastructure.yml
```

See also

▶ You find the source code of Spiceweasel on GitHub at `https://github.com/mattray/spiceweasel`

Index

Thank you for buying
Chef Infrastructure Automation Cookbook

About Packt Publishing

Packt, pronounced 'packed', published its first book "*Mastering phpMyAdmin for Effective MySQL Management*" in April 2004 and subsequently continued to specialize in publishing highly focused books on specific technologies and solutions.

Our books and publications share the experiences of your fellow IT professionals in adapting and customizing today's systems, applications, and frameworks. Our solution based books give you the knowledge and power to customize the software and technologies you're using to get the job done. Packt books are more specific and less general than the IT books you have seen in the past. Our unique business model allows us to bring you more focused information, giving you more of what you need to know, and less of what you don't.

Packt is a modern, yet unique publishing company, which focuses on producing quality, cutting-edge books for communities of developers, administrators, and newbies alike. For more information, please visit our website: www.packtpub.com.

About Packt Open Source

In 2010, Packt launched two new brands, Packt Open Source and Packt Enterprise, in order to continue its focus on specialization. This book is part of the Packt Open Source brand, home to books published on software built around Open Source licences, and offering information to anybody from advanced developers to budding web designers. The Open Source brand also runs Packt's Open Source Royalty Scheme, by which Packt gives a royalty to each Open Source project about whose software a book is sold.

Writing for Packt

We welcome all inquiries from people who are interested in authoring. Book proposals should be sent to author@packtpub.com. If your book idea is still at an early stage and you would like to discuss it first before writing a formal book proposal, contact us; one of our commissioning editors will get in touch with you.

We're not just looking for published authors; if you have strong technical skills but no writing experience, our experienced editors can help you develop a writing career, or simply get some additional reward for your expertise.

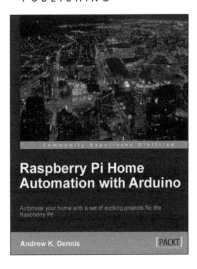

Raspberry Pi Home Automation with Arduino

ISBN: 978-1-84969-586-2 Paperback: 176 pages

Automate your home with a set of exciting projects for the Raspberry Pi!

1. Learn how to dynamically adjust your living environment with detailed step-by-step examples

2. Discover how you can utilize the combined power of the Raspberry Pi and Arduino for your own projects

3. Revolutionize the way you interact with your home on a daily basis

Windows Server 2012 Automation with PowerShell Cookbook

ISBN: 978-1-84968-946-5 Paperback: 372 pages

Over 110 recipes to automate Windows Server administrative tasks using PowerShell

1. Extend the capabilities of your Windows environment

2. Improve the process reliability by using well defined PowerShell scripts

3. Full of examples, scripts, and real-world best practices

Please check **www.PacktPub.com** for information on our titles

Instant AutoIt Scripting

ISBN: 978-1-78216-578-1   Paperback: 60 pages

Learn how to master AutoIt, an open source Basic-like programming language for automating Windows GUI

1. Learn something new in an Instant! A short, fast, focused guide delivering immediate results

2. Read and write apps instantly using the AutoIt freeware programming language

3. Execute or compile scripts and share your own Unic software

4. Organise and automate mundane and repetitive tasks

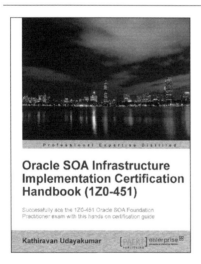

Oracle SOA Infrastructure Implementation Certification Handbook (1Z0-451)

ISBN: 978-1-84968-340-1   Paperback: 372 pages

Successfully ace the 1Z0-451 Oracle SOA Foundation Practitioner exam with this hands on certification guide

1. Successfully clear the first stepping stone towards becoming an Oracle Service Oriented Architecture Infrastructure Implementation Certified Expert

2. The only book available to guide you through the prescribed syllabus for the 1Z0-451 Oracle SOA Foundation Practitioner exam

3. Learn from a range of self-test questions to fully equip you with the knowledge to pass this exam

Please check **www.PacktPub.com** for information on our titles

Made in the USA
San Bernardino, CA
06 September 2014